GA ARCHITECT
世界の建築家シリーズ

現代建築界で活躍している建築家の全貌を、気鋭の批評家書き下ろしの作家論、現地取材の写真、建築家事務所の全面的な協力を得た詳細な図面、簡明な作品解説により立体的に編集した大型サイズの作品集。巻末には全作品リスト、文献リストを収録。変貌をつづける現代建築家の肖像を現時点で正確に把握、記録することを試み、現代建築家全集の最新決定版を意図した。各巻は建築家それぞれの個性を最大限に表現できるよう多彩な構成をとっている。

This is a new series of monographs in which each issue is dedicated to an architect and is a complete chronological account of that architect's works to date. GA ARCHITECT is presented in a large format(300 × 307mm) full of arresting photographs most of which are taken solely for the purpose of illustrating its articles and are heretofore unpublished. A critique by a foremost architectural critic or historian and the architect's own account of his works accompany each volume.

サイズ 300×307mm／総112～250頁，カラー36～54頁
Size 300 x 307 mm/112-250 total pages, 36-54 color pages

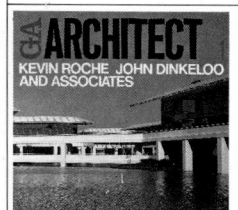

1 ケヴィン・ローチ／ジョン・ディンケルー
KEVIN ROCHE JOHN DINKELOO AND ASSOCIATES *Forthcoming issue* 近刊

論文：ノリー・ミラー　作品：メトロポリタン美術館全体計画／国連プラザビル1,2期／デンバー舞台芸術センター／ディア社西棟／ゼネラルフーヅ本社／ユニオンカーバイド社屋／他、1975年以降完成の最近作を中心に構成　——翻訳：難波和彦

Text: Nory Miller Works: Metropolitan Museum of Art Master Plan/United Nations Plaza Hotel and Office Building/Denver Center for the Performing Arts/Deere West/General Foods Corporation Headquarters/Union Carbide Corporation World Headquarters/and others.

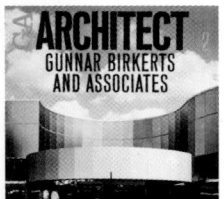

2 グナー・バーカーツ
GUNNAR BIRKERTS AND ASSOCIATES
上製本 ¥12,000　普及版 ¥6,800

論文：ウィリアム・マーリン／グナー・バーカーツ　作品：ミネアポリス連邦準備銀行／ダルース公立図書館／ヒューストン現代美術館／IBM社コンピューター・センター／IBM社屋／コーニング・ガラス博物館／ミシガン大学法学部棟増築　他、全56作品収録。——翻訳：山下泉／難波和彦

Texts: William Marlin/Gunnar Birkerts Works: Federal Reserve Bank of Minneapolis/Duluth Public Library/Contemporary Arts Museum, Houston/IBM Computer Center/Museum of Glass, Corning/and others/total 56 works
36 color pages/206 photos/310 drawings/228 total pages

3 マリオ・ボッタ
MARIO BOTTA
上製本 ¥9,800　普及版 ¥5,800

論文：クリスチャン・ノルベルク＝シュルツ　作品：リヴァ・サン・ヴィターレの住宅／モルビオ・インフェリオーレの高等学校／カプッチーニ修道院図書館／クラフト・センター／フリブール州立銀行／スタービオの住宅　他、全47作品収録。——翻訳：井出章

Texts: Christian Norberg-Schulz Works: One Family House at Riva San Vitale / Secondary School at Morbio Inferiore / Craft Center / State Bank at Fribourg / Office Building at Lugano / One Family House at Stabio / and others
total 47 works 42 color pages / 240 total pages

4 リカルド・ボフィル／タリエール・デ・アルキテクトゥラ
RICARDO BOFILL/TALLER DE ARQUITECTURA

論文：クリスチャン・ノルベルク＝シュルツ　作品：ラ・マンサネラ／ウォールデン7／タリエールのスタジオ／メリトクセルの聖堂／レ・アール計画／湖畔のアーケード・橋／アブラクサス宮殿／他。代表作と計画案を収録。——翻訳：三宅理一

Text: Christian Norberg-Schulz Works: La Manzanera/Walden 7/La Fabrica/The Sanctuary of Meritxell/Le Jardin des Halles/Les Arcades du Lac/ Le Palais d'Abraxas/and others
54 color pages/200 total pages　上製本 ¥9,800　普及版 ¥5,800

5 ザハ・ハディド
ZAHA M. HADID　¥3,900

序文：磯崎新　ザハ・ハディドとの対話：アルヴァン・ボヤルスキー——翻訳：彦坂裕
計画案：マレーヴィッチのテクトニク／19世紀博物館／オランダ議会場増築／アイルランド首相官邸／イートン・プレイス59番地／ラ・ヴィレット公園／ザ・ピーク／トラファルガー広場計画

Introduction: Arata Isozaki Conversations with Zaha Hadid: Alvin Boyarsky
Projects: Malevich's Tektonik/Residence for the Irish Prime Minister/59 Eaton Place/ Parc de la Villette/The Peak/Trafalgar Square Grand Buildings / and others
48 color pages/112 total pages

Key to Abbreviations

alc	Alcove
alcb	Alcove Bed
arcd	Arcade/Covered Passageway
Atl	Atelier
Atr	Atrium
att	Attic
bal	Balcony
bar	Bar
Bk	Breakfast
bnk	Bunk Bed
Br	Bedroom/Children's Bedroom
brg	Bridge/Catwalk
bth	Bathroom
bvd	Belvedere/lookout
car	Carport/Car Shelter
cl	Closet/Walk-in Closet
clk	Cloak
clr	Cellar/Basement
ct	Court
D	Dining Room
den	Den
dk	Deck
dn	Stairs-Down
drk	Darkroom
drs	Dressing Room/Wardrobe
drw	Drawing Room
E	Entry
Ect	Entry Court
Eh	Entry Hall
F	Family Room
fpl	Fireplace
fyr	Foyer
gal	Gallery
gdn	Garden
gm	Game room
grg	Garage
grn	Greenhouse
Gst	Guest Room
gzbo	Gazebo
h	Hall
Ing	Inglenook
K	Kitchen
L	Living Room
Lbr	Library
Lby	Lobby
ldry	Laundry
lft	Loft
lga	Loggia
Lge	Lounge
maid	Maid
MBr	Master Bedroom/Parents' Bedroom
mltp	Multi-purpose Room
msic	Music Room
mud	Mud Room
of	Office
opn	Open/Void
P	Porch/Portico
Ply	Play Room
pool	Swimming Pool/Pool/Pond
pt	Patio
pty	Pantry/Larder
rE	Rear Entry
shw	Shower
sit	Sitting Room
sky	Skylight
slp	Sleeping Loft
sna	Sauna
std	Studio
stdy	Study
Sth	Stair Hall
str	Storage/Storeroom
sun	Sun-room/Sun Parlor/Solarium
svE	Service Entry
svyd	Service Yard
ter	Terrace
tub	Bathtub
up	Stairs-up
utl	Utility Room/Mechanical Room/Heating Room
vra	Veranda
vstb	Vestibule
wc	Water Closet
wrk	Workshop/Work Room

フランク・ロイド・ライト全集　全12巻

〈vol. 1―8：モノグラフ〉

モノグラフ8巻は，完成された建築を撮影した写真と図面を組合せて編集した。初期から晩年に至る400点余の作品を8巻に分け，各時代の特徴を隈無く記録している。特にライトは，近代建築が始まった時点から1959年までの70年余のあいだいつの時代でも第一線で制作し続けてきた唯一の巨匠である。現代建築に彼ほどの影響を他に与えた建築家は類をみない。

彼の作品集は今まで，そのあまりに膨大な作品の数のために，限定されたものとなっており，通史としての作品集は未だに刊行されていない。今回の作品集を通読することによって初めて，ライトの真の偉大さを目の当りに感じることが出来るであろう。また，今までの幾多の誤解や間違いも発見することが出来るだろう。そして，新しいライト像の研究がここから始まることを期待したい。

各巻：サイズ300×307mm／総頁：280～340頁／カラー：30～72頁
図版点数：380～480点／定価：18,000円

〈vol. 9―11：プレリミナリー・スケッチ〉

プレリミナリー・スケッチ3巻は，彼が設計の途中，優れたアイデアやディテールを製図板の上でスケッチしたものを集めたものである。ここでは特に，建築されなかったプロジェクトを中心に編集している。ライトは400点余の建築を完成させたが，それに倍するプロジェクトを設計している。これらの作品は想像力豊かなデザインで，今日でも新鮮な魅力を湛えている。

ここに収録した図面は，今までほとんど発表されなかったものであり，この一枚一枚の図面の中から，ライトの建築に対する考え方や独得のディテール，形，空間が読みとれる。また，完成された建築とは一と味違った姿が発見されるし，そこに幾人もの天才ライトを見い出すことが出来るだろう。

各巻：サイズ300×307mm／総頁：210～240頁／カラー：22～36頁
図版点数：260～300点／定価：18,000円

〈vol. 12：レンダリング〉

フランク・ロイド・ライトのレンダリングは，今日まで20世紀の建築家に深い影響を与えてきた。それは単なる建築透視図というより，芸術作品と呼ぶに相応しい雰囲気を備えている。

レンダリングから読みとれる彼の建築表現のひとつは，特に住宅において自然を重視していることである。地形に対しての建物の配置の妙は天才的といってよい。恐らく彼の設計は，まず自然を読みとることによって進められているのだと思う。またその建築スタイルの変化に伴って，その表現力も多彩を極め，それを年代順に見ていくと非常に興味深い。

この巻は，ライトの全作品の中から特に優れたものを200点選び，特殊紙の選択，製版，印刷の全過程に入念なチェックを行って制作した。

サイズ300×307mm／総頁：288頁／カラー：156頁
図版点数：200点／定価：28,000円

FRANK LLOYD

企画・編集・撮影=二川幸夫／文=ブルース・B・ファイファー
Edited and Photographed by Yukio Futagawa
Text by Bruce Brooks Pfeiffer
訳：安藤正雄，小林克弘

第3回配本 vol.5
MONOGRAPH 1924-1936
総頁：286頁(カラー66頁)
図版点数：397点

第4回配本 vol.4
MONOGRAPH 1914-1923
総頁：282頁(カラー34頁)
図版点数：431点

第5回配本 vol.10
PRELIMINARY STUDIES
1917-1932
総頁：218頁(カラー30頁)
図版点数：272点

第6回配本 vol.6
MONOGRAPH 1937-1941
総頁：334頁(カラー60頁)
図版点数：465点

第7回配本 vol.1
MONOGRAPH 1887-1901
総頁：250頁(カラー30頁)
図版点数：468点

第8回配本 vol.2
MONOGRAPH 1902-1906
総頁：278頁(カラー22頁)
図版点数：480点

第1回配本 vol.12
IN HIS RENDERINGS 1887-1959
総頁：288頁(カラー156頁)
図版点数：200点

第2回配本 vol.9
PRELIMINARY STUDIES 1889-1916
総頁：220頁(カラー22頁)
図版点数：266点

vol.1 MONOGRAPH 1887-1901
vol.2 MONOGRAPH 1902-1906
vol.3 MONOGRAPH 1907-1913
vol.4 MONOGRAPH 1914-1923
vol.5 MONOGRAPH 1924-1936
vol.6 MONOGRAPH 1937-1941
vol.7 MONOGRAPH 1942-1950
vol.8 MONOGRAPH 1951-1959
vol.9 PRELIMINARY STUDIES 1889-1916
vol.10 PRELIMINARY STUDIES 1917-1932
vol.11 PRELIMINARY STUDIES 1933-1959
vol.12 IN HIS RENDERINGS 1887-1959

WRIGHT 12 vols.

A.D.A. EDITA Tokyo

GA HOUSES 21

Global Architecture

GA HOUSES

GA HOUSES 21
Publisher: *Yukio Futagawa*
Editor: *Wayne N.T. Fujii*
Associate Editor: *Satoru Komaki*
Assistant Editor: *Yasuko Kikuchi*
Production: *Takehiko Tanimoto, Mitsuru Gotoh*
Sales Promotion: *Takato Kawahara (Director),
Naoko Tanabe (Overseas affairs),
Kiyoshi Kazama, Eiko Utsuno*
Business Manager: *Yoshiomi Koiso*
Photography: *RETORIA: Y. Futagawa &
Associated Photographers, Yoshio Takase,
Toshiyuki Kobayashi, Ken'ichi Suzuki*

Logotype Design: *Gan Hosoya*

Published in February 1987
© A.D.A. EDITA Tokyo Co., Ltd.
3-12-14 Sendagaya, Shibuya-ku, Tokyo, Japan
Tel.03-403-1581
All rights reserved.

Copyright of Photographs: © *RETORIA:
Y. Futagawa & Associated Photographers*

Printed in Japan
by Nissha Printing Co., Ltd.

《世界の住宅》21
発行者:二川幸夫
編集:ウェイン藤井
編集アシスタント:小巻哲,菊池泰子
制作:谷本武彦,後藤充
営業:川原孝人,田辺直子,風間樹誉志,宇都野英子
経理:小磯義臣
写真:レトリア/二川幸夫,高瀬良夫,
　　　小林俊之,鈴木賢一

ロゴタイプ・デザイン:細谷巖

印刷:日本写真印刷株式会社
製本:(株)丸山製本所

1987年2月20日発行
エーディーエー・エディタ・トーキョー
A.D.A. EDITA Tokyo Co., Ltd.
東京都渋谷区千駄ヶ谷3-12-14
電話(03)403-1581代

禁無断転載

ISBN4-87140-321-1 C1352

Contents 目次

8　*Trip to Epoch-Making*
　JEAN PROUVÉ HOUSE
　Text by François Chaslin
　「エポック・メーキング」再検討⑨
　ジャン・プルーヴェ〈ナンシーの自邸〉
　文：フランソワ・シャスラン

26　BRIAN A. MURPHY
　BAM CONSTRUCTION/DESIGN INC.
　White Tower

34　TOD WILLIAMS & ASSOCIATES
　Eisenberg Residence

42　ANTHONY AMES
　A Garden Pavilion

50　ROB WELLINGTON QUIGLEY
　Jaeger Beach House

58　ROB WELLINGTON QUIGLEY
　Monahan Residence

64　ARNE BYSTROM
　Sun Valley House

74　*Meet the Architect*
　ANTOINE PREDOCK
　作品論⑲アントワーヌ・プレドック
　Rio Grande Valley House
　Fuller House
　Troy Residence
　Lazarus Residence
　Treaster Gray Residence
　The Beach
　Desert Highlands Golf Cottages Project

116　TORU MURAKAMI & ASSOCIATES
　House in Hongo-cho

122　KUNIHIKO HAYAKAWA & ASSOCIATES
　NW House

126　KUNIHIKO HAYAKAWA & ASSOCIATES
　Stratum

131　MARK SIMON
　of CENTERBROOK ARCHITECTS
　Crowell Studio/Residence

134　PAUL RUDOLPH
　Tuttle Residence

142　EDWARD LARRABEE BARNES ASSOCIATES
　ARMAND P. AVAKIAN
　Residence in Dallas

150　GREG MAXWELL
　with CITIGROUP ARCHITECTS & PLANNERS
　Loeken Residence

158　STEVEN EHRLICH
　Buchalter-Friedman Residence

162　CHRISTOPHER H.L. OWEN
　Cummin Residence

Cover: Loeken Residence by Greg Maxwell
pp.4-5: White Tower by Brian A. Murphy
pp.6-7: Lazarus Residence by Antoine Predock
photos by Wayne Fujii
作品解説翻訳：彦坂裕

JEAN PROUVÉ
HIS OWN HOUSE
ジャン・プルーヴェ自邸

Trip to EPOCH-MAKING
「エポック・メーキング」
再検討 9

Jean Prouvé
The Master of Sheet Metal
偉大なる鉄板工

François Chaslin
フランソワ・シャスラン

Jean Prouvé, the "master of sheet metal" from Nancy, had an odd and somewhat sad career. Undoubtedly, he, more than anyone else, epitomized the utter failure of modern architecture to fulfill its ambition to retain complete control over the built form and transform the intricate relationship between art and technology and the ineffectiveness of Le Corbusier's invitation to industry to master the art of building and thereby bring it to a higher stage of development. At the end of a wasted, unfulfilled life, working on menial assignments, Prouvé, who no longer even dreamt of the unachievable new harmony, was a living testimony of the widening gulf between the various professions involved in the building project, the unbridgeable gap between the architect, the engineer and the contractor, all of whose functions used to be performed by the master builder.

Prouvé is seen as the symbol, or almost as the martyr of this fragmentation of crafts and division of labor. He embodies the fundamental failure to understand the developments of the past three decades. "If they refuse to see the light, architects will no longer have a role," Viollet-le-Duc wrote at the end of his *Entretients*," the day of the engineers has come, that is to say, the day of men primarily concerned with building." Today, we have moved beyond even that stage. It is no longer the age-old rivalry between architects and engineers that is under discussion and it is not a question of contrasting those who are "disillusioned and unoccupied, boastful and moody" with those who are "healthy, vigorous, active and useful, conscientious and joyful."

Stated in more serious terms, the problem has now to be seen in terms of the general dissolution of responsibility, the gruelling struggle between mutually disputed areas of competence, in the context of a welter of ill-conceived rules and regulations, or a series of complicated, indescribable and largely absurd formalities involving the piecemeal participation of clashing authorities and wasted talents.

In this context, architecture loses its technical interpretability and its intelligibility; it is all too often littered with botches, barbarisms and poor workmanship and looks for a new raison d'être in the use of symbols and decor. It simply creates forms of realities that have passed it by; it pretends to order that which is already outside its grasp.

Jean Prouvé was born in 1901 in the artistic environment of the Nancy School, which was run by his father Victor and Emile Gallé. He first studied wrought ironwork; the Art Nouveau climate in Lorraine was to make a lasting impression on him. It was strongly influenced by socialism and hostile to stylistic plagiarism, holding skill and craftsmanship in high esteem. Prouvé's first pieces were made in the forge where, working with anvil and hammer, he enjoyed the craftsman's direct contact with his material.

From the outset of his professional life, he was a man of the workshop rather than of the drawing-board; he knew the blacksmith's craft well and had a keen grasp of the ins and outs of metalwork. In 1923 he set up his own firm and in the ensuing years made lamp-stands, railings, gates, door-handles, balustrades and wrought-iron radiator covers and elevator cages.

In 1925, the introduction of electric welding freed him from the forge and allowed him to develop iron and sheet-metal assemblies. "Racked by the idea of building," Prouvé made the main door of the Reifenberg Villa for Mallet-Stevens, joined up with Le Corbusier and Pierre Jeanneret, and played a part in setting up the Union des Artistes Modernes in 1929 with Pierre Chareau, Sonia Delaunay, Eileen Gray, René Herbst, Francis Jourdain, Charlotte Perriand and Mallet-Stevens. He also worked with Tony Garnier and, later, with Beaudoin and Lods, in association with whom he produced works of major significance. These were the prototype of the "BLPS" holiday and week-end home (1935), which could be "erected in the heart of the countryside in a matter of hours" and "transported on any light truck"; the Roland Garros flying club in Buc, which was fabricated in his workshop and bolted together in two weeks; and, most important of all, the Maison du Peuple in Clichy, "a feast of bent sheet-metal," which was erected between 1937 and 1939.

ナンシーの「鉄板細工師」ジャン・プルーヴェの宿命は、何と奇妙で、また悲痛なものであったことか。近代建築は構築物の掌握という野望を抱いたが、見事に失敗し、芸術と技巧の難しい関係を転化するとうそぶいたものの至らず、さらに、建築が一歩前進するためには、工業の手でそれを奪い取る必要があるというル・コルビュジエの呼び掛けも無駄に終わってしまった。近代建築のこれらの失敗を、プルーヴェは他の誰よりも体現している。こうして、彼の人生は損なわれ、中途半端なものと化し、新たな調和も、かなわぬ夢と葬って、彼は晩年を屈辱的な仕事に費やすことになる。

建築作業に携わる各専門分野間の距離は、拡がる一方であり、建築家、技術者、請負業者の間には、埋めつくせない溝が生じている事実をプルーヴェの人生は証言している。前三者は、以前、プロジェクト・ディレクターの名のもとに一体をなしていたのだが。

これは、職業の分離化、作業の細分化と共にこの30年来、文化に対する根本的な無理解がますます増長してきている現況の、象徴的姿といえる。しかし、救済の見込みはある。「建築家が光を求めなくなるとき、彼らが演じる舞台は、もはや存在しない。」とヴィオレ・ル・デュクは『アントルティヤン』(建築講話)の結論で述べている。「彼らにとって代わるのは、技術者、即ち、ただ我武者羅に建設に携わる連中だ。」いや、今日われわれの置かれている状況は、そんなものではない。建築家と技術者の間に存在する昔ながらのライバル意識を問題にしているのではないのだ。「幻滅感に浸り、無為なくせ、大言壮語は欠かさない陰気な連中」を「健全で剛健、活動的かつ陽気な連中」と比較することでもない。問題はより深刻である。盲めっぽうに定められた規範の混淆するなか、無謀で全く無意味なプロセスを経過するうちに、責任観念が全面的に消失する一方、互いに能力を牽制しあい、精根尽き果てる闘いが繰り広げられていることだ。そのうえ、つまらぬ干渉、勢力争い、才能の浪費が、このプロセスのなかで錯綜している。

このような状況下で、建築は技術的平明と明晰を喪失し、不細工、バルバリズム、施工ミスがあちらこちらに顔を出してくる。象徴的なものと外見のなかに、新たなレゾン・デートルを見い出そうと望んでいるのだろう。建築は現実に先を越され、現実を形取るだけに留まっている。手の届かなくなってしまったものを、支配しているような振りをしているのだ。

ジャン・プルーヴェは、1901年、ナンシー派の芸術家の家に生まれた。父ヴィクトールは、ガレと共にナンシー派の指導者の一人であった。ジャン・プルーヴェはまず、美術金属を学んだ。ロレーヌ地方のアール・ヌーヴォーの風潮から受けた影響は、生涯消えることはなかった。社会主義の色濃いこのアール・ヌーヴォーは、様式の剽窃を許さず、技量を重んじた。職人として、素材と直に触れ、鍛冶場では金床と金槌の間に四苦八苦しつつ、彼はこの世界への第一歩を踏み出したのである。

職に入った初めの数年間は、図面台に向かうよりむしろ、作業場(アトリエ)の人間となって、加工技術と慣れ親しみ、金属の取り扱いに必要な所作をものにしていった。1923年、自業を起こし、その後数年間は、電気スタンドの足、鉄柵、扉、把手、欄干、打出し鉄板の暖房器隠し、エレヴェーターの吊台を製作した。

1925年、電気溶接の導入により鉄板および鋼板の接合が可能となり、鍛冶場から解放された。「建築したくて矢も楯もたまらず」プルーヴェはマレ・ステヴァンのために、ライフェンベルグ荘の正面玄関を製作。またル・コルビュジエとピエール・ジャンヌレとも親交を結んだ。1929年には、ピエール・シャロー、ソニア・ドゥローネ、アイリーン・グレイ、ルネ・エルブスト、フランシス・ジュールダン、シャルロット・ペリアン、そしてマレ・ステヴァンと共に、ユニオン・デ・ザルティスト・モデルヌ(近代芸術家同盟)創設に加担し、トニー・ガルニエ、ついでボードワンとロッズとの協力により、彼の主要作品が製作された。1935年、休日と週末の家〈BLPS〉のプロトタイプが完成したが、これは「数時間あれば、野外で組み立てられ」「ライトバンで運搬可能な」家であった。またビュックのローラン・ガロス飛行クラブは、アトリエで製作された後、2週間でボルト継ぎによる組み立てを完了した。なかでも1937年から1939年にかけ建設された、クリ

This striking realization, which was both complex and flexible, combined a covered market and a large, multi-function auditorium provided with sliding partitions, a mobile retractable floor and an opening roof. It had significant repercussions and is still regarded as the high point of industrialized building in the interwar period.

The frame was built in rolled steel sections, much to the regret of its designer who had originally intended to use welded steel sheeting. Assembled sheet-steel elements were employed for the rest of the building, i.e. the partitions, the external walls, the roof and ceilings, the stairs, doors and toilets, canopies and parapets. The facades are often considered to be the first real example of the suspended curtain wall. However, this idea is dismissed by Prouvé, for whom the curtain wall "has no significance unless it is associated with an appropriate structure."

For thirty years, from the start of his working life in 1923 until 1953, Jean Prouvé was a prolific and highly original furniture designer with a preference for sheet metal rather than the nickel-plated steel tubing of the European avant-gardes. His chairs and armchairs are fine examples of his ability to think out his works in practical terms; they reflect an approach that is constantly being renewed and a concern for serviceability and suitability for small-scale manufacture rather than an attempt to achieve a sophisticated form of stylistic expression. In his designs, inventiveness and comfort were always more important than style and form. These pieces of furniture were not designed to look futuristic or chic; rather, they are solid, logical and explicit. Whilst they are nowadays generally regarded as being quaintly old-fashioned, their unvarnished beauty and measured pleasantness still have their appeal. This is equally true of the many other works produced in his workshops such as elevator designs, newspaper kiosks, sketches for car or milk-truck bodies, bicycle forks or the wartime Pyrobal oven.

They were conceived, designed and made with the same materials, the same screws or bolts, the same tapering legs and same studied lack of artistic expressivity or mannerism as his building elements.

Between 1944 and 1954, Prouvé had a successful factory in Maxéville, near Nancy, where he employed up to 250 people in a kind of co-partnership scheme. In this period, he could give full rein to his creative potential, as he had complete control over the technical resources that he needed for his work. During these years, he built nearly fifteen-hundred prefabricated houses, schools, pieces of furniture, building elements, facade panels or framed structures. He also devised a number of remarkable prototypes such as the Meudon houses, the tropical house for Niamey, the "shell house" for the Salon des Arts Ménagers in 1951 and the aluminium and reinforced-concrete Maison Alba. During this period, he also worked on a far greater number of projects with contemporary architects.

This factory was acquired by the Societé de l'Aluminium Français in 1954 at a time when, paradoxically, the implementation of France's rebuilding policy was in full swing. Prouvé's professional life subsequently took a bitter turn. Le Corbusier tried to cheer him up, saying "They've cut off your arms and legs, get along with what's left!" But Prouvé, shut up in the drawing office, without any real contact with the workshop or production line, never really got over the feeling of frustration that was foisted upon him.

His role as architect's adviser, called in as the expert in curtain walls and designer of facades in the 'sixties, simply added to his sadness. His failure to obtain building permission for his prototype "House of Better Days" which was designed in a couple of days and erected in seven hours for Abbé Pierre and his companions at Emmaus, at the height of the housing crisis during the winter of 1956, dashed his hopes of using the light industries to produce single-family dwellings. Le Corbusier, ever friendly, had warmly welcomed this design as "the most beautiful house that I know, the most perfect dwelling, the most brilliant thing ever built...and all that is true, he continued, when it is built and realized, it's the culmination of a life of research."

For twenty-five years, Jean Prouvé was

シーの〈人民の家〉は〈曲げ鋼板の祭典〉といわれた。

間仕切は引き戸式，床は可動の畳込み式，また，開閉式屋根を備えた変形可能な大劇場と，屋内市場とを共存させた特筆すべきこの作品は，複合的で柔軟性に富み，当時，大きな反響を呼んだ。両大戦間における工業的な探索のうち最高峰の作品と評価されている。

骨組みには当初，曲げ鋼板と溶接プレートの使用が予定されていたが，実際には圧延形鋼で施工され，創案者を大いに嘆かせた。骨組み以外の構造部分にはすべて（間仕切，外壁，屋根，天井，階段，扉，便所，庇，そして欄干）接合鋼板部材が使われた。また，ファサードについては，本格的に吊り式カーテンウォールを使った最初の実例とされる。しかしこれは，カーテンウォールは，適格な構造のなかに組み込まれないかぎり，そのもの自体では何の意味ももたないとするプルーヴェの見地を否定するものである。

1923年から1953年，建築家の道を歩み始めてから30年間，数多くの家具を創作したジャン・プルーヴェは，なおも独自の道を歩み続ける。そしてヨーロッパ前衛派の好むニッケル鋼チューブより，相変わらず，鋼板のほうを選んだ。彼の手になる椅子，あるいは肘掛け椅子は，心憎いほど日用性に心が配られ，決して改良の手をゆるめない。また，洗練された様式表現よりむしろ，使い易さ，少量生産の便宜の点に工夫が凝らされている。流儀あるいは様式より，創意性や快適さが常に先行しているのだ。彼の家具はまず，頑丈で合理的，また明瞭であり，未来を先取りするとか，粋を利かせるということは二の次にされた。今日，そのほとんどは，なんとなく流行遅れになってしまったものの，簡素な美しさを保ち，地味ではあるが好感を呼ぶ。彼のアトリエから出された作品がえてしてそうであるように——エレヴェーター設計，キオスク，乗用車あるいは牛乳運搬トラックの車体デザイン，自転車の前輪支柱，戦時下に普及したピロバル・オーヴン。

これらの製品は，構築物の構成部材として創案，設計，製作された。また，材料，ねじ釘，ボルト，流線形のぬきは，同一タイプのものが使われ，芸術的表現やわざとらしさを意図的に排除してある。

1944年から1954年に至るまで，プルーヴェはナンシー近郊のマクセヴィルに工場を得た。一種の共同経営というかたちで，250名の工具が一体となって従業し，効率が高かった。必要な技巧手段を存分に使えたこの時期，彼の才能は迸った。そして，約1500軒を数えるプレファブ住宅，校舎，家具，建設部材，ファサード・パネルまたは骨組みのパーツが製作された。さらに，各種の卓抜なプロトタイプが創造された。たとえば，ムードンの住宅，ニアメイのトロピカルハウス，1951年度家庭用器具展示会（サロン・デ・ザール・メナジエ）におけるシェル構造の住宅，アルミニウムと鉄筋コンクリートのアルバの家が挙げられる。そして現代建築家との共同製作をつぎつぎと重ねていったのである。

1954年，工場がフランス・アルミニウム社により買収された結果，活動手段を奪われたプルーヴェの建築家としての道は，これを境に険しいものとなってゆく。奇しくも，フランスでは再建政策たけなわの頃であった。「臓物を切り取られたっていうなら，残されたもので，なんとかやりぬくんだ！」というル・コルビュジエの励ましもむなしく，プルーヴェは設計事務所に閉じ籠るばかりで，アトリエや製造ラインより遠ざかり，強いられたこの欲求不満の状態から完全に抜け出すことはなかった。

建築家の相談役，カーテンウォールの熟練者，60年代のファサード屋という役どころに甘んずるよりほかなかったプルーヴェを決定的に悲嘆に沈ませた出来事がある。1956年冬，住宅難の深刻化を背景に，ピエール神父とエマウス派の仲間のために，数日間で設計を仕上げ，7時間で建設した〈より良き日々のための家〉のプロトタイプが不成功に終わったのだ。その結果，個人住宅の少量生産化に托した希望が，儚なく消え果ててしまった。この住宅には，遂に認可が下りなかった。ル・コルビュジエは，相変わらず友情に厚く，この作品についても，「これまで私の見てきた家のうちでもっとも美しい建物である。住宅としても完全無欠であり，ついぞ見たことのない，きらめくばかりの建築だ。」と，

virtually no more than an architect's assistant; he who had hoped to embody all the qualities of the master builder was not even accorded professional status. This all-round stylist and ingenious handyman was expected to give his "colleagues" the benefit of his materials, such as stainless steel, aluminium and sheet metal (in rolls, welded, bent, swaged, punched, seamed) and, later, the extruded aluminium sections and the structural forms that he had personally designed (porches, door handles, shells, sheet metal designs and three-dimensional reticulated tablecloths) and, needless to say, his facade panels.

Despite his reluctance to become involved in complex projects, he placed his grasp of modern techniques at the service of French architecture. During this period, he was associated with projects designed by Lurcat, Laprade, Le Couteur, Pouillon, Dubuisson, Remondet, Zehrfuss (CNIT de la Défense and Unesco), Dufau, Andrault and Parat (Orléans-la-Source), Novarina (the elegant Vittel spa and the Grenoble town hall), Mailly (tour Nobel de la Défence), Joly and Folliasson, Belont and Silvy (his faithful disciples), Candilis, Josic and Woods (the Free University of Berlin), Niemeyer (the facade of the Communist Party headquarters) and, more recently, Willerval (the ungainly Les Halles complex in Paris).

He worked with nearly everybody, from mandarins to newcomers; what is more, some of this work was extremely successful.

For a period of thirteen years, beginning in 1957, he gave a course at the old Conservatoire National des Arts et Métiers. Hundreds of students who were unhappy with the teaching at the Ecole des Beaux-Arts and a good number of young professionals flocked to hear him. Once a week, he stood at the blackboard in a dreary lecture hall, where he slowly drew, with a masterly hand, brilliantly clear figures that were carefully copied by his devoted audience. In a cogent analysis of building techniques, he dissected buildings, machines and mechanisms with the kind of consummate pedagogical skill exhibited in the exploded views of Viollet-le-Duc or in the drawings of the old anatomists. His courses dealt with materials, the appropriate ways of assembling and working them, the proportioning of loads and the need for accurate jointing (essential for connecting the frame and the shell, the structure and the walls, the roof and the facades). He emphasized the need to economize on materials and explained the ways of solving details and the extent to which "a building takes on greater character the more it is simplified." His lectures were attended in reverential silence; he was frightened to death!

Prouvé's whole message was based on his conviction as to the power of intuition, the unity of the different stages in the building project, and the damage caused by techniques involving the fragmentation of building work. For him, the "built idea" had to be immediate, essential and pure, with the shortest possible time between conception and completion. It had to be perceived immediately as a complete and coherent piece of work, which had not been produced by trial and error and approximations. He told his audience that, in his workshops, a chair would go into production as soon as its design was on the drawing-board: the prototype would be brought to him the following day. "Monday's pencil stroke was a finished product by Tuesday morning." This provided an immediate opportunity to examine mistakes, design faults and any production problems that may have arisen; with this procedure, no one could have any illusions about the design. Quite the opposite happened in conventional architectural production where a design took months and often years to complete; and even then it was hardly recognizable in relation to the original concept, while the built form sometimes bore only a vague resemblance to what was on the drawing board.

For Jean Prouvé, "the only conceivable place for the architect's site office is the factory producing the materials." This is the only way of ensuring complete control of detailing and remaining fully in charge of the building work. But this means "rolling up one's sleeves," knowing something about the materials and tools required for the job and working closely with the workers and technicians at every stage of the project. It also means absolutely sound decision-

温かく敬意を表し，さらに，「この家は，現実に建てられ，製作された。いわば，探究に捧げられた人生の帰結といえる。」とことばを続けた。

それに続く25年間，ジャン・プルーヴェは建築家の共同製作者の役に踏み留まることになる。プロジェクト・ディレクターの全素養を，一挙に併せ持とうとした彼であったが，建築家協会への登録も許されなかった。プルーヴェは工業デザイナーとしてあらゆる分野を手掛け，大工仕事では天才的な手腕を見せた。そして，系列下の同業者のために，彼の馴染みの材料であるステンレス・スティール，アルミニウム，帯鋼，溶接鋼板，曲げ鋼板，バックル・プレート，穴あきプレート，フック・プレート，その後，押し出しアルミニウムを，また自分で開発した柱廊，支柱，シェル，引っ張り鉄板，ハング・プレート，ヴォールト・プレート，腰掛け，網状立体羽目，そして勿論，ファサード・パネルを提供した。

作業プロセスを超越しようと試みたものの，結局はそのなかに封じこまれてしまったプルーヴェは，この年代のフランス建築に，技術面における近代性——表面的ではあったが——を与え，数々の共同プロジェクトに携わった。リュルカ，ラプラード，ル・クトゥール，パビヨン，デュブュイソン，ルモンデ，ゼールフュス（デファンス地区のCNITとユネスコ），デュフォー，アンドゥローとパラ（オルレアン・ラ・スルスにおいて），ノバリーナ（ヴィッテルのエレガントな小酒場とグルノーブルの市役所），ド・マイイ（デファンス地区のノーベル・タワー），ジョリーとフォリアソン，彼の愛弟子であるベルモンとソルヴィー，カンディリス，ジョジックとウッズ（ベルリン自由大学），ニーマイヤー（共産党本部の洗練されたファサード）と，より最近では，ウィレルバル（パリのレアル地区の不細工な建物）との仕事が挙げられる。

彼は大物から若者に至るまで，あらゆる人々との共同製作に取り組み，そのいくつかは見事な成果をみせている。

1957年より13年間，古くからある国立工芸学院で講義を持ち，ボザールの授業に不満な学生たち数百人や，大勢の若い建築家が傾聴した。週に一遍，陰気な大教室のなかで，ゆっくりと懇切丁寧に，黒板にしっかりと極めて明快な図形を描くと，聴講生は注意深くそれを写すのだった。建築工程は理路整然と分析され，ヴィオレ・ル・デュクの分解図面による完璧な教育法，あるいは昔の解剖学者の流儀で，建設物，機械，または機械工学がつぶさに解明された。彼はそこで，材料接合，板金加工，そして支柱と外皮，構造部と外壁，および屋根とファサードの連接部の微妙な取り扱い方と，引っ張りのバランスについて話し，「まさに道義的問題」である素材の倹約，ディテールの解決法について教示した。また「建築というものは，単純化してゆくうちに，個性がはっきりと出てくる。」ことについて語った。まるで，荘厳なミサの儀式に参列しているような敬虔な沈黙が教室に漲っていた。彼もすっかりあがってしまうのが常だった。

プルーヴェのメッセージのすべては，つぎの信条に要約できる。即ち，勘の持つ力，プロセスの統一，作業の細分化の進展による支障，である。彼の見解によれば，建築創案とは直観性のものであり，本質的で純粋であるから，ただちに施工されるべきである。それは，非の打ちどころのない調和ある精神から生まれ，手探りや漸近法によって得られるものではない。「私のアトリエでは，ひとつの椅子が考案され，その設計が完成するとすぐに製造にとりかかりました」と，彼は語っている。翌日には，プロトタイプが完成されていたのである。「月曜日に設計されたものは，火曜日の朝，現物化していました。」と言う。こうすれば，誤ち，設計ミス，製造過程における難点が即時，判別され，線描による錯覚が回避できる。これに対し，従来の建築製作では，設計段階から製作にこぎつけるまで数ヶ月，いや，数ヶ年もの年月が必要とされる。その結果，設計図とは似ても似つかないものができ，設計図の指示と建造物との関係は曖昧となる。

ジャン・プルーヴェにとり，「建築事務所の所在地が，材料製造工場以外にあるとは，考えられない。」こうして初めて，ディテールが完璧にコントロールでき，建築を意のままに進められるのだ。だがそれには「そのなかに身を投じ」な

making. Prouvé believed in "getting on with the job." He maintained that, just as the builder does not usually knock down and rebuild a newly finished building, the designer should be prepared to stand by his own design instincts and not water them down at a later stage.

Prouvé never had any time for the formalities surrounding the building project. He had a deep-seated dislike of the whole decision-making process. As far as he was concerned, this killed off the good idea or took all the interest out of the project, whether it involved the architect, building contractor, the engineers, the technical consultants or the building inspectors. For him, the whole process amounted to a battle of wills that offered little hope of the people concerned ever working together as a real team. It was simply a succession of interventions in which everyone altered or touched up his "partner's" contribution.

This old builder had little sympathy for architects: he had known too many of them and had first-hand experience of their arrogance, their artistic pretensions, their futile attempts to impart a sacrosanct character to frequently inept drawings and their outmoded attachment to the fringe elements of society. He criticized their apparent lack of interest in the economics of building and felt more at home with contractors, who were constantly faced with the realities of the balance sheet, "who weren't simply paid a percentage and ran the risk of going bankrupt."

He gave the impression of being a man weighed down by many years of bitter anger and a hatred of the bare-faced "Now-build-me-that" mentality. He frequently contrasted the industrialist's pride in his products with the architect's constant complaining and readiness to blame others for the inadequacies in his designs.

Poor Prouvé. He declared himself to be both "disorientated and bewildered." He could not accept that the building trade, to which he had devoted his life, had been able to take so little advantage of the inventiveness, technical advances and development of industry and had remained so far behind the times.

Looking out of the train, on his weekly journey from Paris to Nancy, he saw an untidy assortment of buildings haphazardly constructed using outdated methods. They formed a striking contrast with the custom-designed gleaming, stainless-steel railway carriages.

In the last years of his life, this inventor, whose mind had constantly been occupied with construction and engineering problems, simply lost his patience with the way things were going. A fall on the treacherous slope leading up to his hillside home had forced him to give up skiing. He died on the night of 22-23 March 1984, the first night of spring. He was almost as old as the century, almost as young as the modern movement.

HIS HOUSE

In March 1954, Jean Prouvé was forced out of his workshops at Maxéville which, for thirty years, had been run on a co-partnership basis. He decided to build himself a house on a very steep hill on the outskirts of Nancy: "fifty meters of steep path" on loose soil that was quite unsuitable for building. The land was bought in May and the house was built at full speed by the whole Prouvé family between June and September. In that month, they moved in, although the house was still in a fairly basic state and the interior partitions still had to be finished off.

The house was built from lightweight elements which were transported to the site on a jeep owned by Prouvé's father and assembled by the family with some outside help. It was, in fact, mainly built with materials obtained from his old factories with the connivance of his former workers. "It was made of left-overs," he explained: windows, facade panels, a porch originally intended for an industrialized school model, while the second house at the bottom of the garden was built from the former offices of the company, which had themselves been constructed from the frame of a prototype of a prefabricated house with a central porch.

In terms of layout, the house was linear, built on a concrete slab cast level with the soil (the "best form of temperature control"). This slab is reinforced with a

---

ければならぬ。素材や，道具，手段に精通し，絶えず職人や技術者の世界と，密着した共同作業を営まなければならぬ。また，決断に際しては，絶対的な確信に基づいた時のみ下すべきだ。現場にしろ工場にしろ，後には戻れない。構築されてしまったら，それで終わりだ。プレスされてしまえばもう，元の状態には還せない。創案というものは，精神のなかから鮮明な姿で現われなければならない。完璧な姿で，毅然として。

プルーヴェは，建設プロセスを飽くことなく告発する。アーキテクトから請負業者の間に，エンジニア，技術設計室，さらに現場管理事務所を通さなければならないデシジョン・メイキングの手順は，創案を破壊し，設計図を褪色させる。敵意や反感が滝のように落ちてくる状況のもとで，調和ある仕事が生まれるだろうか。介入，干渉は後を断たず，各人がパートナーの貢物を粗悪にし，加筆訂正するのだ。

この経験豊かなコンストラクターの好意は，アーキテクトの方へは向けられない。この職業についてはあまりにも知りすぎていた。その尊大ぶり，芸術をひけらかし，ともすれば愚鈍な設計を神聖化しようと足掻いたり，時代錯誤の疎外感覚を大事にしたりする連中だ。彼は，アーキテクトに経済観念の不足を咎め，損益勘定という現実を，常に踏まえている請負業者の方に好意を寄せた。「業者への支払いは歩合制ではなく，破産に追いやられるのは彼らだ。」

長年，鬱積してきたアーキテクトへの恨み，「こういうものを建ててくれ」とぶしつけに注文してくる彼らへの憎しみが，ここに感じられる。常に上機嫌で，自分の仕事に誇りを抱いている企業家とは対照的に，満足することを知らず，愚痴っぽく，仕事の不全をすぐ他人になすりつけるアーキテクト。彼はこの二者をよく比べたものだった。

哀れなプルーヴェ。彼は昨今，「みじめで途方に暮れている。」と告げていた。人生を賭けた建築が，創意工夫，技術進歩，そして工業発展をほとんど活用しないで，いまだに旧式な状態に滞っていることが納得できなかった。

ナンシーからパリに毎週のように通う汽車の窓の向こうには，既に廃れた工法で，無計画に建てられた雑然とした世界があった。それに反し，車両の方は，ステンレス・スティール製で，光り輝き，完璧な仕上げを見せていた。

昔は，ボルト締めやジョイントおよび型打ちの問題が，一時も頭を離れたことの無かった発明の才人，プルーヴェも，晩年の数ヶ年は苛立ちを覚えていた。そして，丘の上の自宅に続く，あの憎らしい急坂でころんでしまい，80歳位まで好きで続けたスキーも断念せざるを得なかった。1984年3月22日から23日にかけた夜半――折りしも立春であったが，最期の息をひきとったのである。一世紀を生きてきたといえるほど歳はとっていたが，近代性と同じくらい，若かった。

□プルーヴェの自宅
1954年3月，13年間を共同経営のかたちで過ごしたマクセヴィルのアトリエから追われたジャン・プルーヴェは，ナンシー周辺にある丘の中腹に自宅の建設を決めた。土砂崩れが起き，建設はほとんど不可能といえる「険しい小径が，50メートルほど続いている」場所だった。5月に土地が買取られ，6月から9月まで家族全員が参加して，速やかに工事が進められた。9月になると間仕切の組み立ての仕上げをしながら，かなり不便な状況ではあったが，一家の生活が始まった。

この家は工具たちの暗黙の合意を得，前の工場から回収した材料が主に使われた。軽量部材は，父親のジープで運搬し，組み立ては幾人かの手を借りながら家族で取り組んだ。「この家は残り物で建てました。」と彼は説明する。窓，ファサード・パネル，柱廊がそれである。柱廊は本来，規格化校舎のモデルタイプ用につくられたものである。庭の下方に建設された第2の家は，取り壊された会社の事務室の部材が用いられた。この事務室にしても，もとは中央ポルチコ付きのプレファブ住宅のプロトタイプ用の骨組みを活用したものだった。

家は，地面に直接流されたコンクリート・スラブ上に建設され，一直線をなしていた。（温度調整には最適である。）金属製小梁の骨格による鉄筋で，中央暖房システムの蛇管が通された。傾斜部分を削り取った，一種の水平段丘は，一面

framework of small girders and incorporates the coils of a built-in central heating system: it is a kind of smooth terrace, cut out of the slope, backing onto the hill with a 27-meter-long solid wall, which appears to serve to retain the earth. This wall is lined on the inside with a long row of wall-cupboards, which are built into the metal framework and are fitted with sliding doors made of bent sheet metal and wood. "I love wood," Prouvé told Dominique Clayssen; "the door slides at a simple push. People are always looking for complications, but it's only a matter of respecting the proportions. The Japanese always have a hole at the exact height at which pressure is applied horizontally." Jean Prouvé's house is a tribute to his admirably practical approach, which is fostered by an incomparable technical intuition and a consummate sense of elegance. "For me," he said, "the most important thing in building a house is to have a spontaneous idea of how it should be built." And, as Le Corbusier recognized, "everything he touches and designs immediately takes on an elegant plastic form, while at the same time he provides brilliant solutions to the problems concerning the strength of the materials and fabrication."

The house on rue Augustin-Hacquart is practically windowless and doorless on the side of the hill and on its northern side, but has a very open, glazed frontage on the southern side. This is provided by a series of alternating aluminium panels punched with "porthole" windows, wooden breast panels accomodating lightweight sliding metal shutters and, below the porch roof which offers shade in the summer, large glazed surfaces that serve to light up the living-room and allow plenty of sun into the back of the room in the winter.

This living-room was built with the family's large number of visitors in mind (Prouvé called it "the inn"). It has bookshelves, a fireplace and, in one corner, a beautiful date palm, which has grown in the soil from one of the dates placed during building thirty years ago in a hole left in the concrete slab.

In contrast, the other rooms are tiny: the children's rooms measure three by two meters (with room for a bed, a desk, an armchair and a small bookcase), while the parents' room is three by three meters. As in many of Prouvé's houses, the "sanitation block" forms a separate unit, which is built in non-loadbearing masonry. Although Jean Prouvé generally used various systems of monoblock shells for the roofs of his small buildings, for this house he used large laminated board panels, which were both stiff and very flexible, "like a fishing rod." These panels were placed on steel supports and covered with strips of aluminium on the outside. Inside the house, they were left exposed.

This patently simple solution was altogether typical of this inventor's approach to building. "Everything I'm explaining to you," he told Isabella Costa, who persuaded him to recount the story behind this house," was not drawn; it was the product of observation. It was necessary to take advantage of the available materials. Without handling it, one could never imagine that a wooden panel could actually be pliant. Thus, the movement in this roof has never been represented on the drawing-board. Well, the whole house is like that. The rest is nothing more than internal partitions."

We should like to express our gratitude to the Nancy architect, Isabelle da Costa who has kindly allowed us to reproduce her drawings. She was a frequent visitor to Jean Prouvé's home during the last months of his life when she was preparing her excellent article on his house. Part of this article was published in the *AMC* magazine (No. 4, June 1984).

の無窓の壁により，丘に背をもたらせているかのようだ。全長27メートルのこの壁は，土を支えているように見えたが，その内側には，金属製骨組みを内蔵する長い戸棚が付けられ，壁を二重構造にしている。戸棚には，曲げ鋼板と木製の扉が付けられ，ほぞがつくられ，引き入れ式になっている。「私は木材にとても惹かれます。」と彼はドミニック・クレセンに打ち明ける。「この扉なども，軽く押すだけで滑ってゆきます。皆，難しく考えすぎるんですよ。ただ均衡だけに注意を払えばよいのです。日本人は，圧力が水平にかかる，正確な位置に穴をあけています。」

ジャン・プルーヴェのこの作品は，無類といえる技巧への直感と，優美に対する完璧なセンスを貯えた，彼の見事な経験主義を再認識させてくれる。彼は語る。「私にとって，一軒の家を建てるということは，取りも直さず，その家に対する建築概念を一瞬のうちにもつことを意味します。」なるほど，コルビュが認めているように，「彼が触れ，思い付くすべてのものは，ただちに優雅な造形美をもってしまう。しかも，材料の耐久性や製造過程で起こる問題も一括して，見事に片付けてしまうのだ。」

オーギュスタン・アックアール街の家は，従って，丘陵に面した側と北側は薄暗いが，南向きにつくられている。南側は，ガラス張りの大きく開いたファサードで覆われている。ファサードには，円形窓の付いたアルミニウム・パネルと，木製の窓台付きのパネルが変化を与えている。窓台にほられた溝の上を，金属製の軽量の雨戸が滑るようにつくられている。夏には，屋根の庇が影を提供してくれる。庇の下は，大々的なガラス張りであるから，居間を明るくし，冬には，ガラス壁を通して太陽の光が部屋の奥まで，充分に照らす。

プルーヴェが，〈田舎風レストラン〉と呼んでいたこの居間は広かった。訪問客が多かったからだ。本棚，暖炉が設けられ，片隅には，自然科学博物館の温室であるとばかりに，しあわせそうに，美しいやしの木が置かれていた。この木は30年以上も前，工事現場のコンクリート・スラブ用の穴のなかに捨てられたやしの種子が芽ぶいたもので，それ以来，地面に根を張り成長し続けてきた。個室は，居間とは対照的に狭い。子供用の個室は，2メートル×3メートル（ベッド，テーブル兼勉強机，肘掛椅子，小さな本棚），両親の部屋は3メートル×3メートルである。プルーヴェの住宅によく見られるのだが，衛生設備の一画は別扱いで独立した一式となっていて，石工事（この場合，耐力ユニットではない。）でつくられている。彼は小規模の建屋の屋根には，たいてい，多様なシステムの単一ブロックのシェルを用いるのだが，ここでは大版の木製パネルが使われた。木製パネルは，薄片の張合わせでできたもので，硬質かつ「釣竿のように，きわめてしなやか」である。そして，「単なる台架」のように，さまざまな種類の金属製柱廊の上に設置され，アルミ箔のテープで被い，留め金で固定されている。屋内側は，生のまま，むきだしになっている。

これは，清澄な簡素さという解答だ。この創造者の建築虚構の世界の特色が，明白に出されている。イザベル・ダ・コスタは，彼にこの家について語ってもらった。「私が説明することは，設計図には全く記載されていません。観察しているうちに分かったことですから。」と彼は明言する。「使用材料を生かす必要があったのです。木製パネルのしなやかさなど，手に取ってみなければ，想像さえつかないものです。それに，この屋根の流れも，設計図には全く描かれませんでした。この家のポイントは，屋根にあるというのに。あとは，内部に設置した間仕切でしかありません。」　　　　　　（翻訳：デルマス・柚紀子）

図面資料は，その作成者であるナンシーの建築家，イザベル・ダ・コスタの提供による。彼女は，(優れた)論文準備のために，死も間近にせまったプルーヴェに，数ヶ月間，頻繁に面会した。その論文の一部は，1984年6月発行のAMC誌，第4号に掲載されている。

JEAN PROUVÉ
Jean Prouvé House
Nancy, France
1954

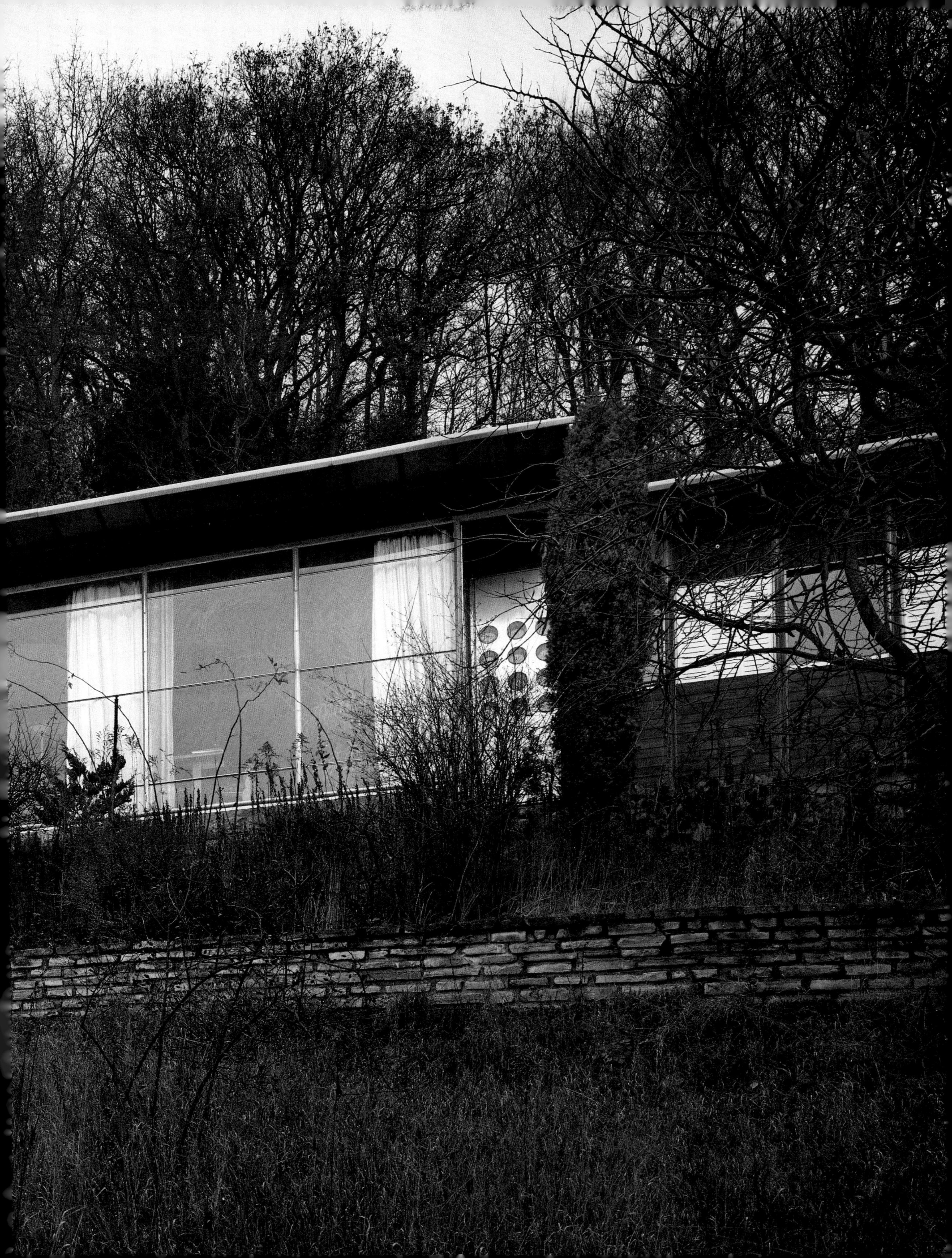

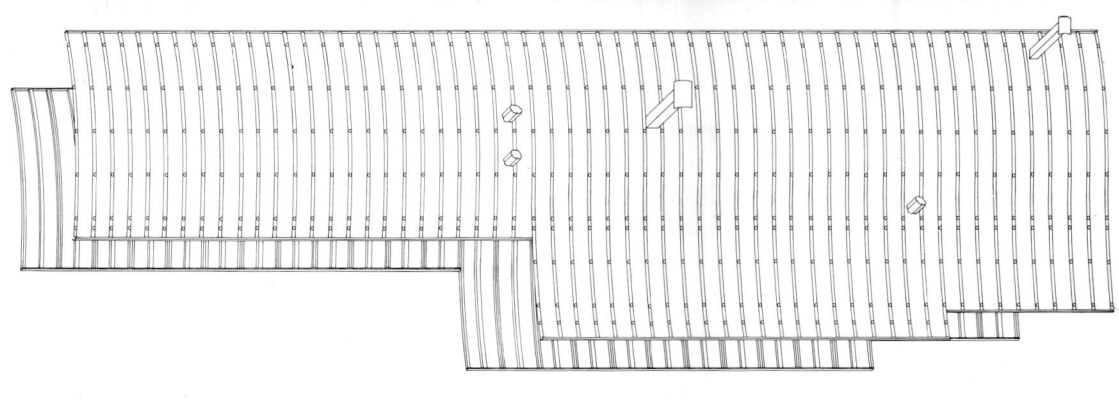

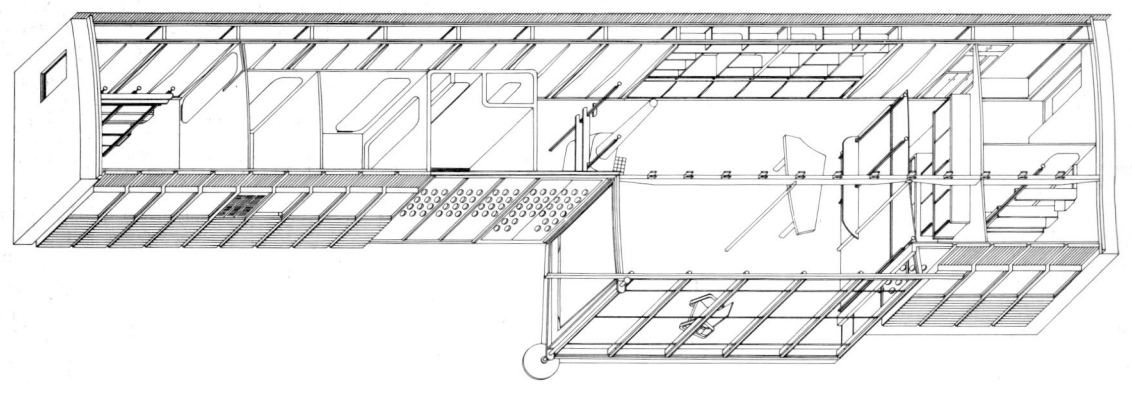

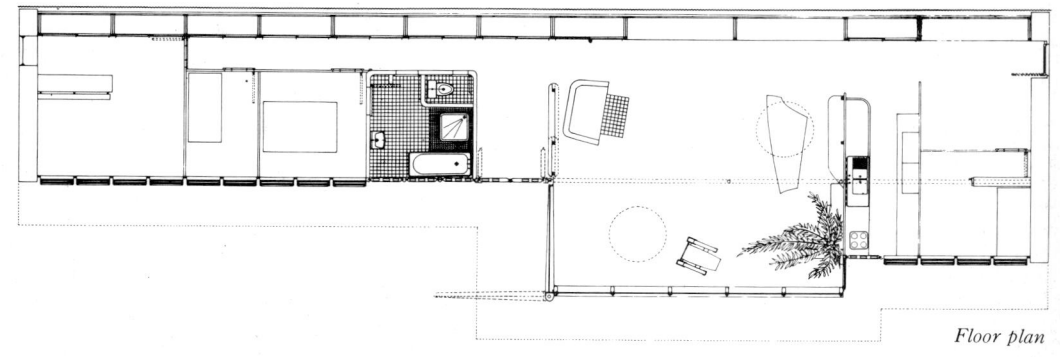

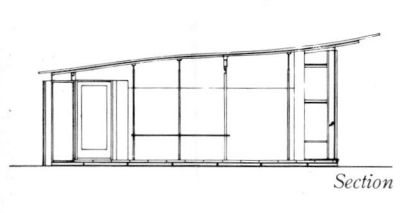

Section

Floor plan

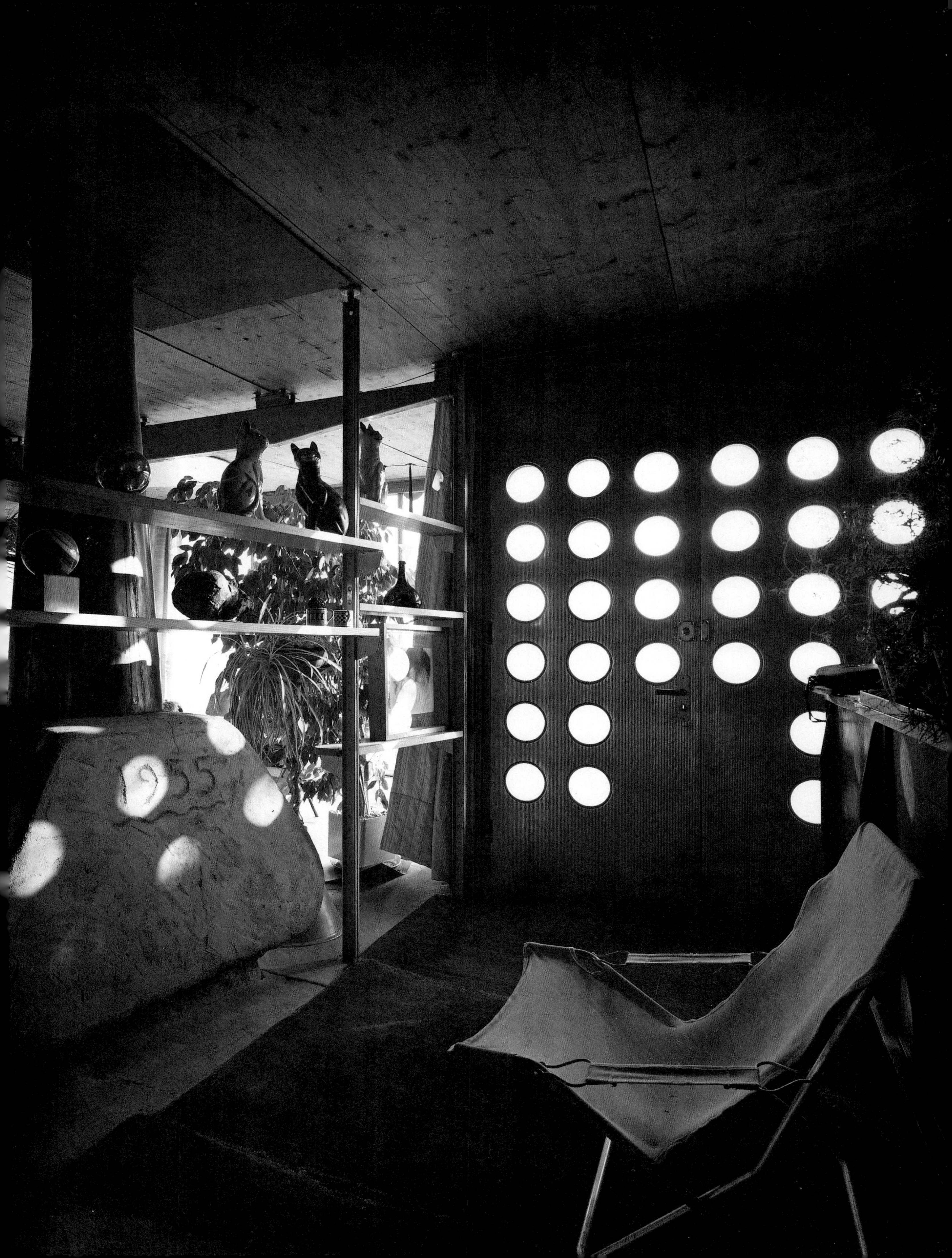
1955

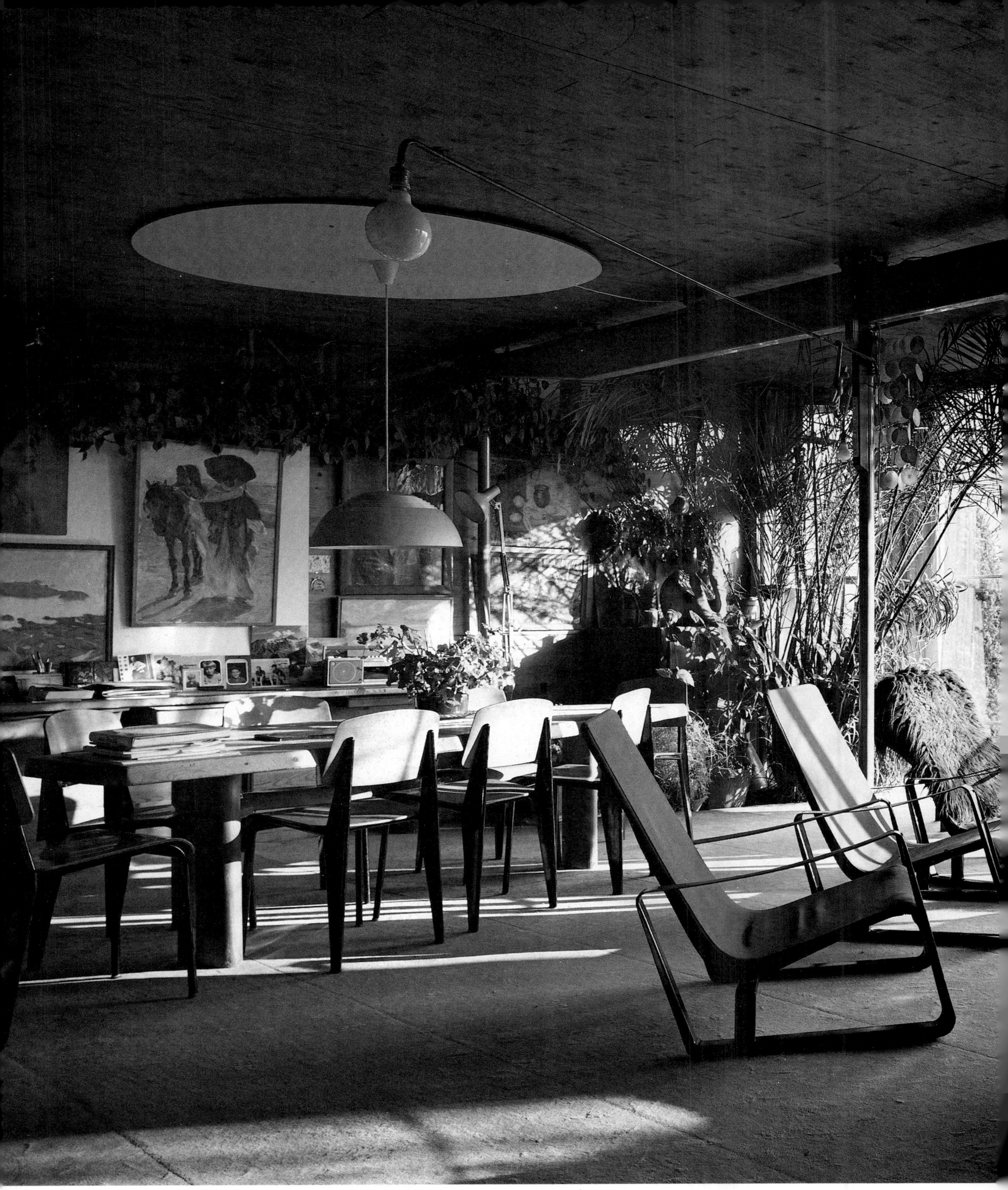

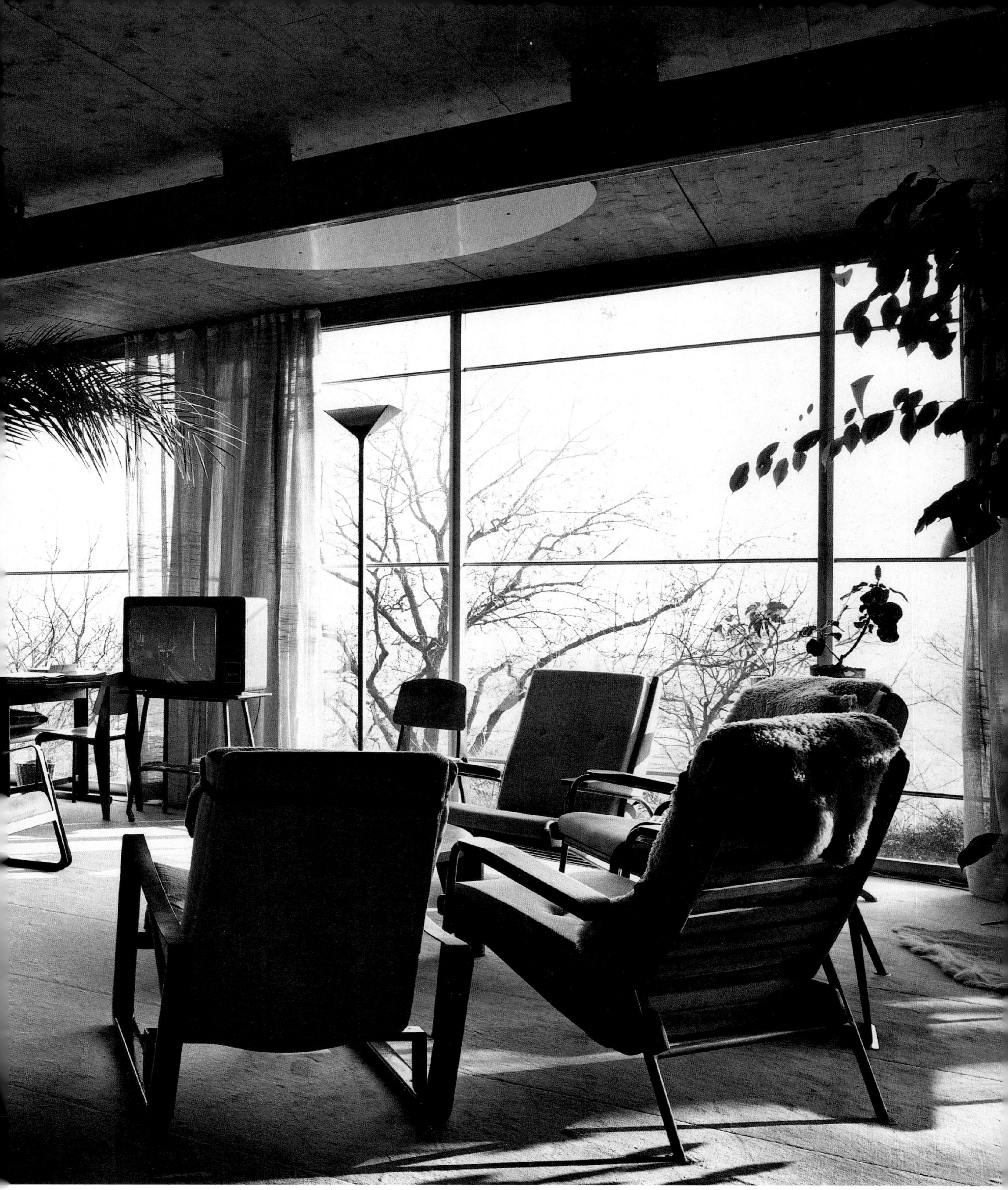

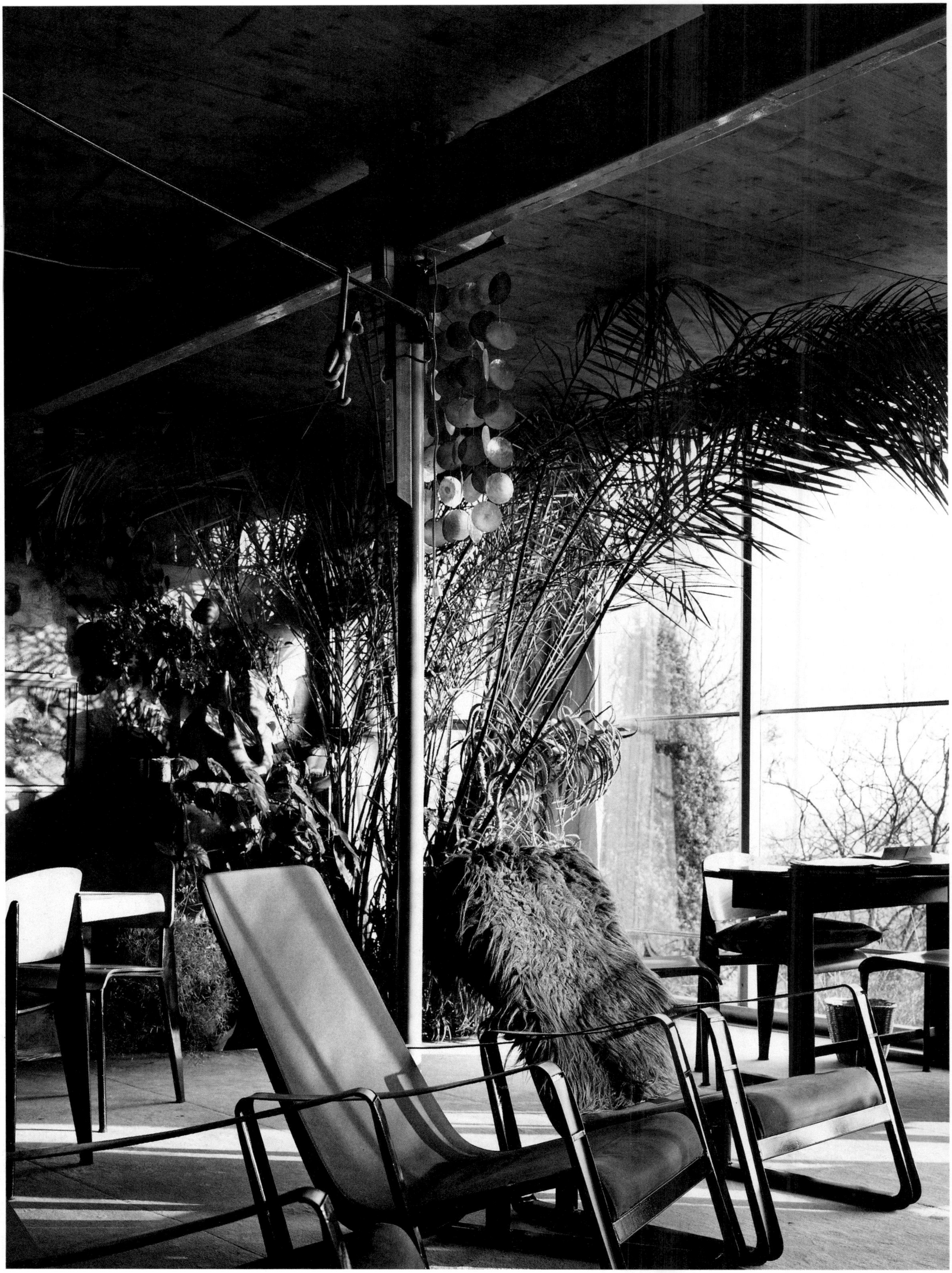

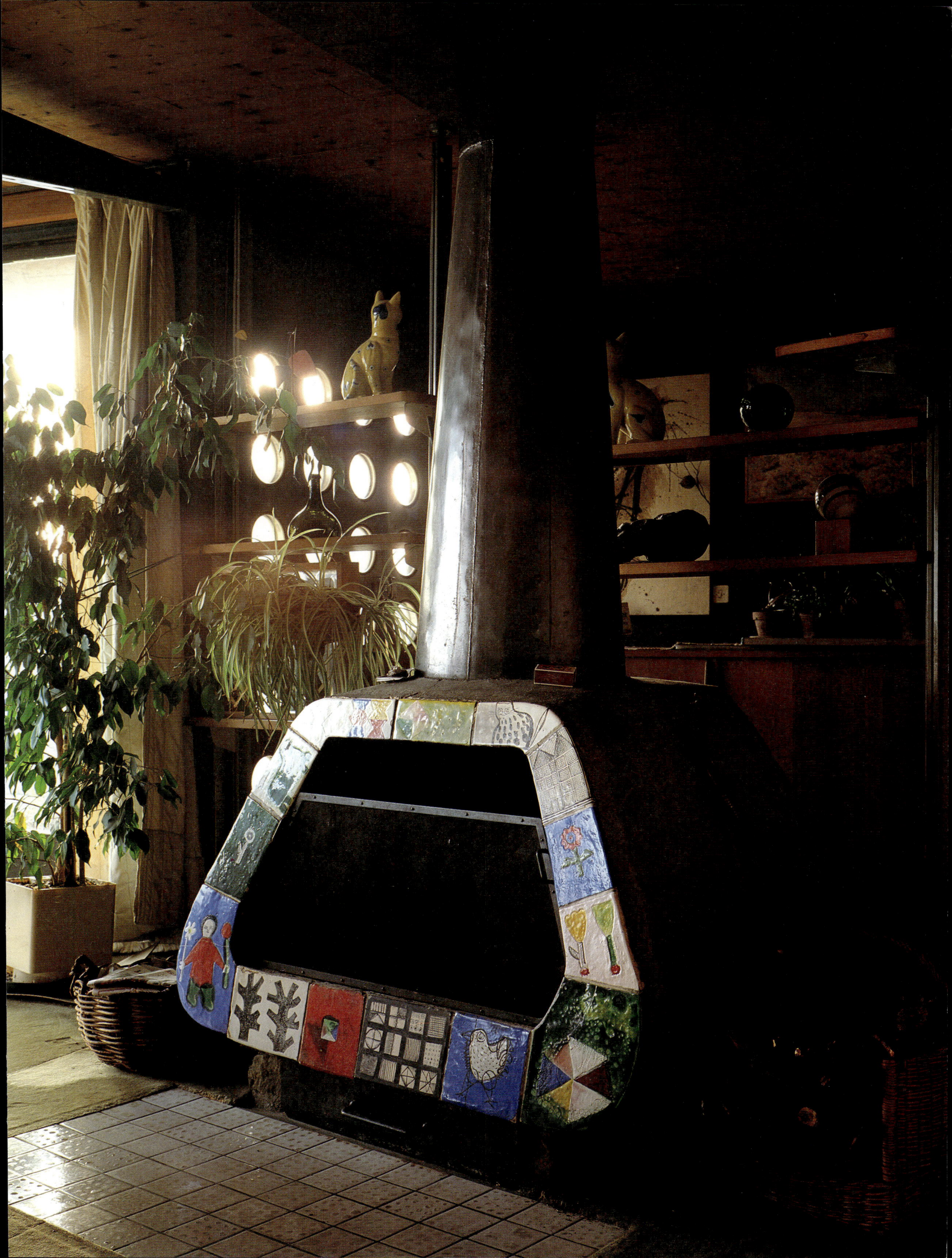

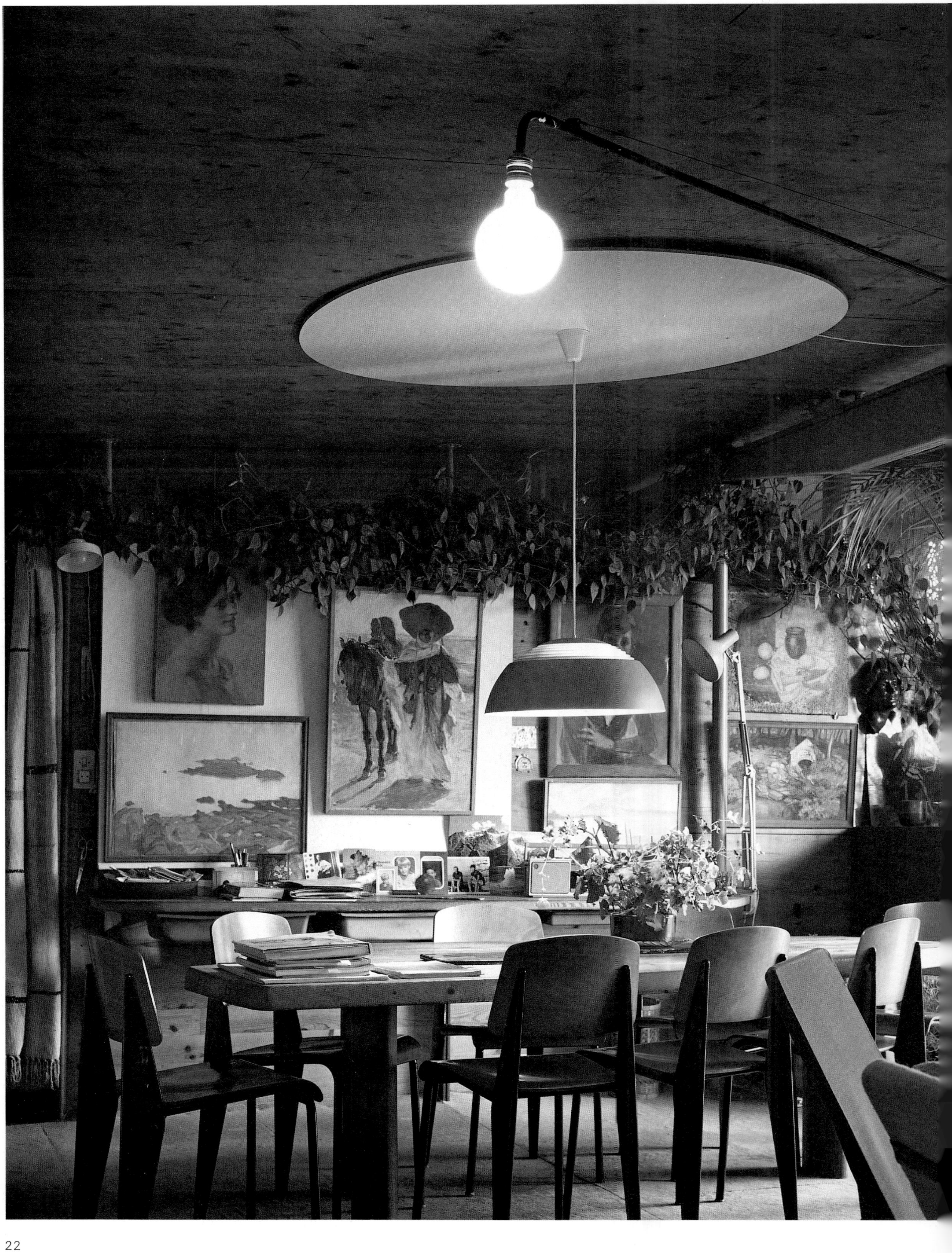

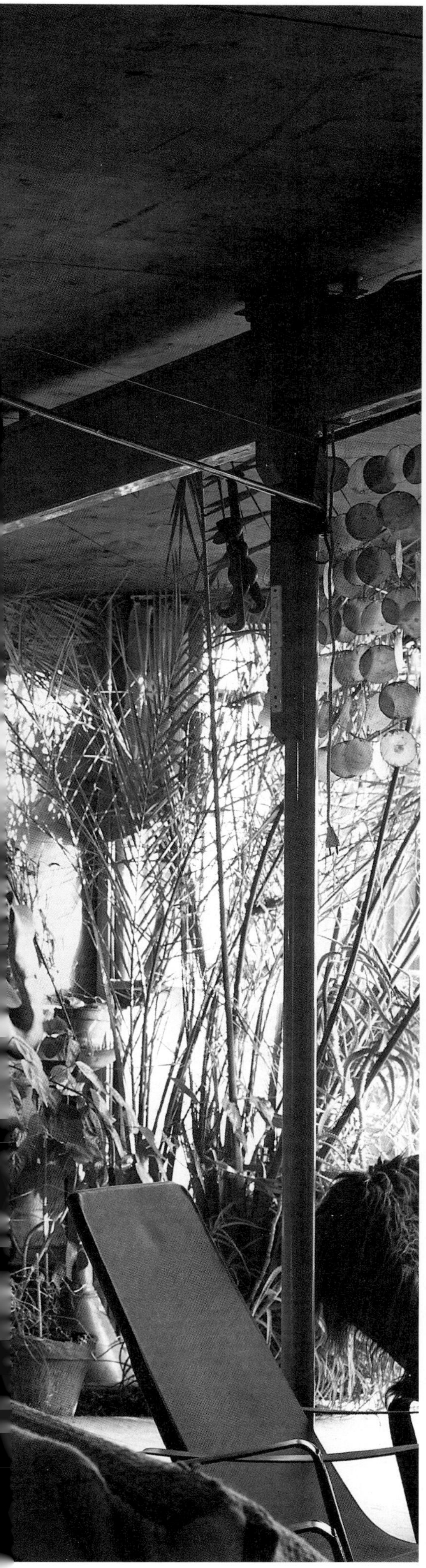

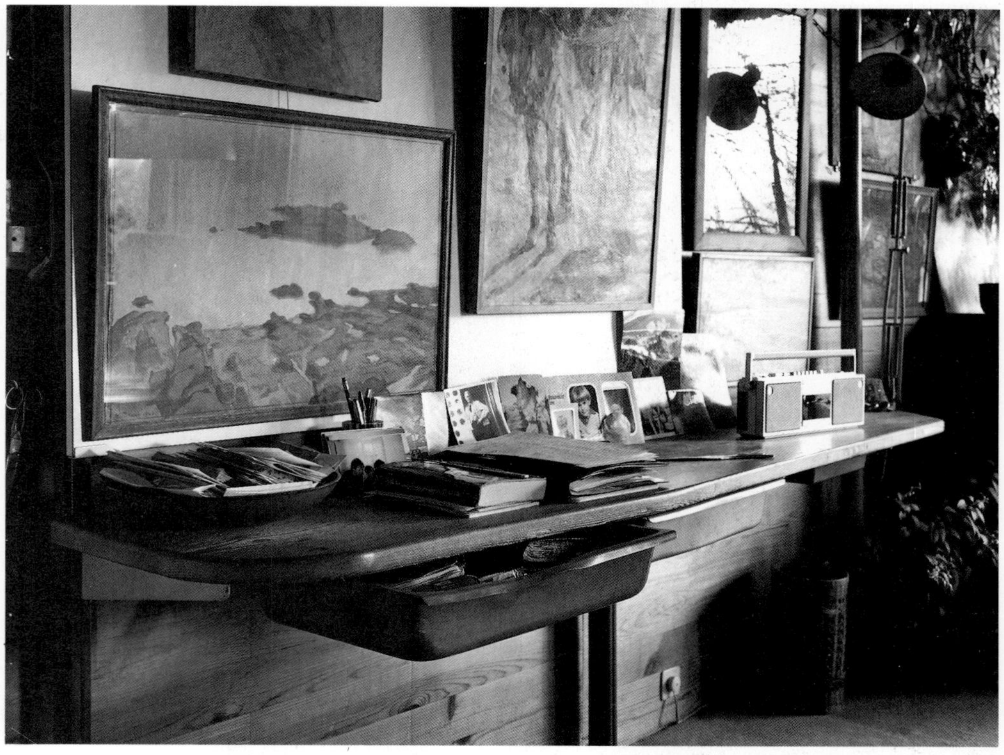

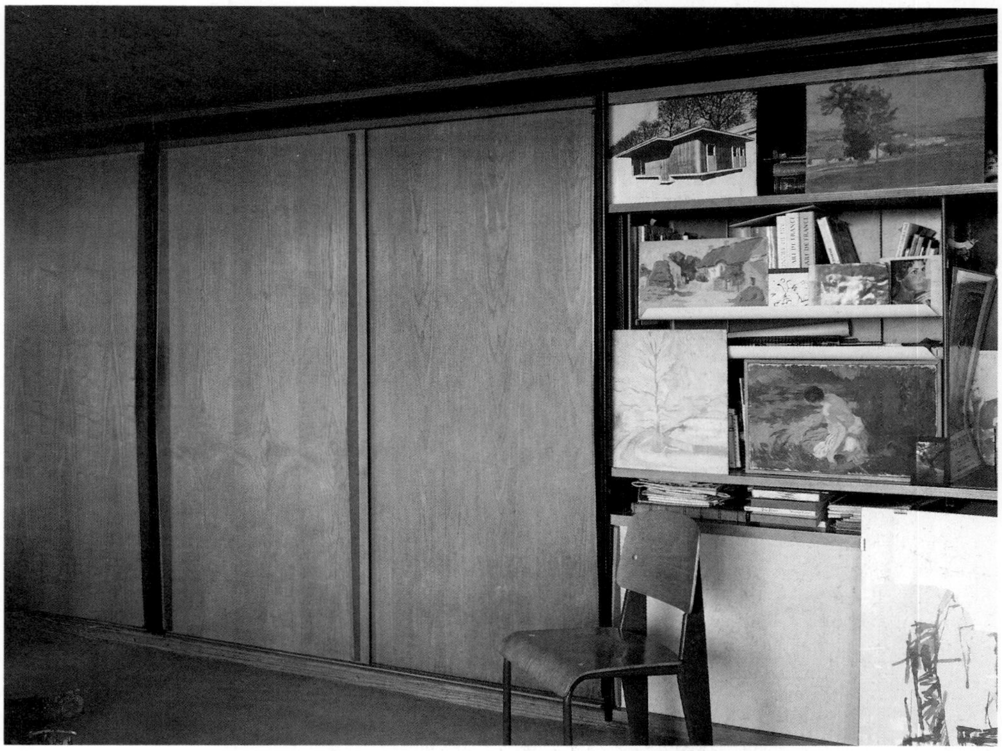

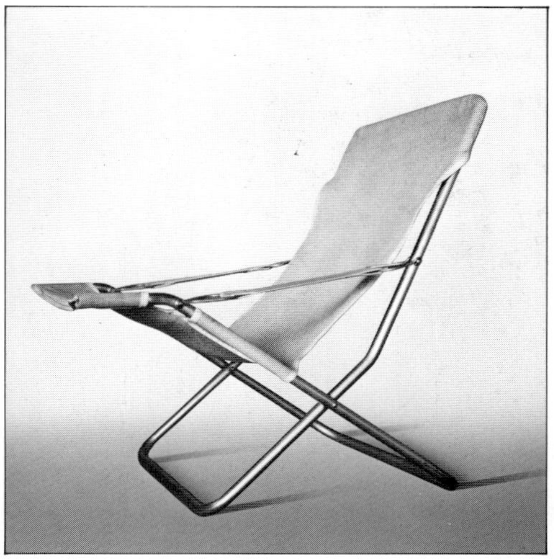

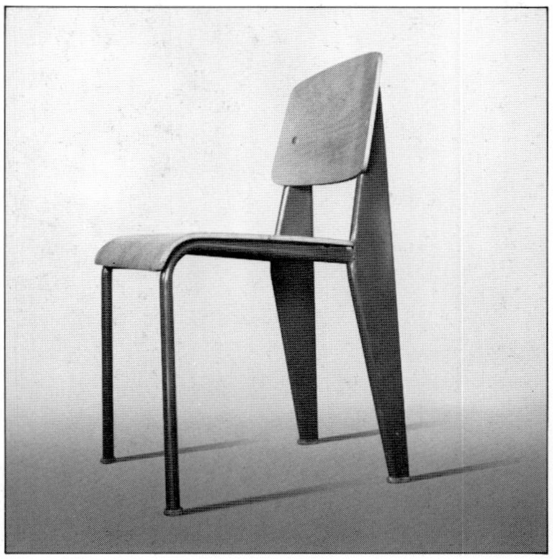

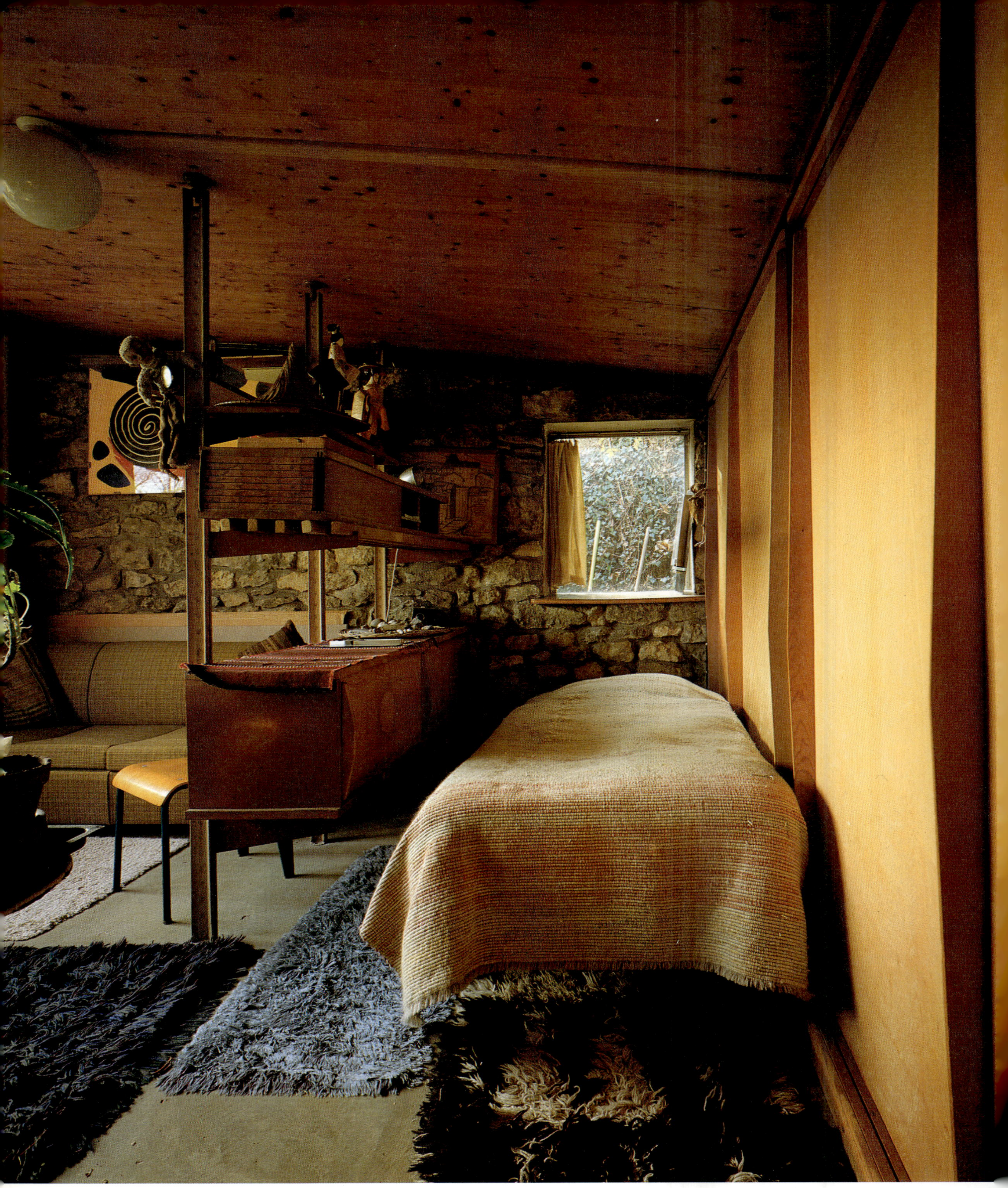

25

BRIAN A. MURPHY
BAM CONSTRUCTION/DESIGN INC
White Tower
Santa Monica, California
1985-86

Photos: W. Fiuii

A white 5-story cantilever from canyon floor attached to the slope with 4 bridges. House sits on footprint of existing structure to minimize damage to landscape.
 Circulation: all floors accessible from outside with decks for a.m. and p.m. sun.
 Decks and bridges of expanded metal grating to allow maximum solar penetration to lower floors.
 Wood floor joists act as white reflectors of p.m. sunlight. Thin cables to minimize shadows.
 Walking path by Tim Murphy made of rubble from previous structure. Landscape of indigenous plants all volunteers. Special thanks to Craig Krumwiede.
BAM

4本のブリッジによって傾斜地と結ばれたキャニオン・フロアから、白い5階建てが張り出している。住宅は既設の脚部の上に立ち、ランドスケープへの侵害を最小限なものにとどめている。
　サーキュレーションに関していえば、すべての階が日中陽光の下にあり、屋外デッキからアクセス可能。
　エクスパンデッド・メタル格子のデッキとブリッジは、最大限に太陽光を落とそうとする配慮から。木材床が反射板。午後の陽光を白く効射させるものとして働き、細いケーブルは日影を最小限度にするものとして。
　ティム・マーフィーによる小径は、先在した構造物の栗石でつくられた。土地に固有な植物をもつランドスケープは、すべて自生のものである。クレイグ・クルムウィーデ氏にはとくに謝意を表したい。

Consultants: Joseph Perazelli, structural; Susa Frenz, Barbara Helton-Berg, Seth Reed, Kaye Secomb, architectural consultants at BAM
General contractor: BAM Construction/Design Inc.

Floor plans

LEVEL 5

Site plan

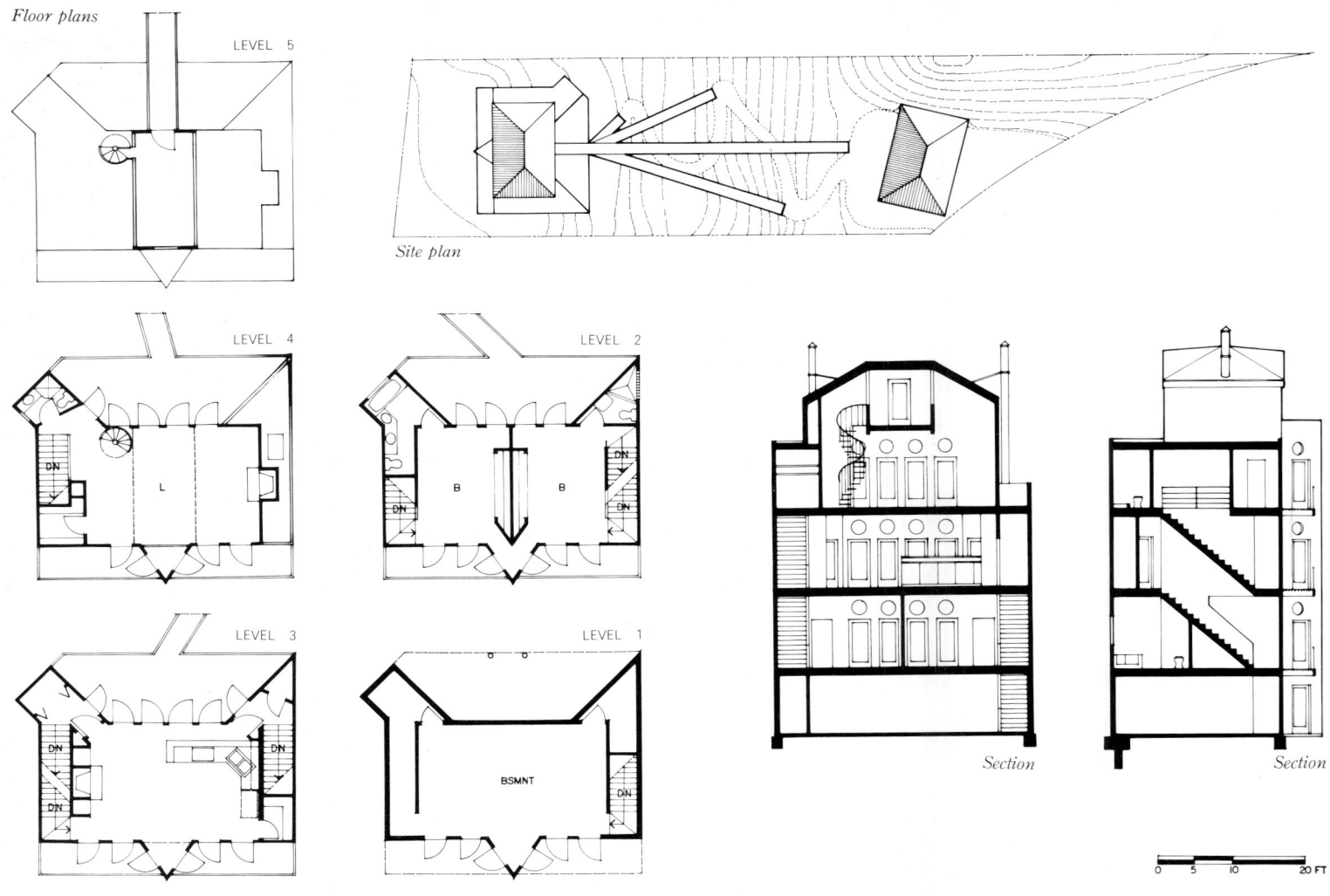

LEVEL 4
LEVEL 2
LEVEL 3
LEVEL 1

Section *Section*

0 5 10 20 FT

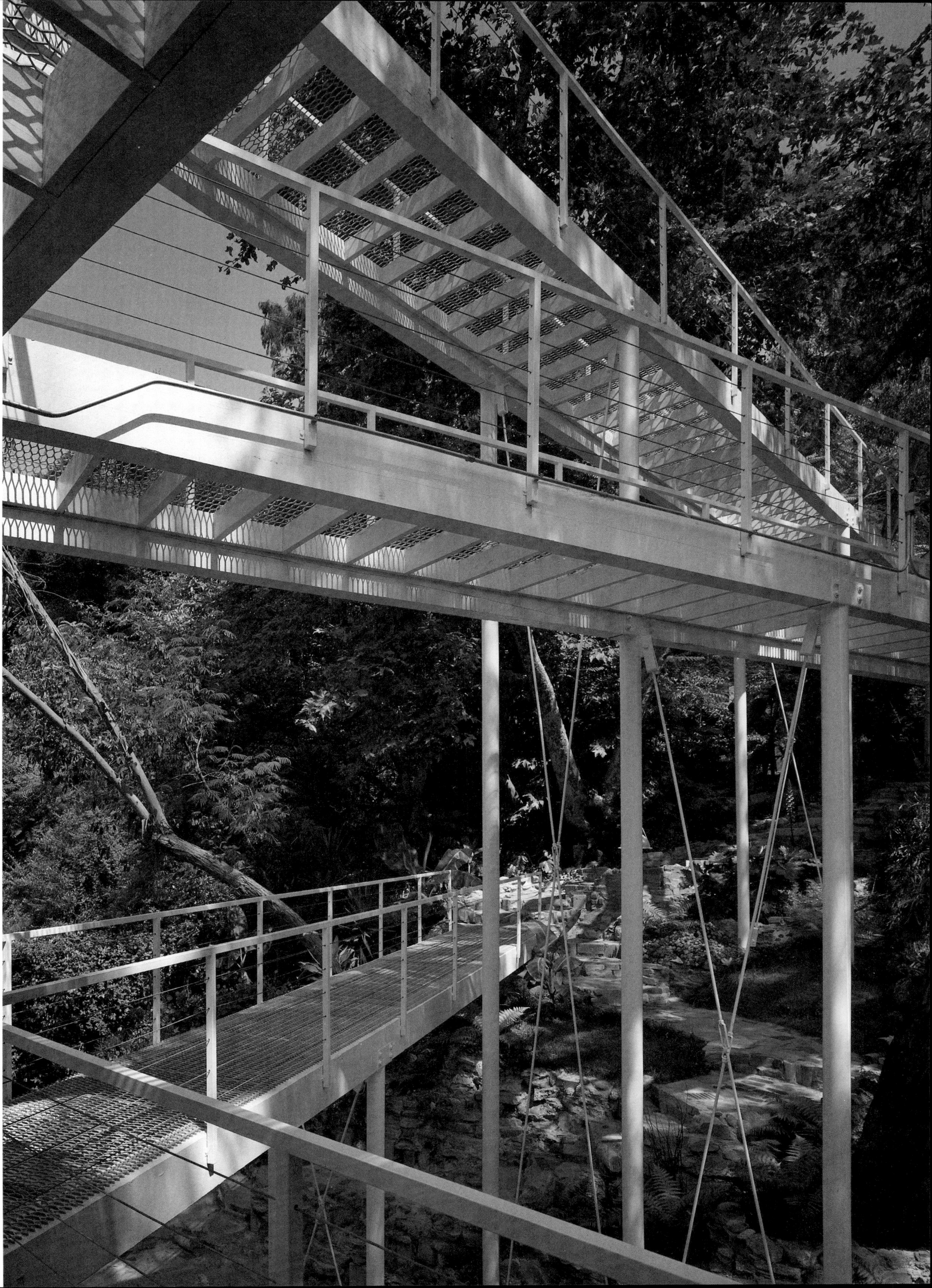

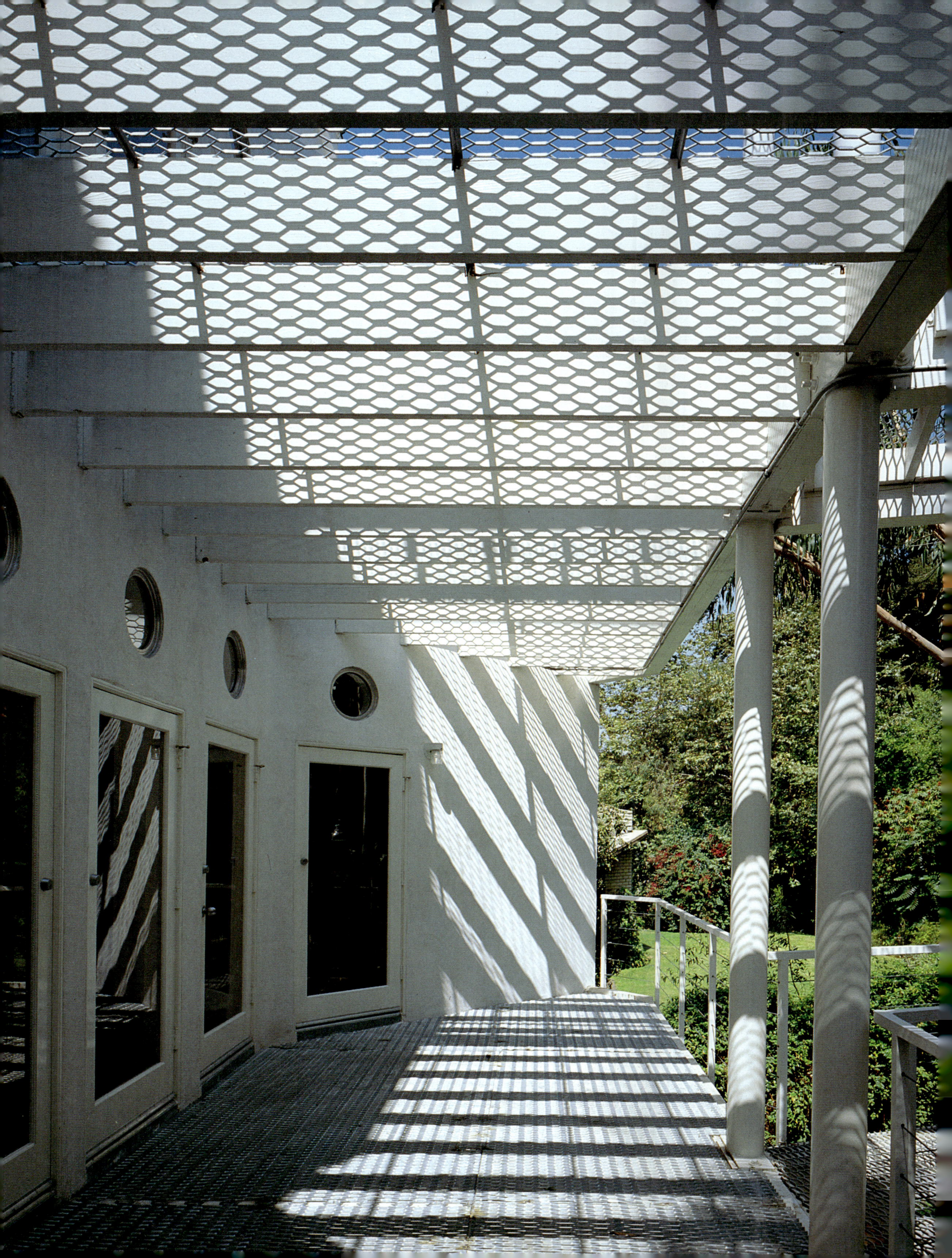

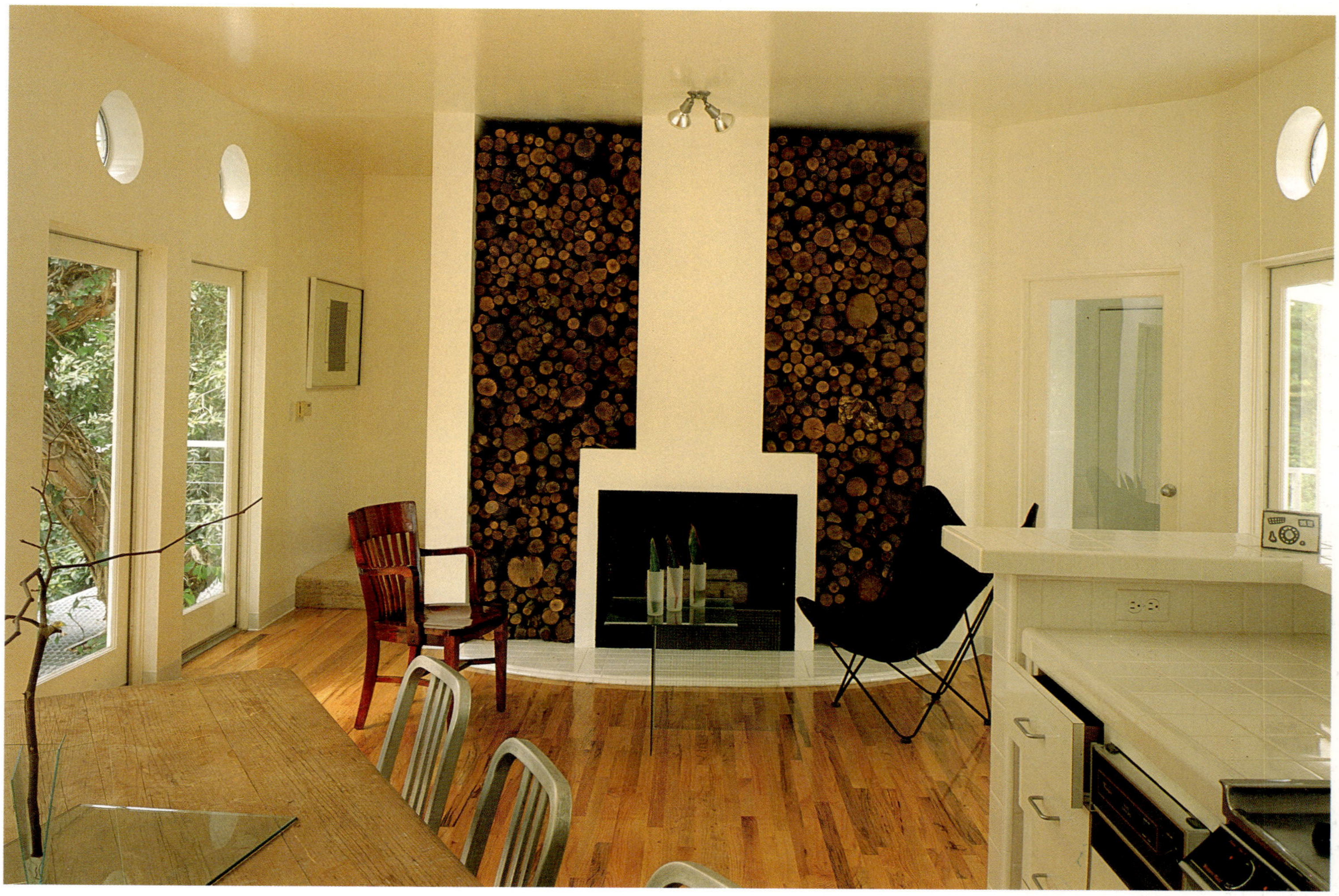

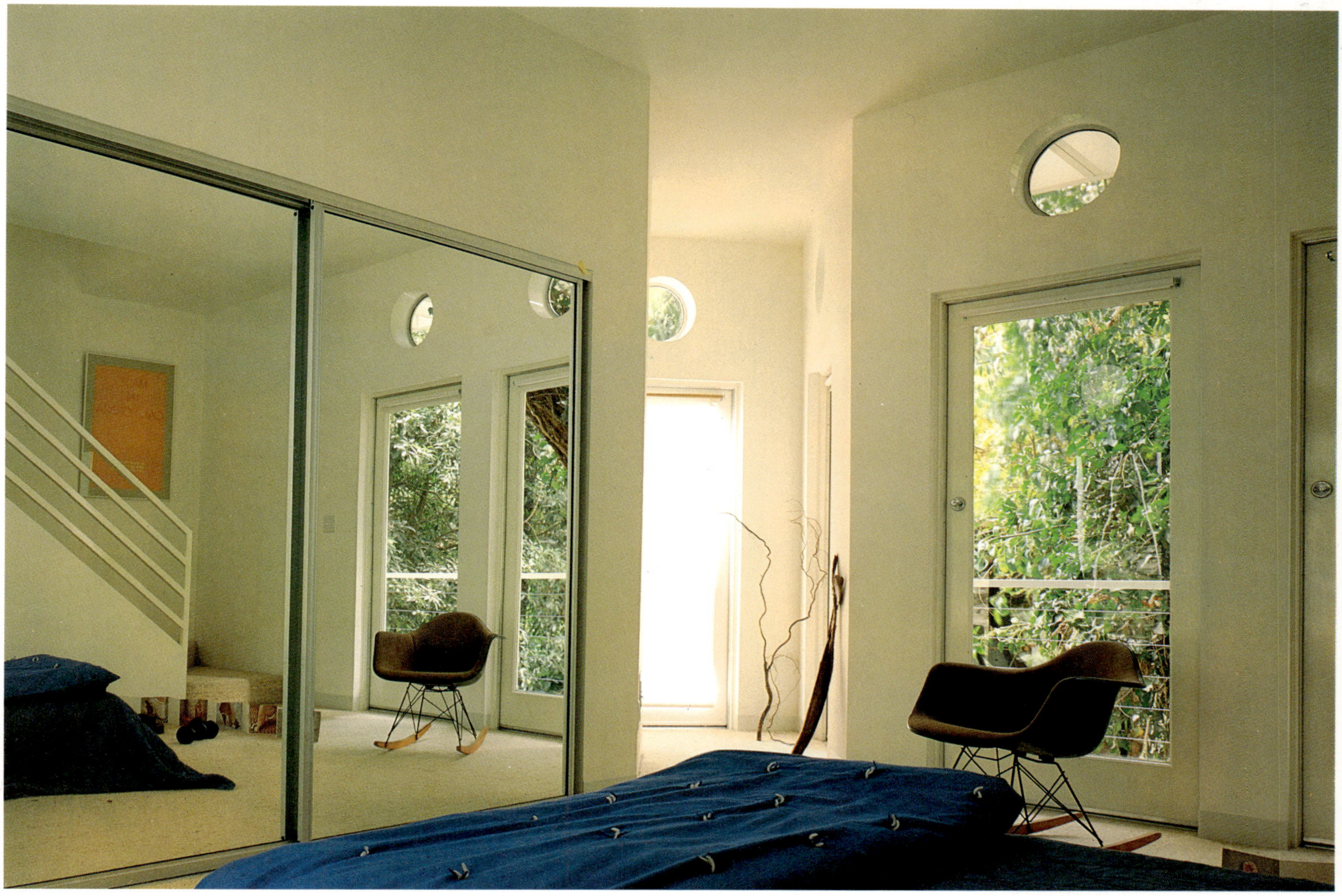

32

33

TOD WILLIAMS & ASSOCIATES
Tod Williams and Robert McAnulty
Eisenberg Residence
Southport, New York
1984-85

Photos: W. Fujii

Floor plan with site

The program is a summer home to become a place to retire for a couple with grown children.

The house was conceived as three separate building blocks which identified three uses; these were the central room, the stair tower, and the bedroom wing. Each block is essentially the same kind of construction (wood frame) and the same color tone but has been finished with different materials...stucco, metal paneling and wood.

The first volume (living, dining, and kitchen) is a half cube, creating a room of grand proportions with a coffered ceiling and pilastered walls. The corners are glazed and the highly structured room suggests both an idealized pavilion and a free plan. Special pieces of cabinetwork were designed to bind yet differentiate the various functions of the block.

The stair tower is both the middle block used for entry, a stairway and a bridge. A red metal canopy over hangs the front door. Just before entering, one can catch a glimpse of the great room's ceiling. It is here where one realizes that all living functions are at the upper level on the piano nobile. Just past the front door on the right a long shelf supports a tall mirror set on an angle. Its reflection causes the axial space to become dynamic and gives a second glimpse of the great room above. A shaft with multiple perforations is symbolically an isolated tower and the stairwell itself. All vertical movement and all horizontal movement is through this space.

The third volume is more conventionally rendered. At the lowest level is the entry with garage and storage, at the middle level is the master bedroom with dressing, bath and laundry, and at the uppermost level are a small living room, guest bedrooms, baths and balconies. The feeling here is of intimacy and warmth and views from these spaces are more personal.

Outside there is a walled entry courtyard carved from the site and above it the deck with pool set not toward the grand view but to the south where it orients itself to the presence of a small pond.

Winner of an AIA Distinguished Architecture Award for 1986, we believe that this house defies every categorization on a simple response. This is a house which celebrates nature by presenting a subtle opposition. Its forms are simple, clearly manmade ones; its details reflect a clarity of thought and thoughtful attention. The first gesture is one of strength but the memory that persists is of delicacy and pertinance.

Consultants: Frank Taffel and Associates, structural; A.E. Bye and Associates, landscape
General contractor: Kurt Anoreassen Construction

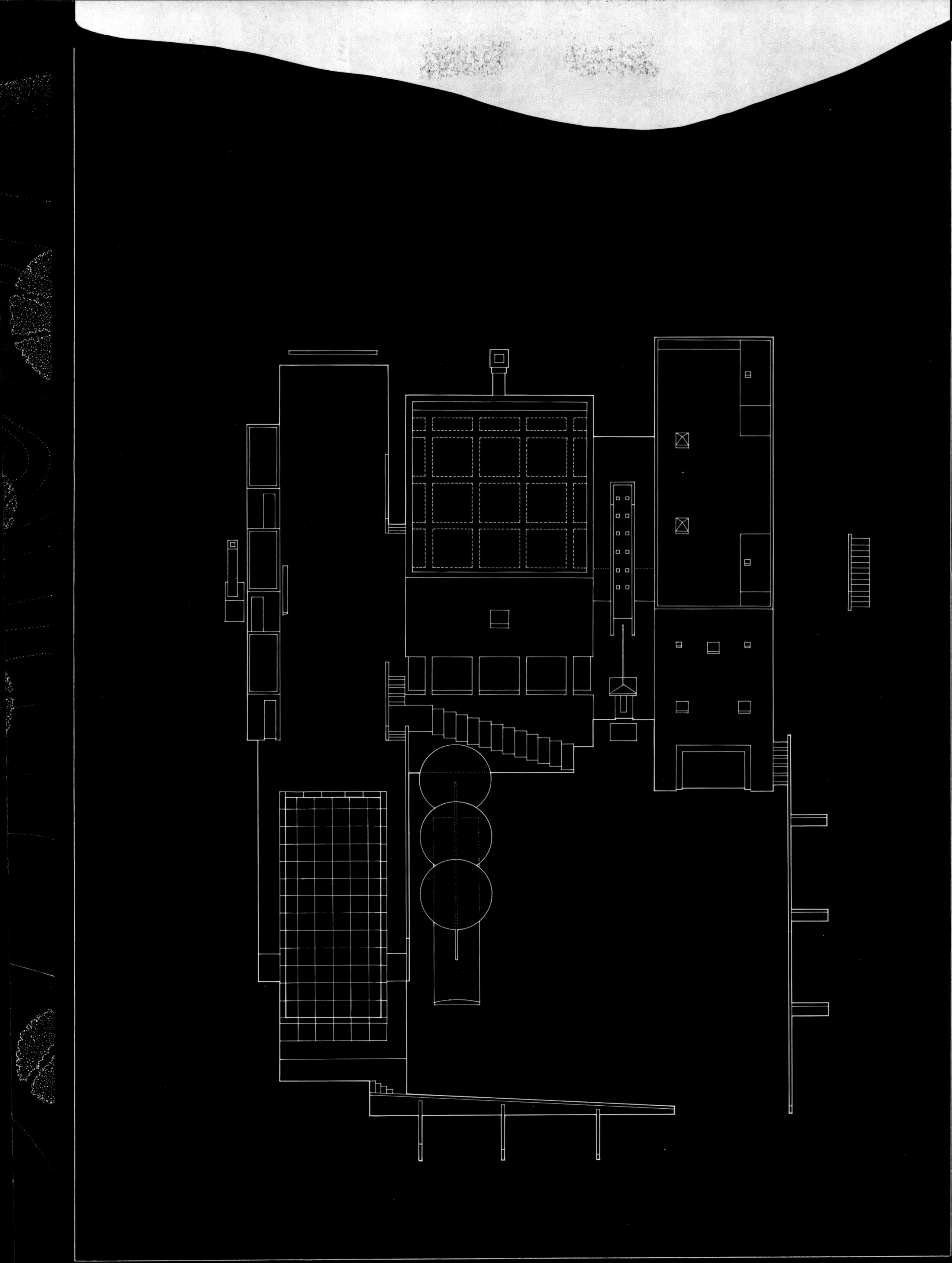

プログラムは，成人した子供たちと夫婦の老後の場所となる夏期住居である。
　住宅は3つの分離された建物として考えられた。それぞれの建物は3つの異なった用途をアイデンティファイする。すなわち，中心となる部屋，階段のタワー，そしてベッドルームのウィングである。本来的に各ブロックは同種の構造（木枠組）で同じ色調をもつが，スタッコ，メタルパネル，木という異なった材料で仕上げられている。
　第1のヴォリューム（リヴィング，ダイニング，キッチン）は半立方体で，格間天井とピラスターをもつ壁面で構成されたグランド・プロポーションの単一部屋をつくりだしている。隅部にはガラスが嵌めこまれ，高度に明快な構造をもった部屋は，理想化されたパビリオンの自由なプランを暗示する。特別に造作された家具類が，ブロックの異なった機能を差異付けながらも結びつけている。
　階段タワーは入口としても使用される仲介的なブロックで，階段とブリッジをもつ。赤の金属キャノピーは正面ドアの上にせり出している。建物に入る寸前に，人は主室の天井を一瞥できるようにもなっている。あらゆる居住機能が上階のピアノ・ノービレのレヴェルにあることを気づかせるのもここである。正面ドアを入るとすぐ右手に細長い棚が丈高い鏡のセットを支えているのを人は見つけるだろう。それによって，軸性をもつ空間がダイナミックなものとなり，上階の主室をふたたび一瞥し得る仕掛けだ。複数に貫通するシャフトが，象徴的に，分離されたタワーと井戸状になった階段それ自身となっている。すべての垂直的な動き，すべての水平的な動きは，この空間によって生じてゆく。
　第3のヴォリュームは，より因習的に考案されて

いるといってよい。最下レヴェルにはガレージと倉庫をもつ入口，中間レヴェルはドレッシングルーム付きのマスターベッドルーム，浴室，洗濯室，そして最上レヴェルには小規模なリヴィングルームとゲスト用のベッドルーム，浴室，バルコニーがある。ここには，親密さや暖かさの感覚があり，これらの空間からの眺めはすこぶる個人的な色彩に彩られている。

外部には，敷地を穿ってつくられた壁面に囲われている入口の中庭があり，その上方にはプールをもつデッキがしつらえられている。そこからは壮大な眺望は開けないが，小さな池のある南への眺望が確保された。

1986年度のAIA建築優秀賞を受賞したとき，私たちは，この住宅が単純な反応がつきもののカテゴリー化を拒むものであることを確信した。これは微妙な対立性を表現することによって自然を祝祭する住宅にほかならない。その形態は単純で明快な人工的なそれであり，またそのディテールは思想や思索的配慮の明晰さを反映する。主要な身振りは強靭そのものである一方，そこに生残する記憶はデリケートでかつ適切なものである。

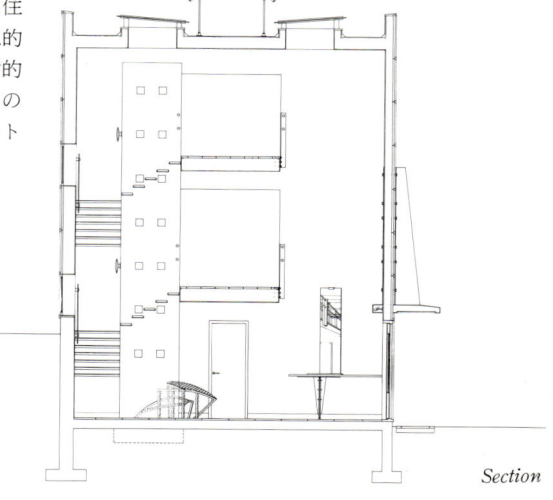

Section

38

39

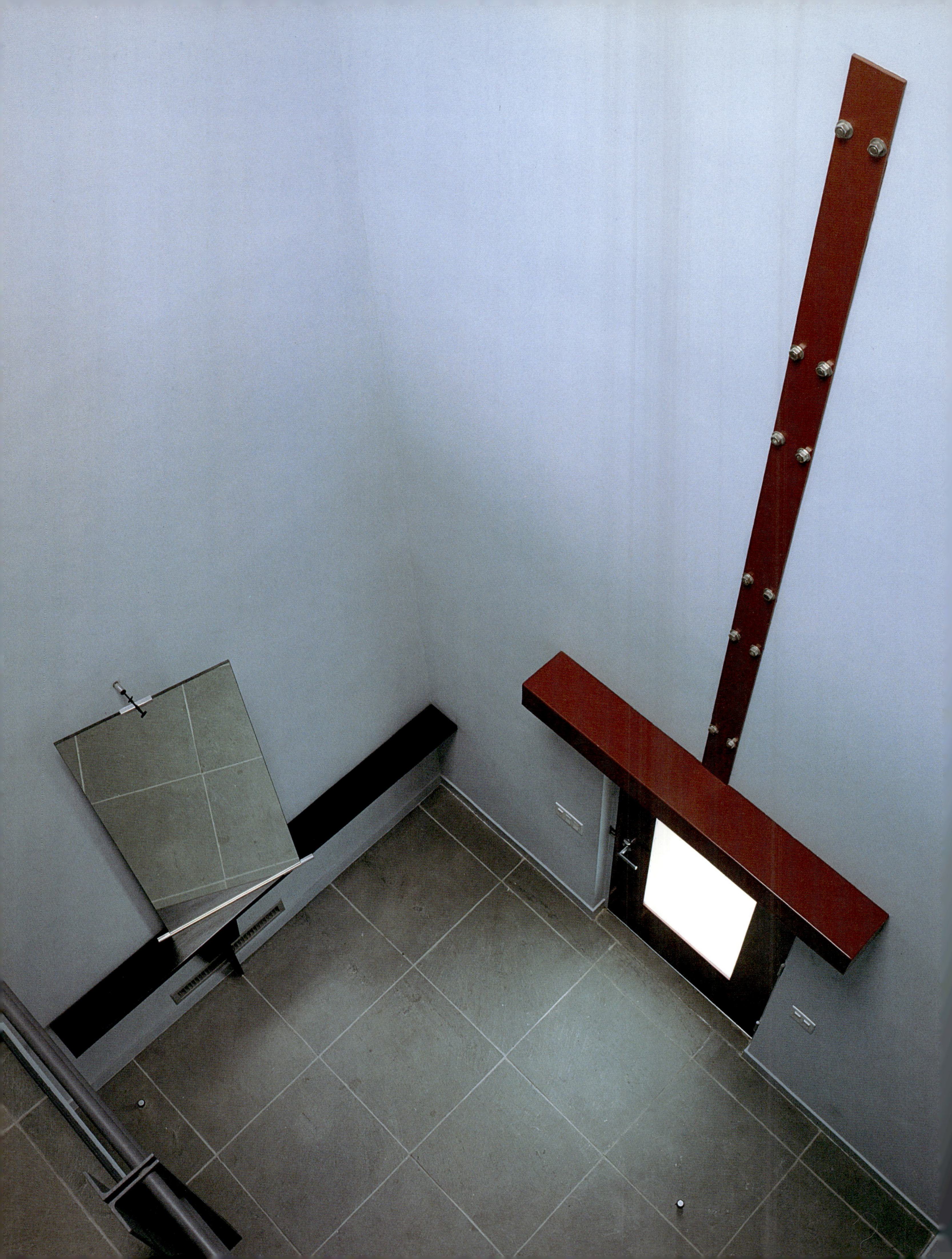

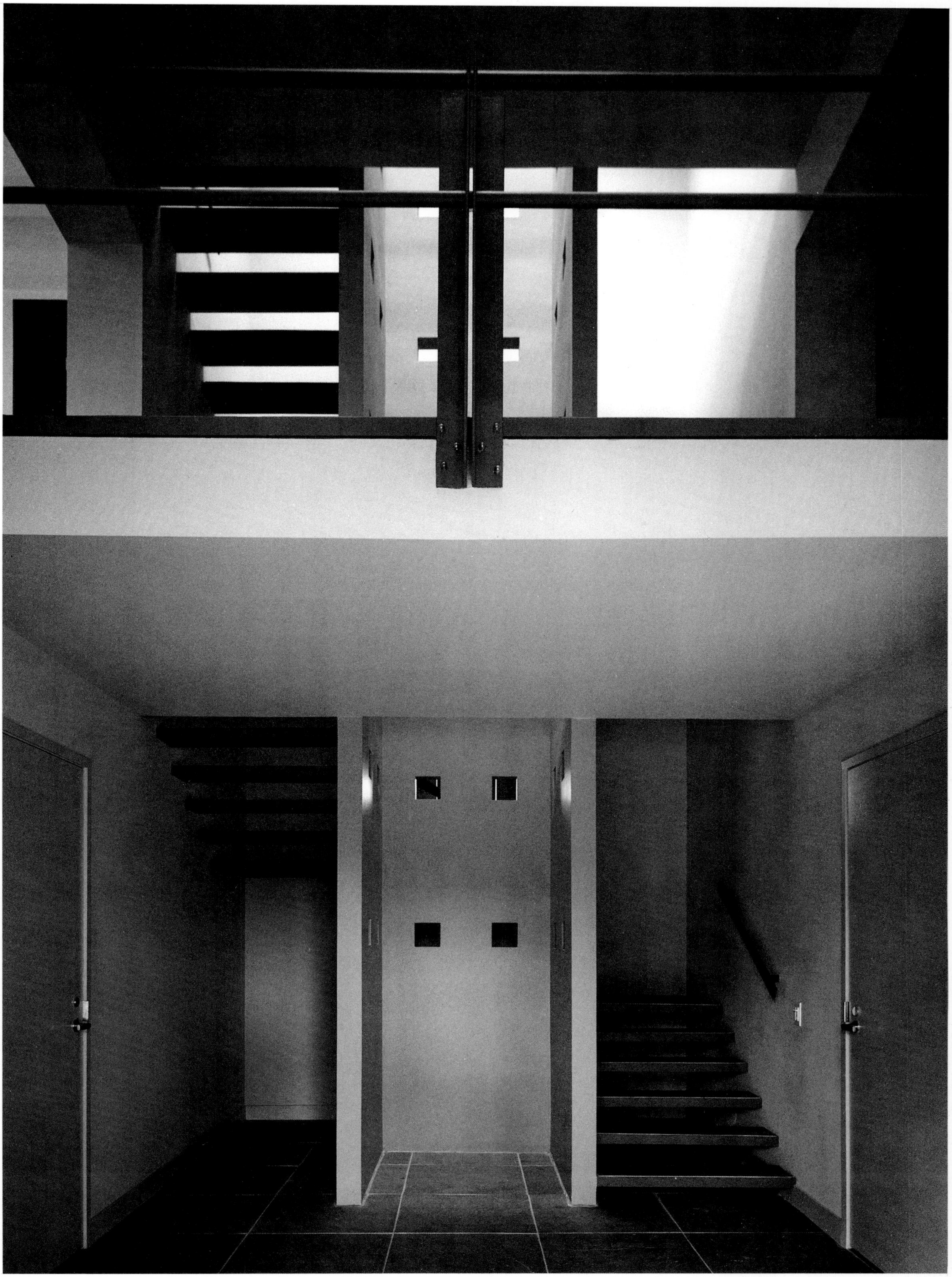

ANTHONY AMES
A Garden Pavilion
Atlanta, Georgia
1980-86

Photos: W. Fujii

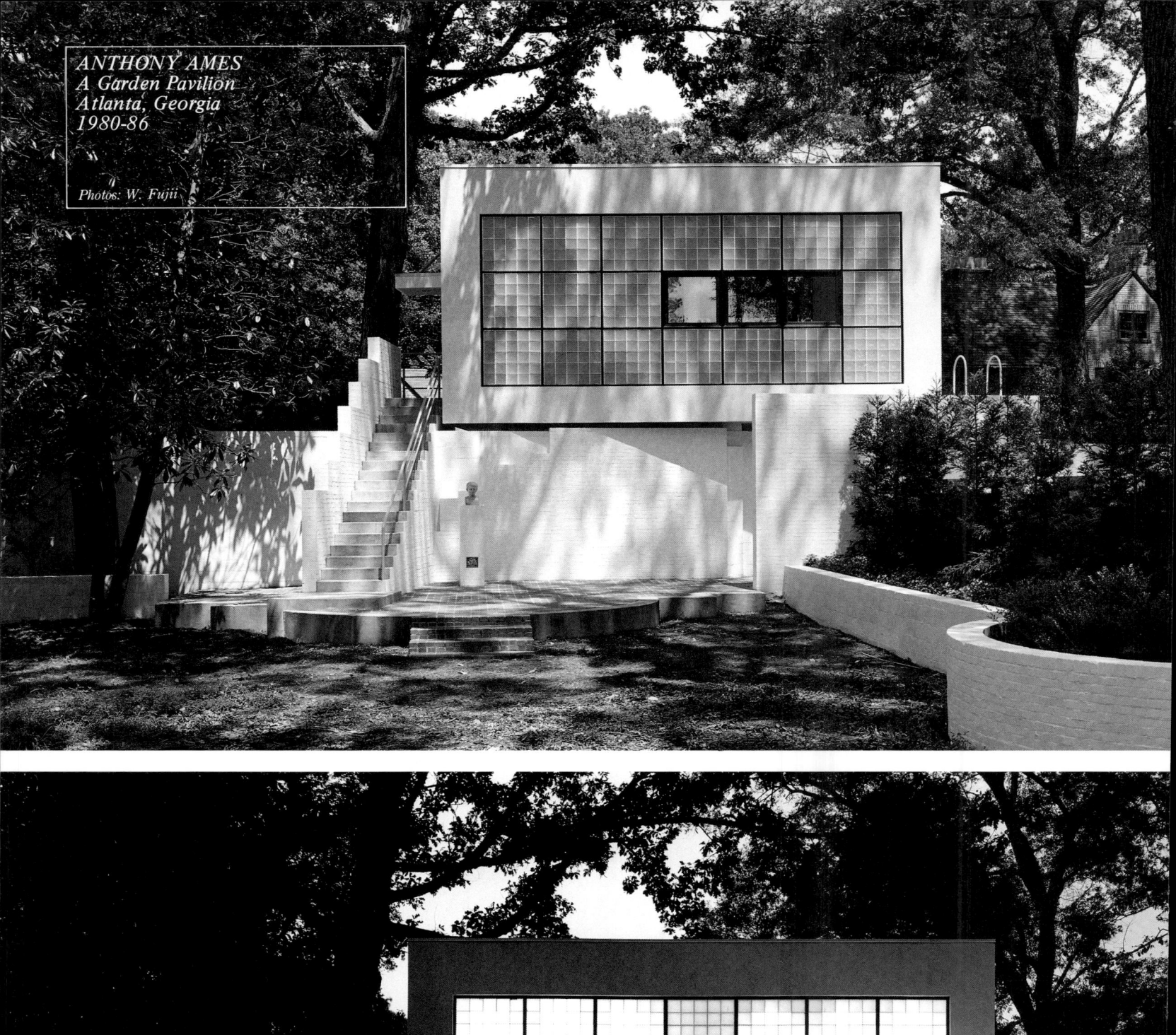

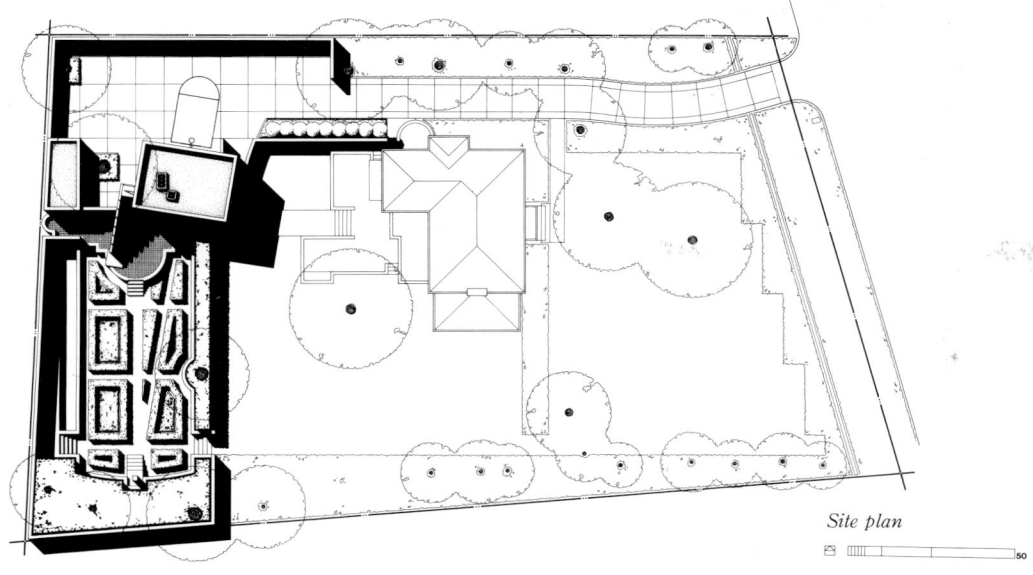

Site plan

家庭がもつ忙しく慌ただしい混乱から肉体的にも精神的にも避難したい，そんな場所を求めるクライアントの要求にしたがって，既存の住宅の背後に付属する建築として，この書斎／ゲストハウスはつくられた。パビリオンを哲学的に探究することによって，慎重な観察者を刺激し，喜ばせる細部の強度が獲得されている。

建物は，先在する住宅の確固としたグリッドから振られ，なおかつピロティ上に立ち上げ（それによってシェルター化された駐車場がつくられる），周囲の環境との物理的・精神的断続が試みられた。2つの主立面は，まったく異なって扱われている。やや閉鎖的で公共性をもつ中庭側のファサード，そこには学者が退屈しないようにバスケットの輪がとりつけられている。もうひとつは木洩れ日を捕らえる庭園に向けられた半透明のガラス壁，「巨大な細胞質の幕」となったファサードである。

この控えめで露出度の少ない箱の内部に，密実なコアの方向性によってより大きな先在する住宅を参照したプライヴェイトな領域がある。件のコアは，オープンプランの中におけるその形象的特質によって孤立したオブジェとしても，また本来の位置から動いてしまった，反転された空間のエッジとして貢献するためにつくられたポケットとしても読むことが可能だ。図としての建物／地としての建物といった都市プランニング的観点への参照は，全体構造物のもつ形象的特質によって反復されてゆく。

3面で理想的な空間を境界づけるポケットの緊密でコンパクトな形態や，この密実で自立したコアは，プログラムの機能的な要求を充たしている。

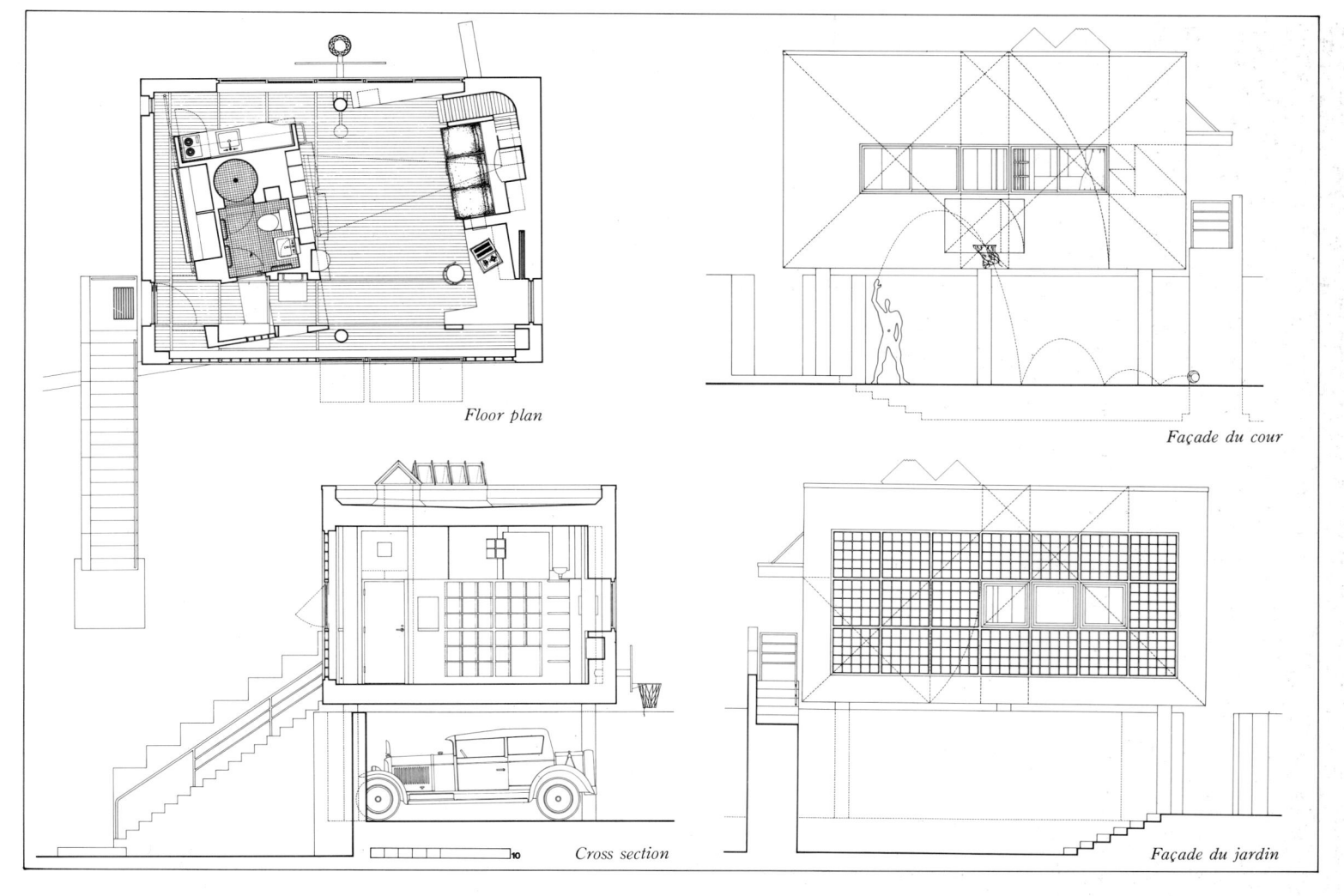

The client's need for a physical and mental retreat from the numerous distractions of a busy household led to the creation of this study/guest-house as an ancillary structure behind the existing house. The pavilion's philosophical pursuits allowed for an intensity of detail which stimulates and rewards the careful observer.

The structure is rotated off the established grid of the residence and then elevated on pilotis (creating a sheltered car park) to dissociate it physically and spiritually from its surroundings. The two major facades are then treated quite differently: a rather closed public courtyard facade, with a basketball hoop to engage the weary scholar, and "une grande toile cellulaire," a translucent wall of glass facing into the garden, capturing the sunlight as it filters through the trees.

Within this spare and relatively unrevealing box is a private domain which refers back to the larger residence through the orientation of its dense core. This core can be read both as an object isolated by its figural qualities in an open plan or as poche creating and serving as edge for the negative space from which it has been removed. These references to aspects of urban planning — building as figure vs. building as ground — are reiterated by the figural qualities of the entire structure.

The tightly compacted form of the poche that borders the ideal space on three sides and this dense free-standing core accomodate the functional necessities of the program.

Floor plan

Façade du cour

Cross section

Façade du jardin

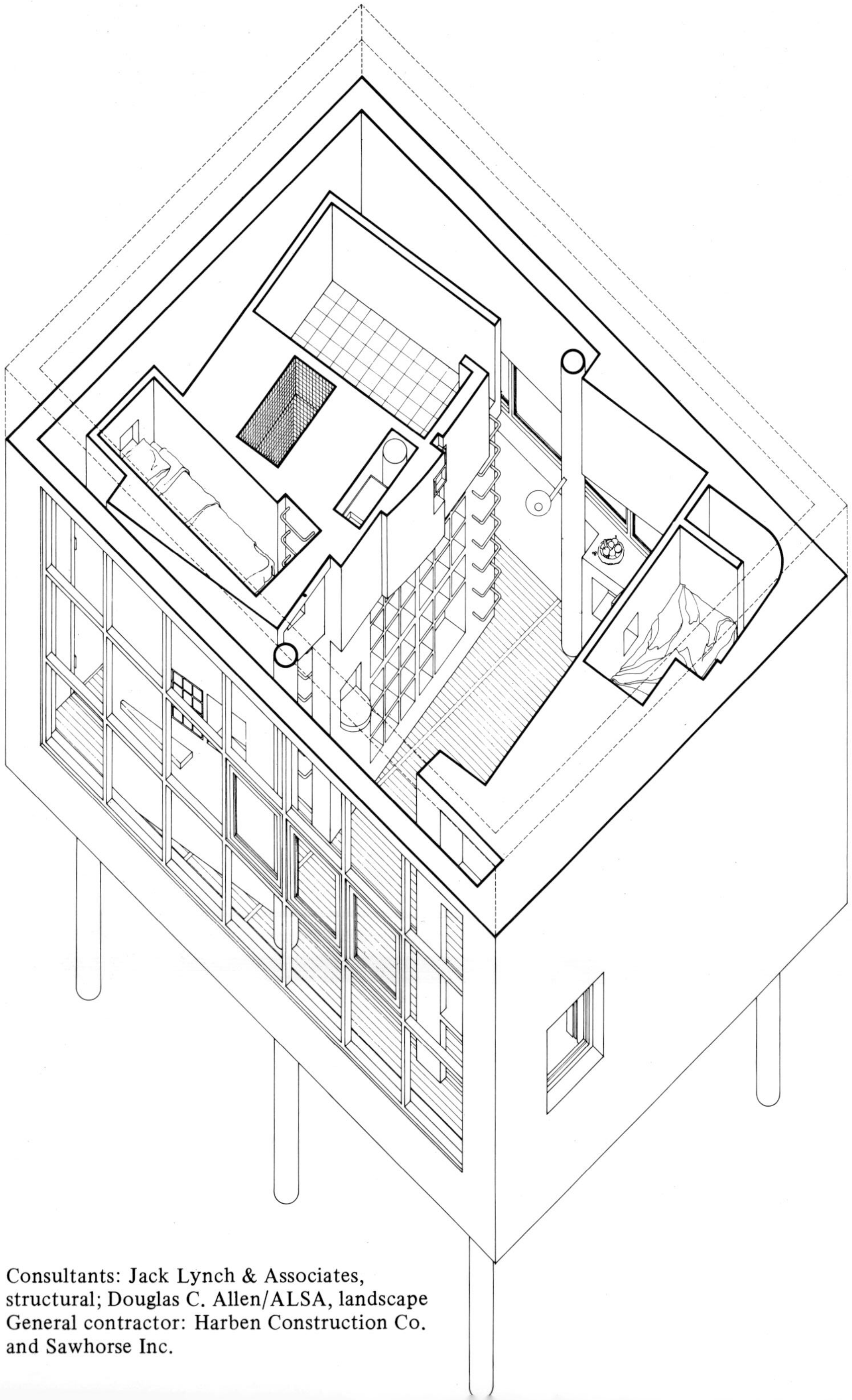

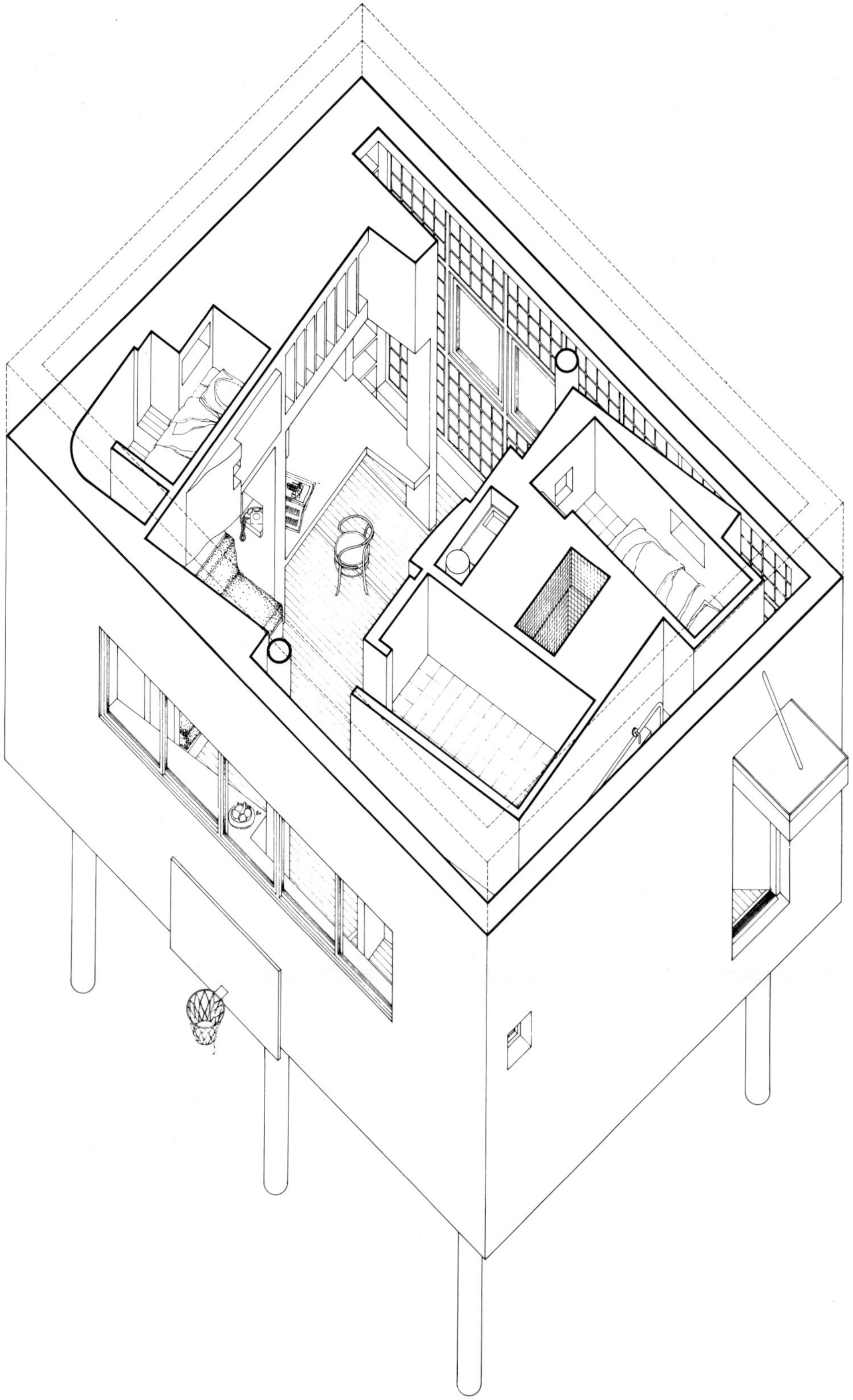

Consultants: Jack Lynch & Associates,
structural; Douglas C. Allen/ALSA, landscape
General contractor: Harben Construction Co.
and Sawhorse Inc.

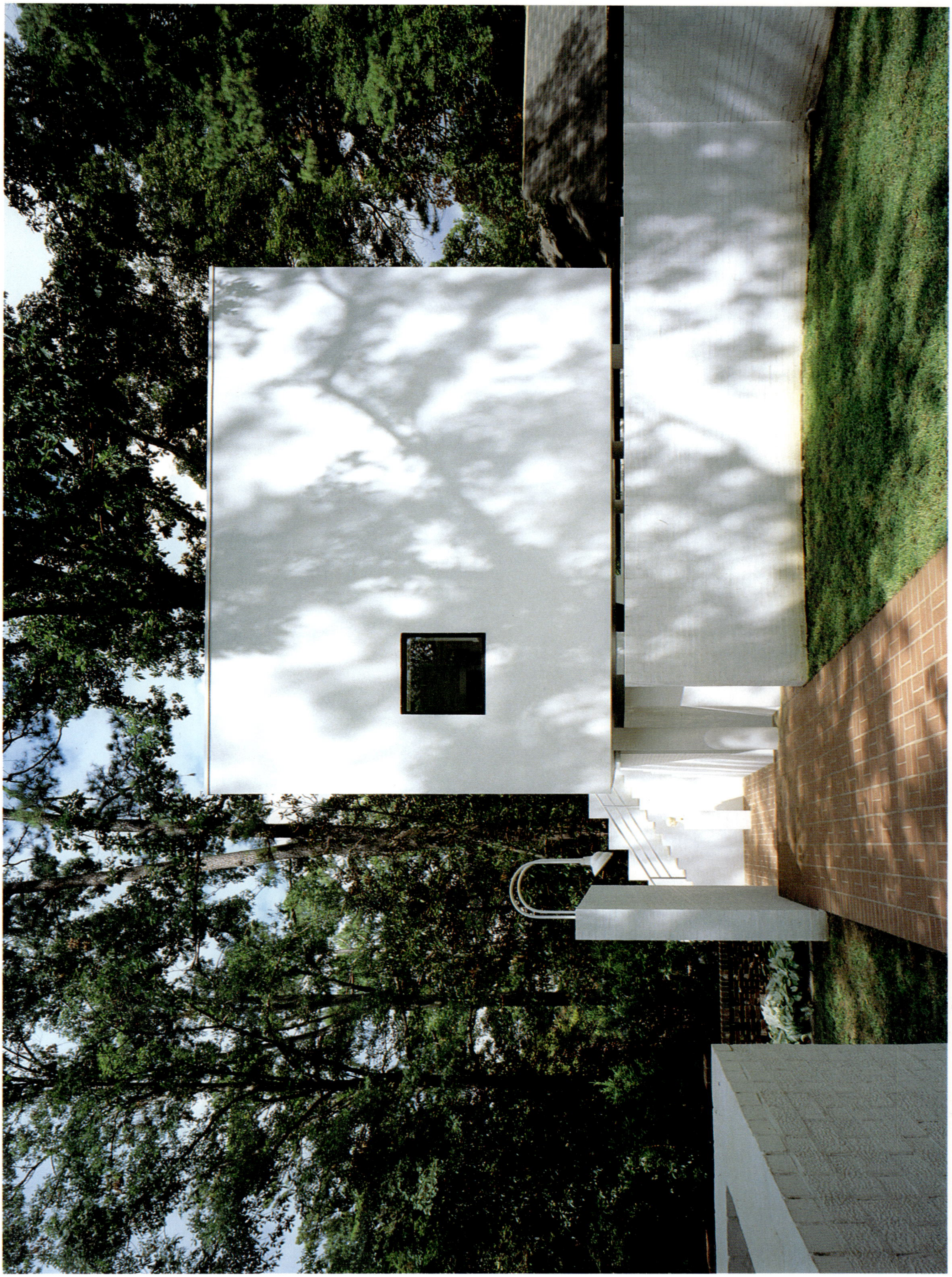

Longitudinal section

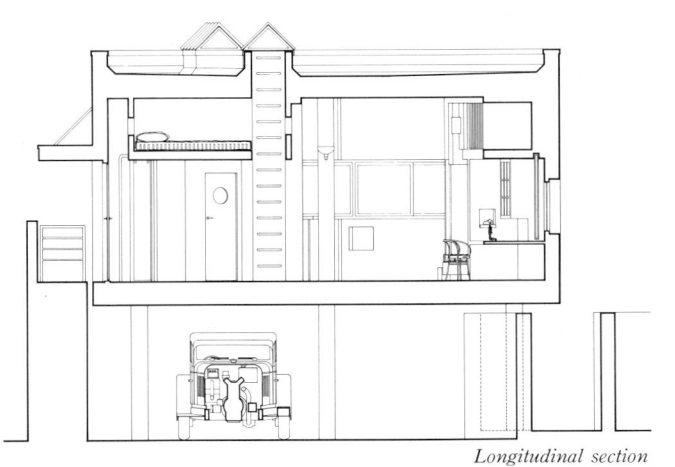

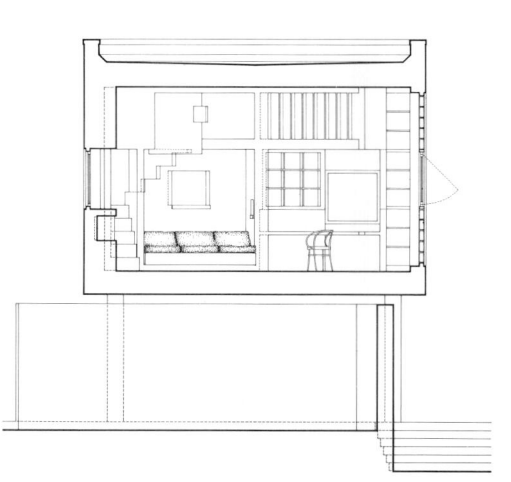

Cross section

Longitudinal section

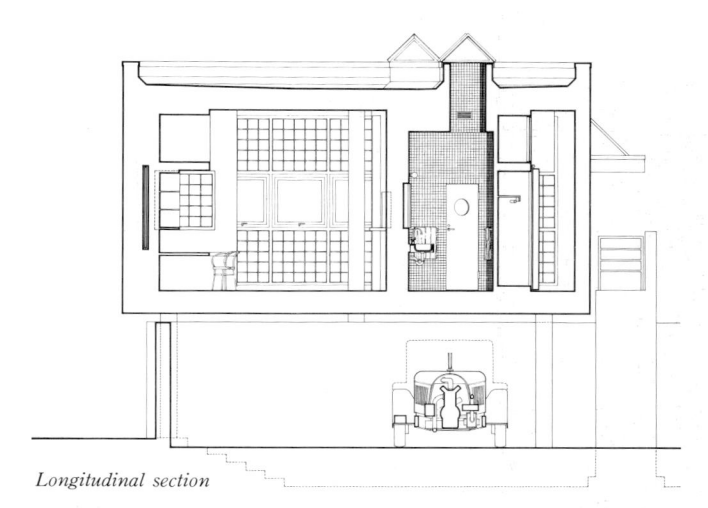

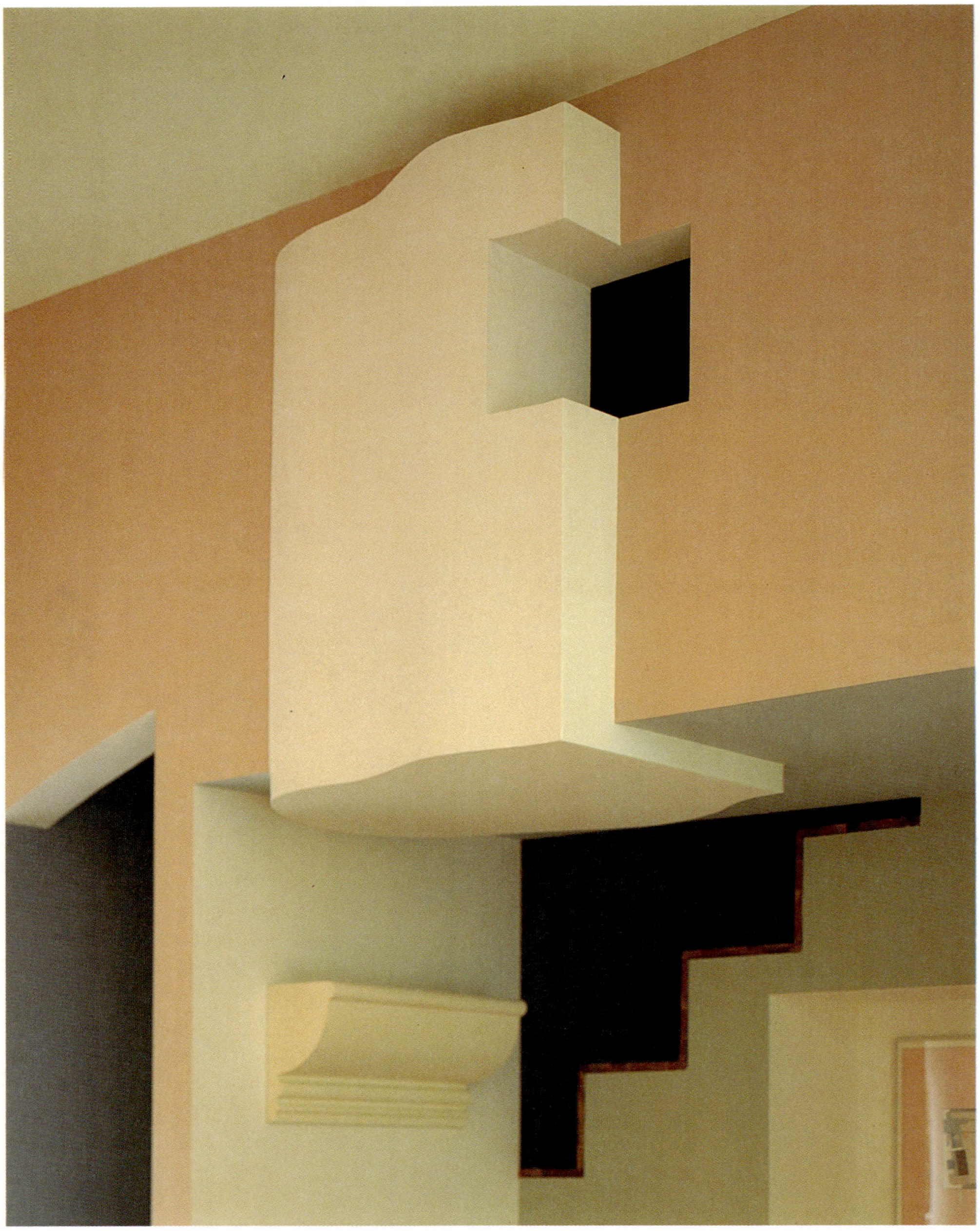
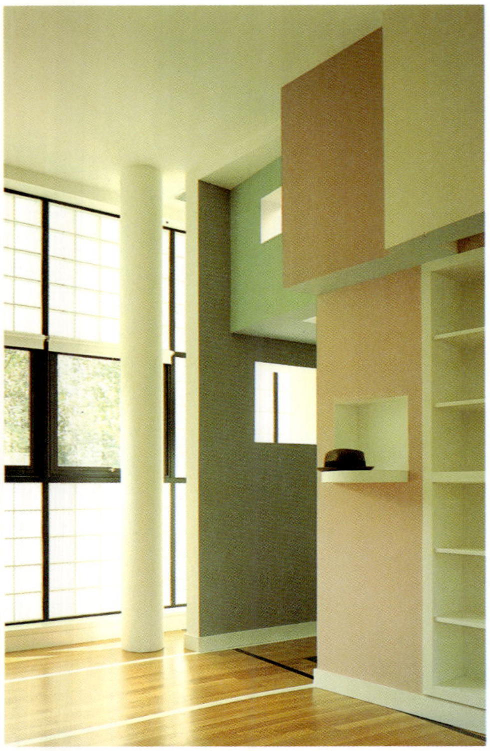
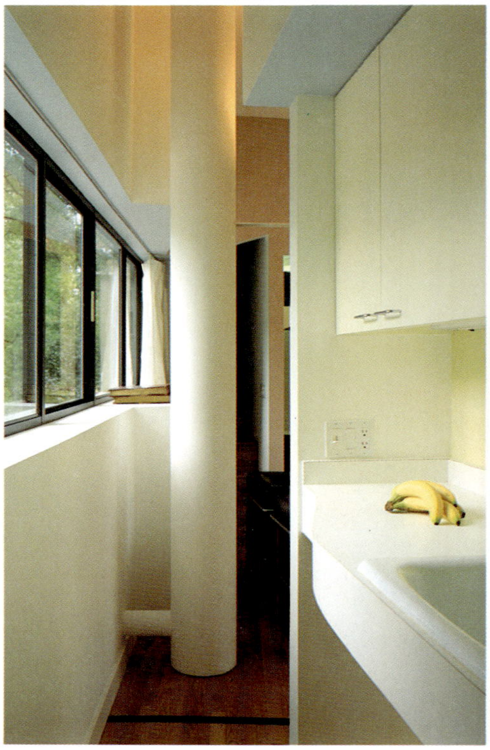
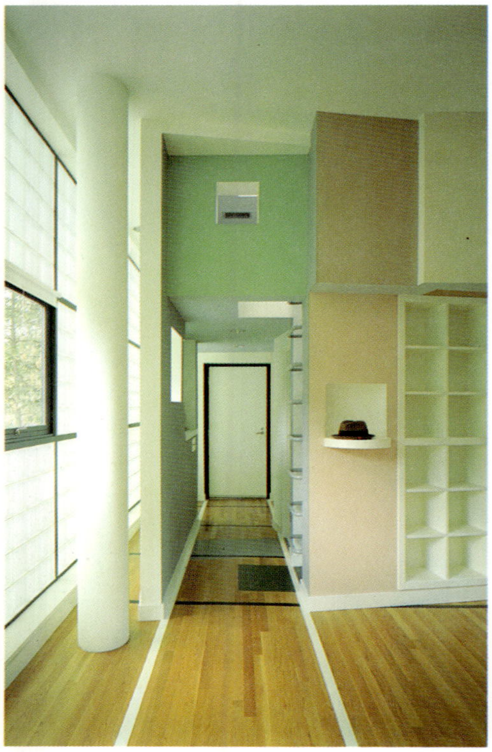

49

ROB WELLINGTON QUIGLEY
Mel McGee, project architect
Jaeger Beach House
Del Mar, California
1982-84

Photos: W. Fujii

The clients desire a get-away beach house. The Southern California site is 150 feet from the beach but is surrounded on three sides by wide asphalt drives. It is isolated from the sea by a continuous wall of dwellings on the west. Immediately on the east is a four lane highway.

The pavilion-like structures rise from this unfortunate reality, optimistically seeking the ocean views and turning inward on themselves away from the encircling rear facades and fences. Locally nostalgic imagery celebrates the wonderful duality of a beach life: sea views/harsh glare, cool wind/hot sun, quiet rest/constant ocean pounding, beach bum lifestyle/elitist location, private retreat/group activity.

The buildings are organized not by geometry but by the natural forces of the sea... a symbolic aquatic event leaves in its wake an intimate urban village, magical and faceted in its asphalt setting. This narrative is a design device used to give the landlocked house a rapport and immediacy to the sea. The exploration is not into "natural" architecture, but the interface between man-made objects and nature.

The resulting beach house investigates the idea of permanence in a transient Southern California society.
Rob W. Quigley

Consultants: Bob Sowards, structural; Burton W. Adams, mechanical; Steve Adams, landscape; Evie Avinante, interior
General contractor: Wodehouse & Associates

クライアントは隠れ家としてのビーチハウスを望んだ。

南カリフォルニアにある敷地は、海岸から150フィートの近さだが、3方を広いアスファルトの自動車道に囲まれている。西側は家々の壁が続き、海とのあいだを遮っている。東側には間近に4車線の高速道路が走っている。

あづまや風の構造は、こうした好ましからざる現実のもたらしたもので、海の眺めを積極的に取り込み、建物の背面を塀で囲い、内側に向き合わせることになったのである。このあたり特有のなつかしいイメージが、海岸での生活のもつ素敵な二重性をさらに盛りあげる——海の景色とまばゆい光、涼しい風と照りつける太陽、静けさと絶え間ない波音、海辺の怠惰な生活と類稀な地形、ひそやかな隠棲と仲間と連れ立ってのにぎやかさ。

建物群は幾何学ではなく、海のもつ自然の力によって編成されている。つまり、水のひきおこす現象を象徴的に想定し、水の引いた跡、アスファルトにつつまれた背景のなかに残された、魔法のような、宝石のように刻まれたいくつもの小面をみせる、こぢんまりとした都市の村。この物語は、陸に封じ込められたこの家に、海への直接的で、親密な関わりを与えるための工夫なのである。この試みは、「自然」建築へと向かうのではなく、人工物と自然とのあいだに横たわる界面を探ろうというものである。

結果としては、このビーチハウスは、移ろいやすい南カリフォルニアの社会で、永遠という観念を求めたものとなった。

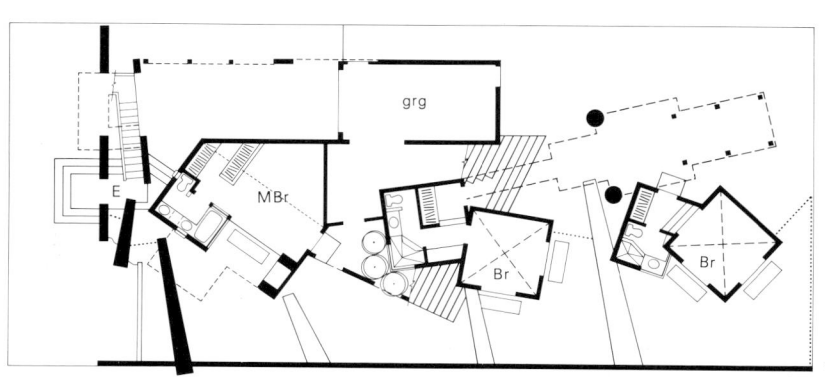

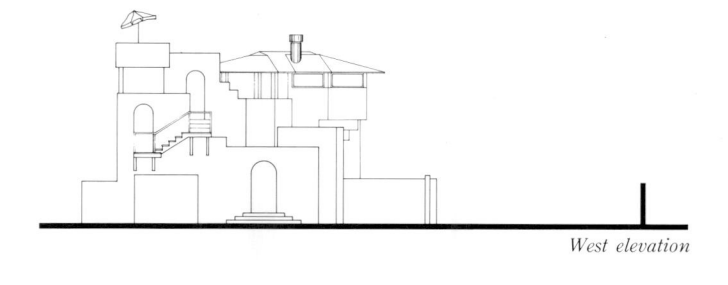

First floor

West elevation

52

North elevation

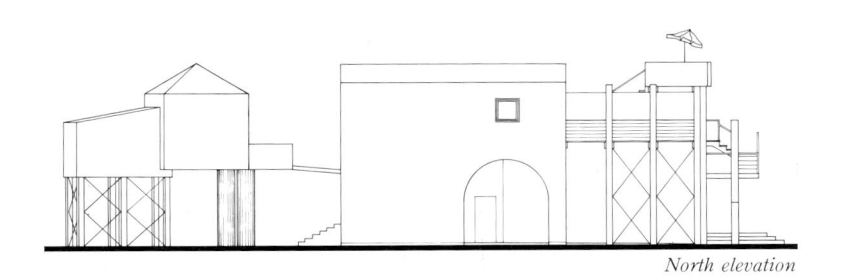

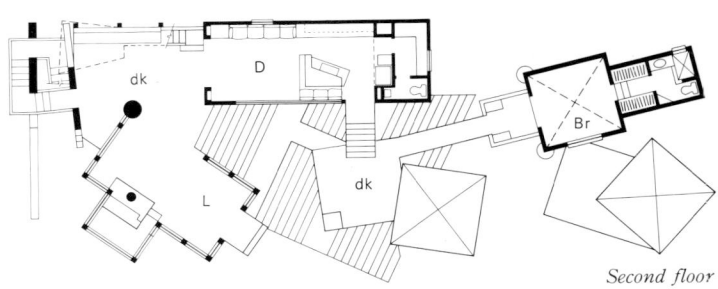

Second floor

54

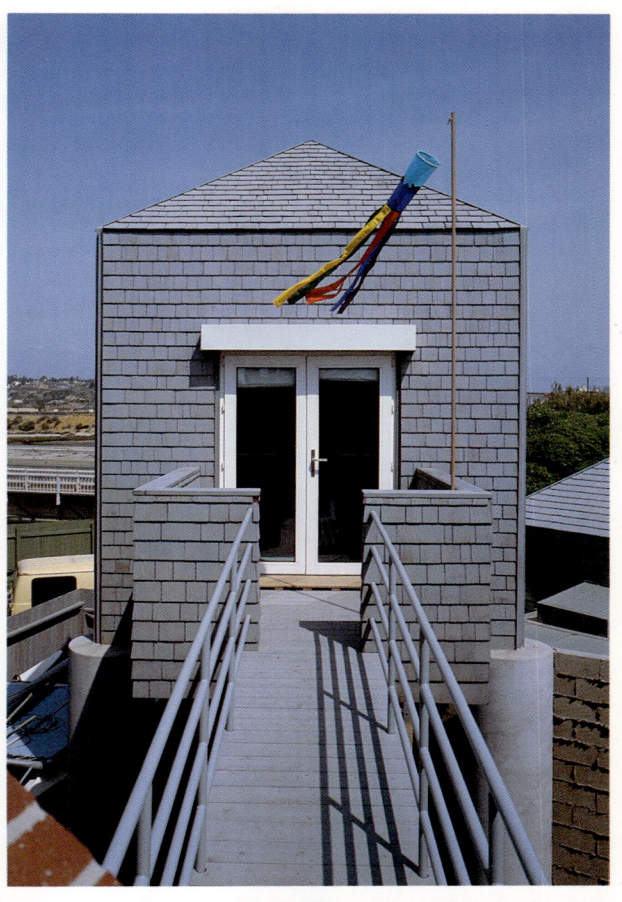

Section through site

56

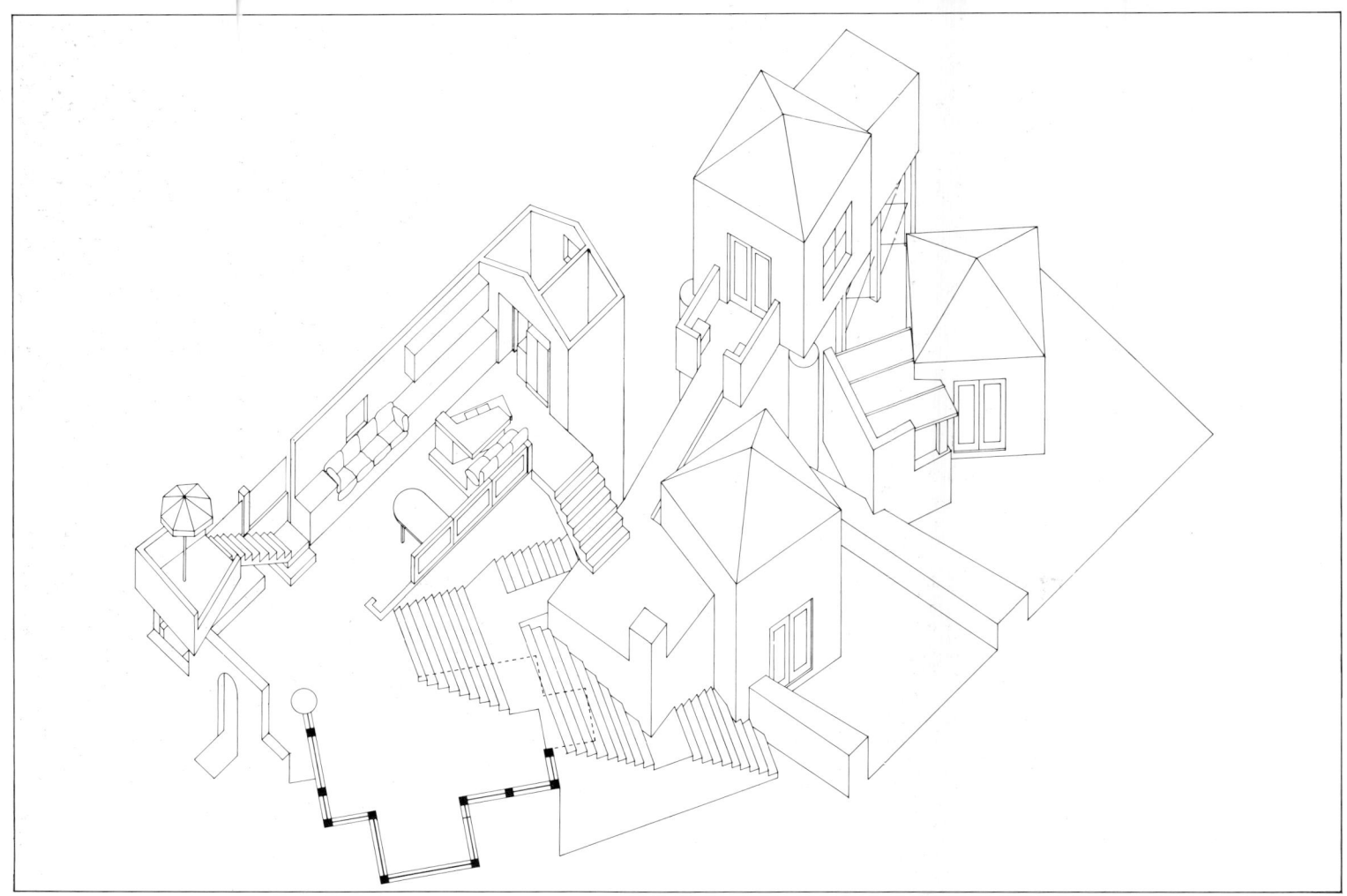

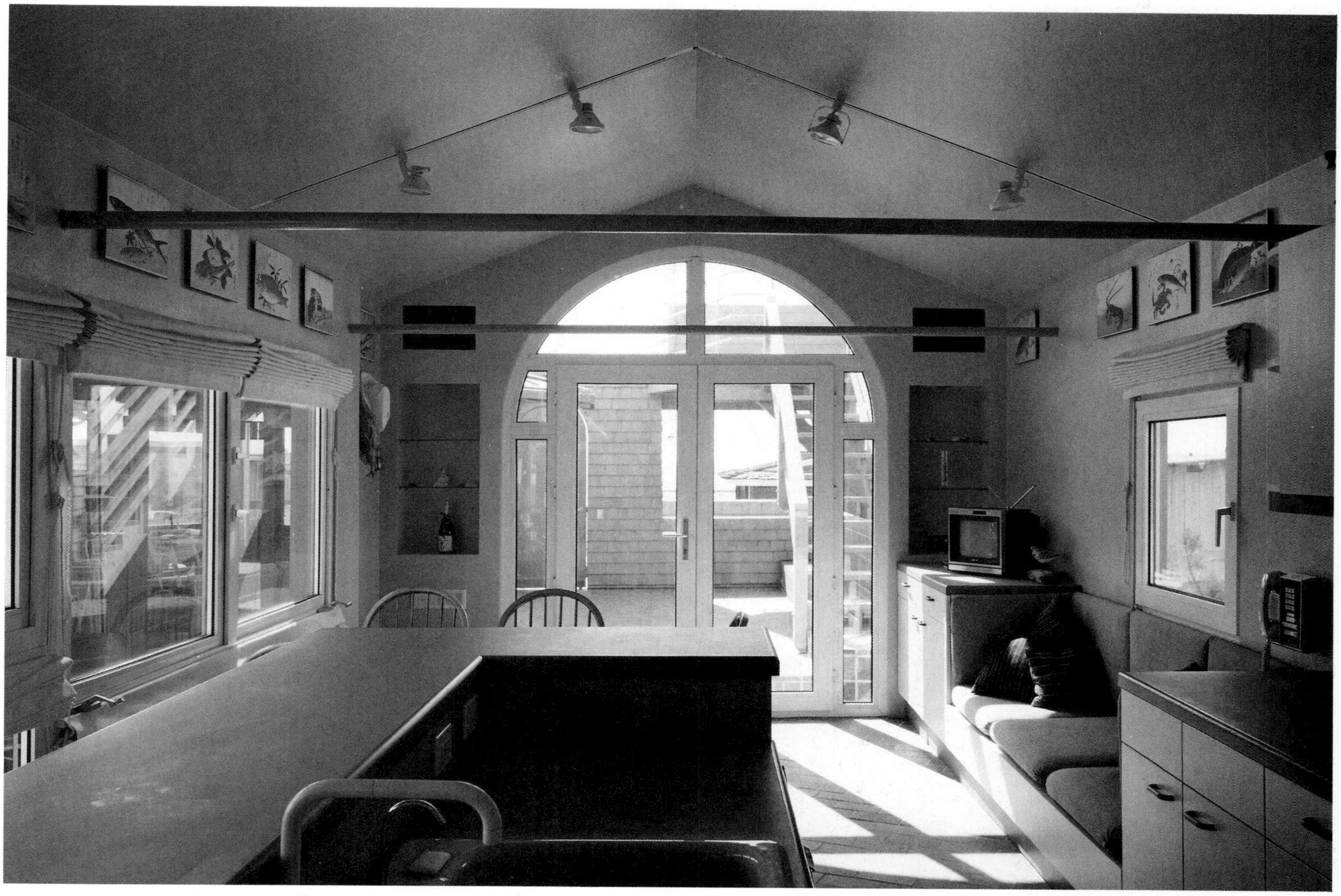

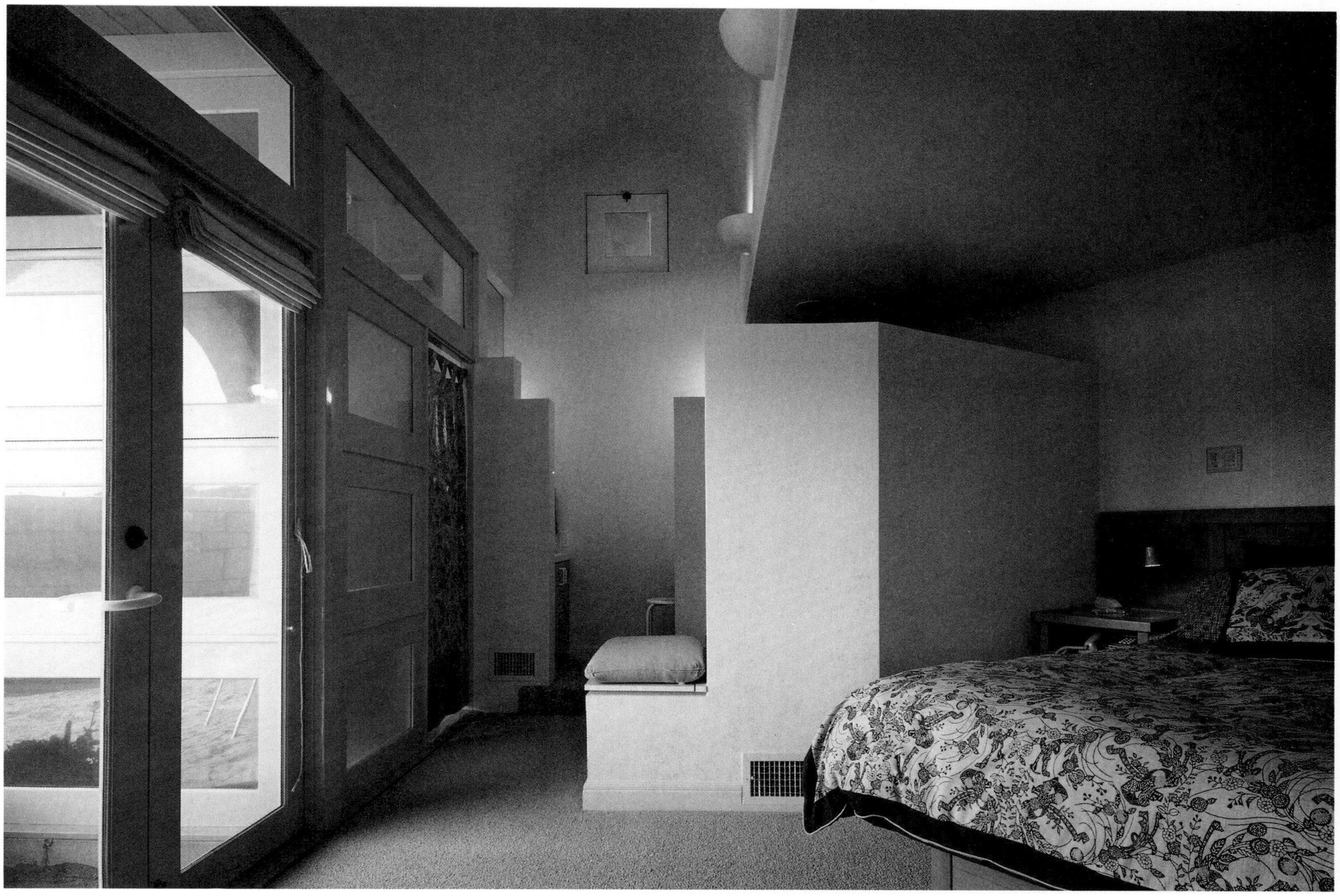

ROB WELLINGTON QUIGLEY
William Behun, project architect;
Kathleen McCormick, color and interior
Monahan Residence
La Jolla, California
1980-86

Photos: W. Fujii

This three bedroom, 2000 sq.ft. house addresses the dilemma of the three piece suit formality required of a prominent lawyer living in a Casual Arcadia. The classical Palladian plan is challenged by California modernist concepts of informal open plan living.

Concerns for privacy, prevailing winds and access to the sun distort the biaxial symmetry.

The long coastal view is framed by the dining/entry axis and the raised living platforms allow for ocean views from every room.

Consultants: South Bay Engineering, structural; Steve Adams/Adams, Wyckoff & Brown, landscape; Patrick B. Quigley & Associates, lighting
General conractor: Don Bauhoffer

3つのベッドルームをもつこの2000平方フィートの住宅は、「カジュアル・アルカディア」(気楽な理想郷)に住もうと望む著名な法律家が要求した3組の形態性をめぐるディレンマを処理している。古典的なパラディオ風平面は、インフォーマルで開放的な平面に居住するというカリフォルニアのモダニストのコンセプトによって挑発的に喚起されている。

プライヴァシー、風の流れ、太陽への接近、こうしたことがらへの関心が、2軸シンメトリーを歪めている。

長い沿岸への眺望はダイニング／入口軸によって枠取られ、居住面を立ち上げることにより、すべての部屋から海原を眺めることができる。

Site plan

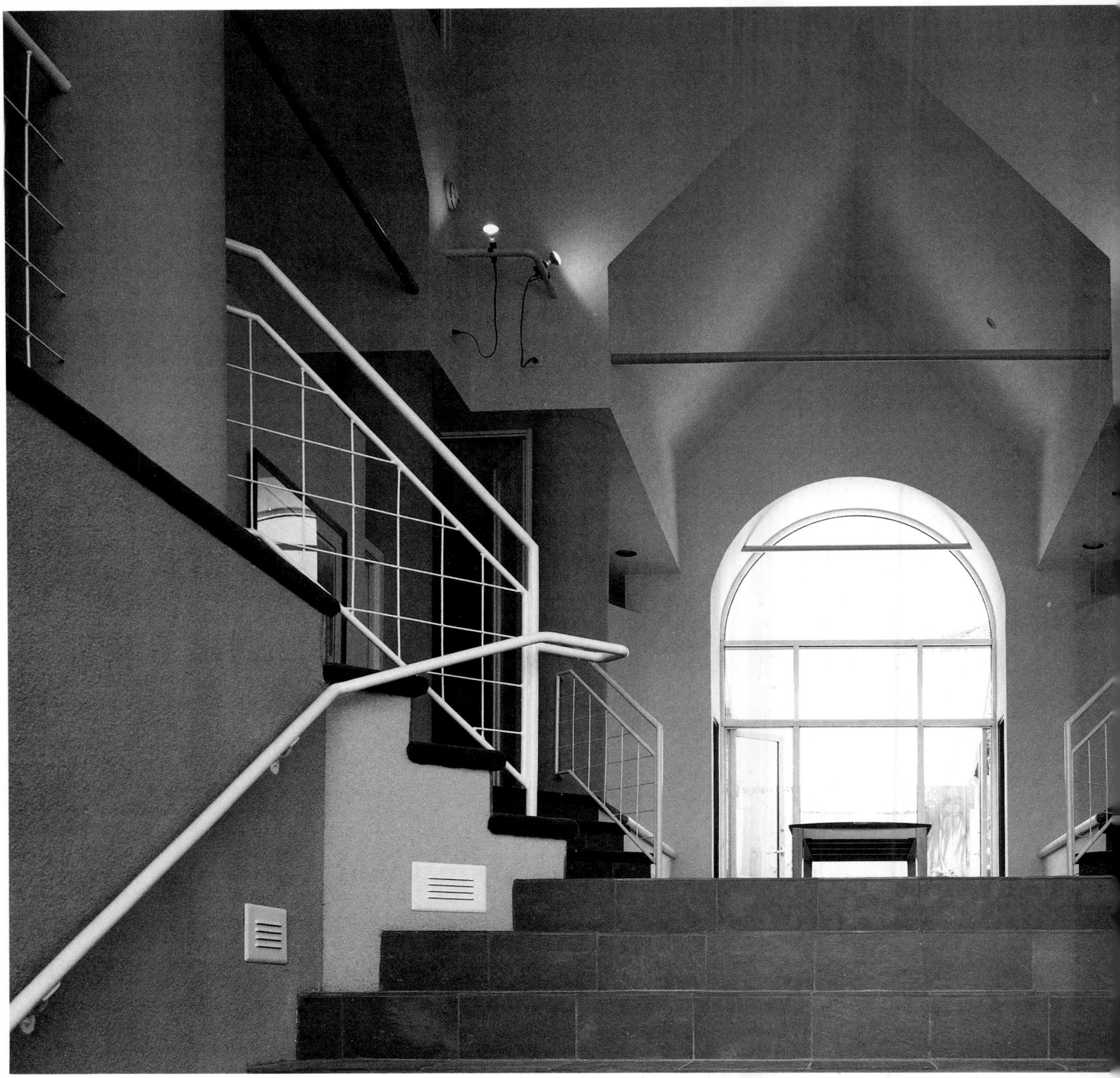

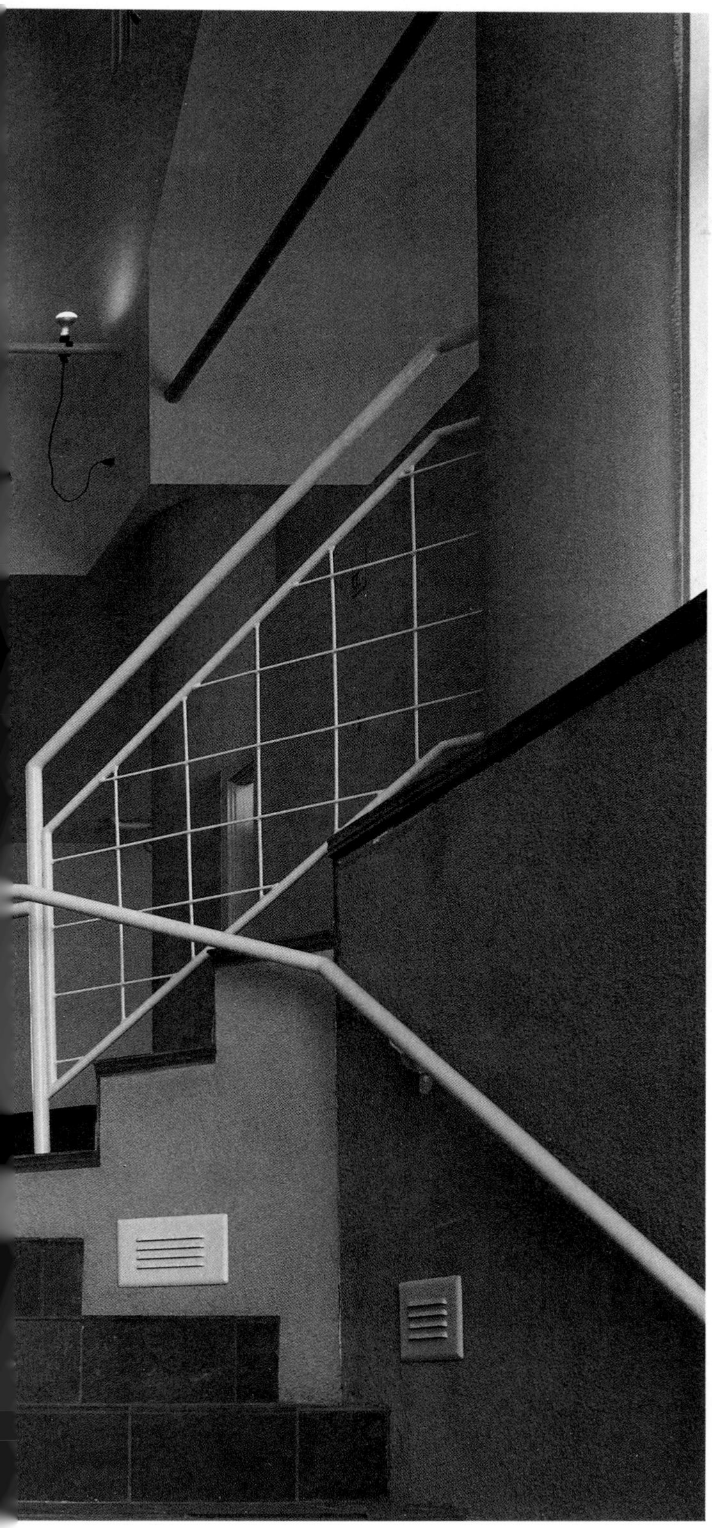

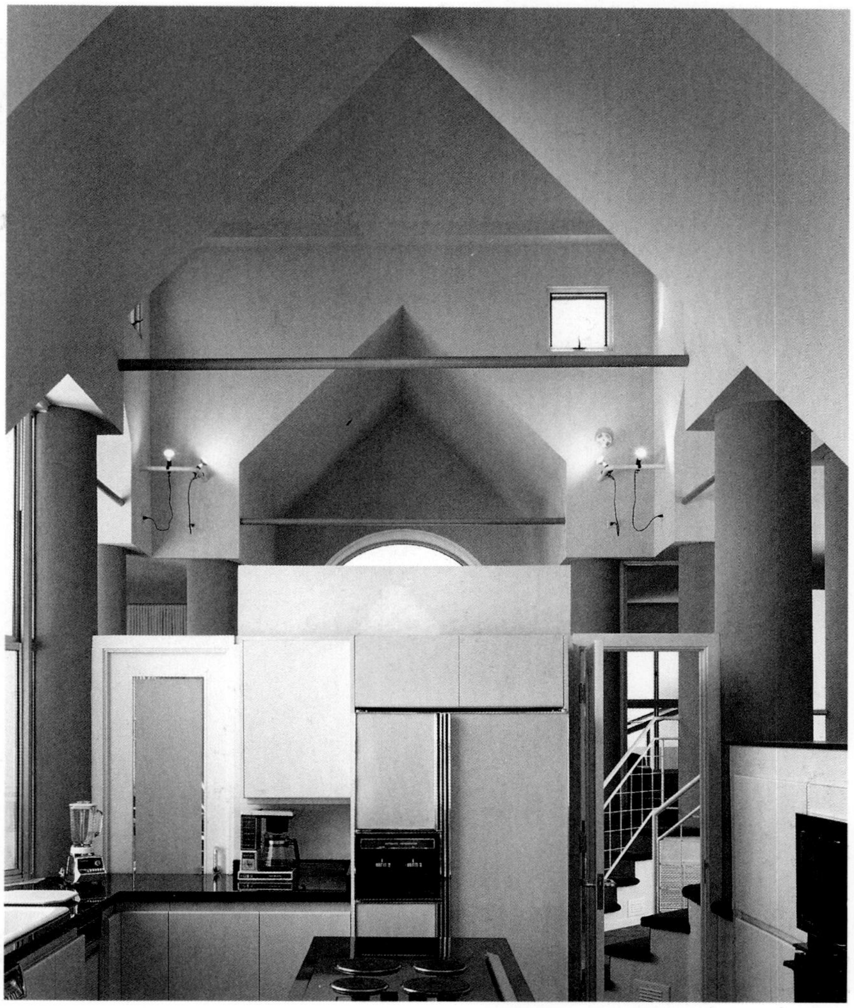

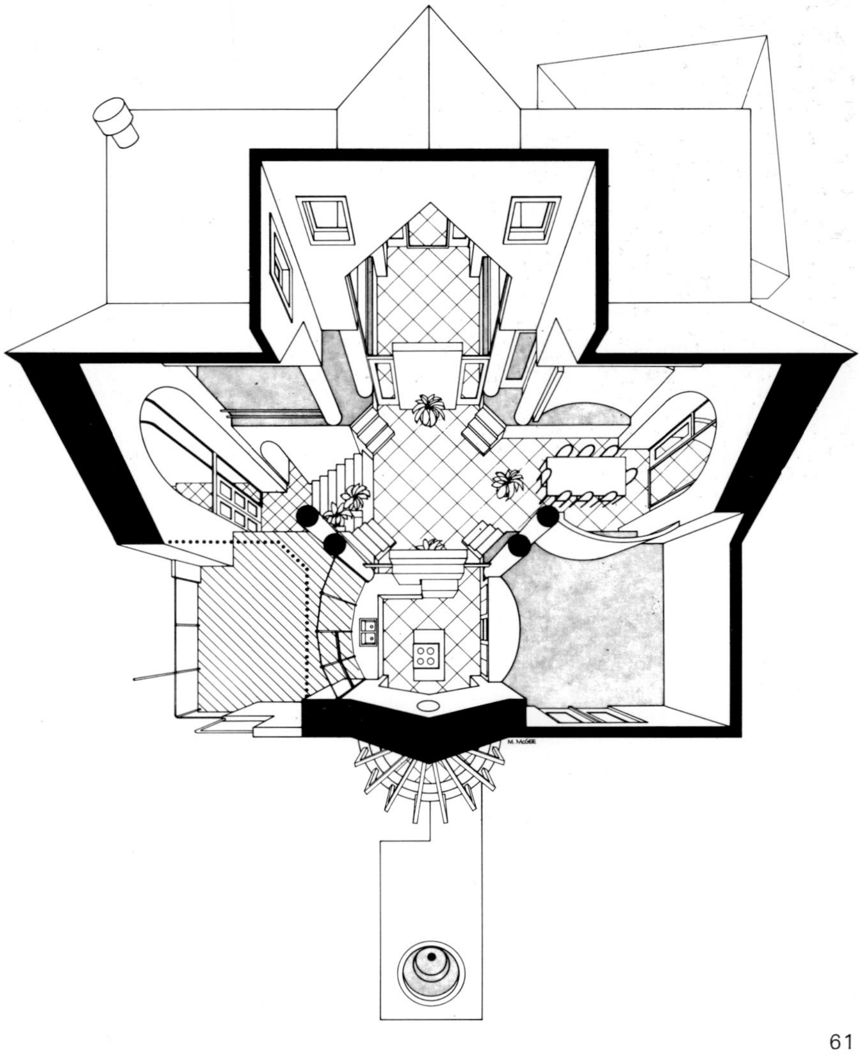

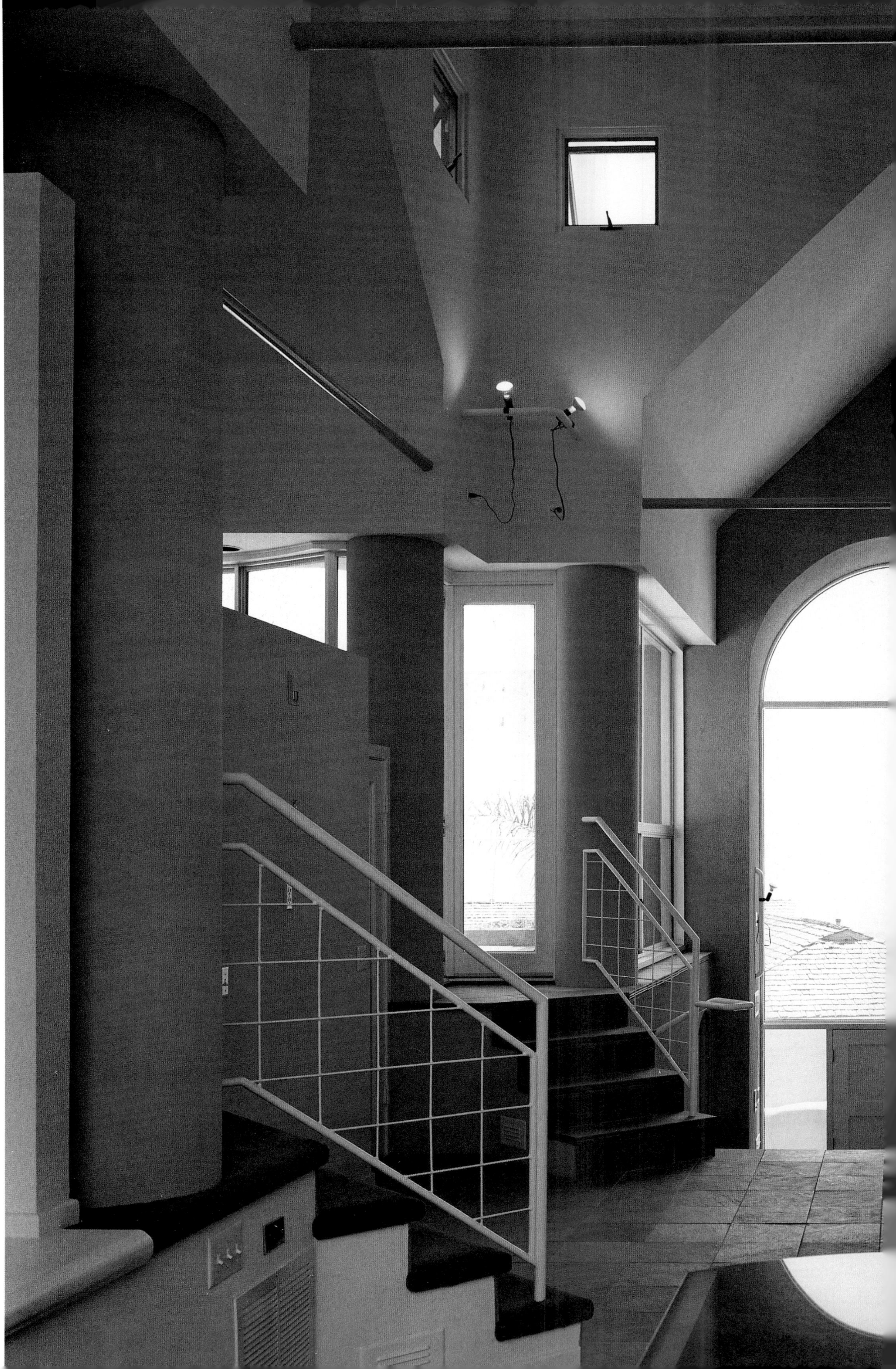

63

ARNE BYSTROM
Sun Valley House
Sun Valley, Idaho
1982-86

Photos: W. Fujii

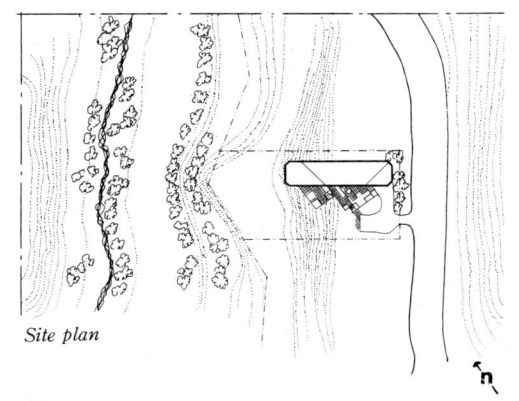

Site plan

Program
To design a mountain house that integrates the latest state-of-the-art solar technology with the warm tradition of wood structuralism. The plan is programed by functional priorities into three areas: a garage, studio, and storage zone; a family-grandchildren zone with four bedroom suites adjoining a solar gallery that opens onto a sunken pool and garden; and a "basehouse" containing a master bedroom, kitchen, dining, and living area which provide the nuclear residential functions.

Site
The site is along a residential road surrounded by wilderness area on three sides. It is located on Trail Creek and is divided into an upper and lower bench by a 30 foot grade change. The site elevation is 6000 feet and the vegetation is transitional high-prairie/alpine.

Solution
The idea of house is shelter, as realized by the roof. With its great overhangs, layered beams, and bracketed column supports, the roof structure is reminiscent of traditional Asian houses, the great houses of the Swiss Alps, the mast-framed stave churches of Norway, and of course, the residences of architects Greene and Greene. On a subjective level, the roof and bracketed columns reference a protective forest canopy covering the "understory" or layered interior living spaces. The roof is also carefully shaped so that the winter snows are diverted away from the out-door living areas and entrances to the house and the snow build-up harmlessly slides away from the people spaces.

The idea of house as shelter is also realized by the shaping, cutting, and berming of the earth, as well as the concrete terracing which form extensions of the interior spaces. Here the sources are deeply Wrightian and influenced by the detailing work of Carlo Scarpa. Berms on the north and east give privacy from the road and protection from winter draughts down Trail Creek Valley. After the garage, the house is sunken four feet into the ground forming an enclosed courtyard which contains a reflecting pool with an abstract water wheel, used both for cooling and enjoyment.

Entry into the house affords a series of spatial and visual experiences down a constructed stairway to the fore entry of the southern terraces, under the solar collectors, through the great glass wall into the house, and through the second glass wall, until reaching the final "cave like" recesses. Throughout this progression, the scale continually decreases as the detailing increases.

Ultimately, the house cascades down the slope to the lower bench, and the projection of the walls form gardens and terraces. The floor plan is structurally independent from the roof canopy and is oriented west-south in opposition to the northwest-southeast roof. The zig-zag circulation pattern runs through the solar gallery which functions as a spa/game room, a hallway, and a passive/active solar energy collection area. The solar heat is stored in rock bins located beneath this gallery.

The roof slope matches the angle of the December sun, allowing maximum winter sun penetration, while its overhang shades out the June sun. The unique evacuated tube collector arrays are suspended from the roof on pipe and cable space frames. Unbacked and visually transparent, the collectors allow some sun penetration to heat the gallery and rock bin storage. The solar energy collected from this active system is piped to hydronic slabs that suppliment the rock bin storage system. All glazing is R-5 Argon "heat mirror" c.

The visual play between the "high-tech" collectors and the natural elements of the house provide a fascinating, but unresolved hierarchy.

プログラム：
木構造の暖かい感じの伝統を伴いつつ，最近アート的色彩をもつようになったソーラーテクノロジーを統合した山荘をデザインすること。平面計画は，機能上の優位性に従って以下の３つに分けられている。第１にはガレージ，スタディオ，倉庫のゾーン，第２には家族と孫のためのゾーンで，サンクンになったプールと庭の上部に開かれたソーラーギャラリーと結びつく４つのベッドルームのスイートをもっている。第３にはマスターベッドルーム，キッチン，ダイニング，そしてリヴィング領域を含む「ベースハウス」で，核となる居住機能を提供する。

敷地：
敷地は，３面を野原に囲われた宅地道路に沿っている。トレイル・クリークに位置するここは，30フィートの勾配で変化しながら高低の段丘に分割されている。敷地は6000フィートの高度で，植栽は高原植物と高山植物の過度的なものである。

解決：
この住宅の理念は，屋根によって実現されるシェルターとして表現されている。大いなる突出を示し，多層化する梁，持ち送り柱の支持をもつ屋根構造は，伝統的なアジアの家々やスイス・アルペンの大住宅，ノルウェーに見られるマストで枠取られた桟をもつ教会，そしてもちろん建築家のグリーン＆グリーンの作品を想起させるものだ。主題の観点からすると，屋根と持ち送り柱は，「下階」あるいは積層されたインテリアの居住空間を覆う保護的な森のキャノピーを参照している。屋根はまた注意深く形付けられ，冬の雪は住宅へのエントランスやリヴィング，屋外の領域からどけられ，積もった雪は人の行動する空間から危険なく滑り除かれることになる。

シェルターという住宅の理念は，インテリア空間から伸延するコンクリート製のテラスだけでなく，大地を形付け，掘削し，小径をつけることによっても具体化された。ここでの源泉はライトに多くを負っていると共に，カルロ・スカルパのディテールに影響されていると言ってよい。北と東の小径は道路からのプライヴァシーとトレイル・クリーク狭谷を吹き降ろす冬風からの防護を確保してゆく。ガレージの後ろで，住宅は４フィートほど地面から沈み，抽象的な水車をもつリフレクティング・プールのある閉ざされた中庭を形成しつつ，冷涼や娯楽に寄与する。

住宅への入口は，前方の南テラス入口へと構成的な階段を降りるひと続きの空間的かつ視覚的体験を得ている。それはソーラー集光器の下に，住宅内の大きなガラス壁やもうひとつのガラス壁を通して確保され，最終的には「ほら穴状の」奥の院に達する。こうした進行過程のあいだ，スケールはだんだんに落ちてゆく一方ディテールは増加してゆくことになる。

究極的には，住宅は低い方の段丘への勾配を段状に下降し，壁の突出が庭やテラスを形成する。フロアー平面は，構造的には屋根キャノピーから自立し，北西－南東を向いた屋根と対立して西－南に方向付けられた。ジグザグのサーキュレーションのパターンは，温泉／ゲーム室，廊下，パッシヴ／アクティヴのソーラーエネルギー集光器領域としての諸機能を横切って走ってゆく。このギャラリーの下，岩盤蓄熱室内部にはソーラー暖房が貯えられている。

屋根勾配は12月の太陽と直交する角度に合わせられ，最大限に冬の陽の光を採り込む一方，その突出部は６月の太陽に影を落としてゆく。ユニークな中空チューブ集光器の配列群は，パイプやケーブルでできたスペースフレームで屋根から宙吊られている。支持がなく透明であるため，集光器が多少の陽光によってもギャラリーや岩盤蓄熱室を暖めることができるのだ。このアクティヴシステムから集められたソーラーエネルギーは，注水スラブへパイプで導かれ，岩盤蓄熱システムの補完となるのである。ガラスはすべてR－5アルゴン型「熱線反射ガラス」になっている。

「ハイテク」な集光器と住宅の自然エレメントのあいだの視覚的遊戯は，魅力的な，しかしかたくるしくはないヒエラルキーを実現するのである。

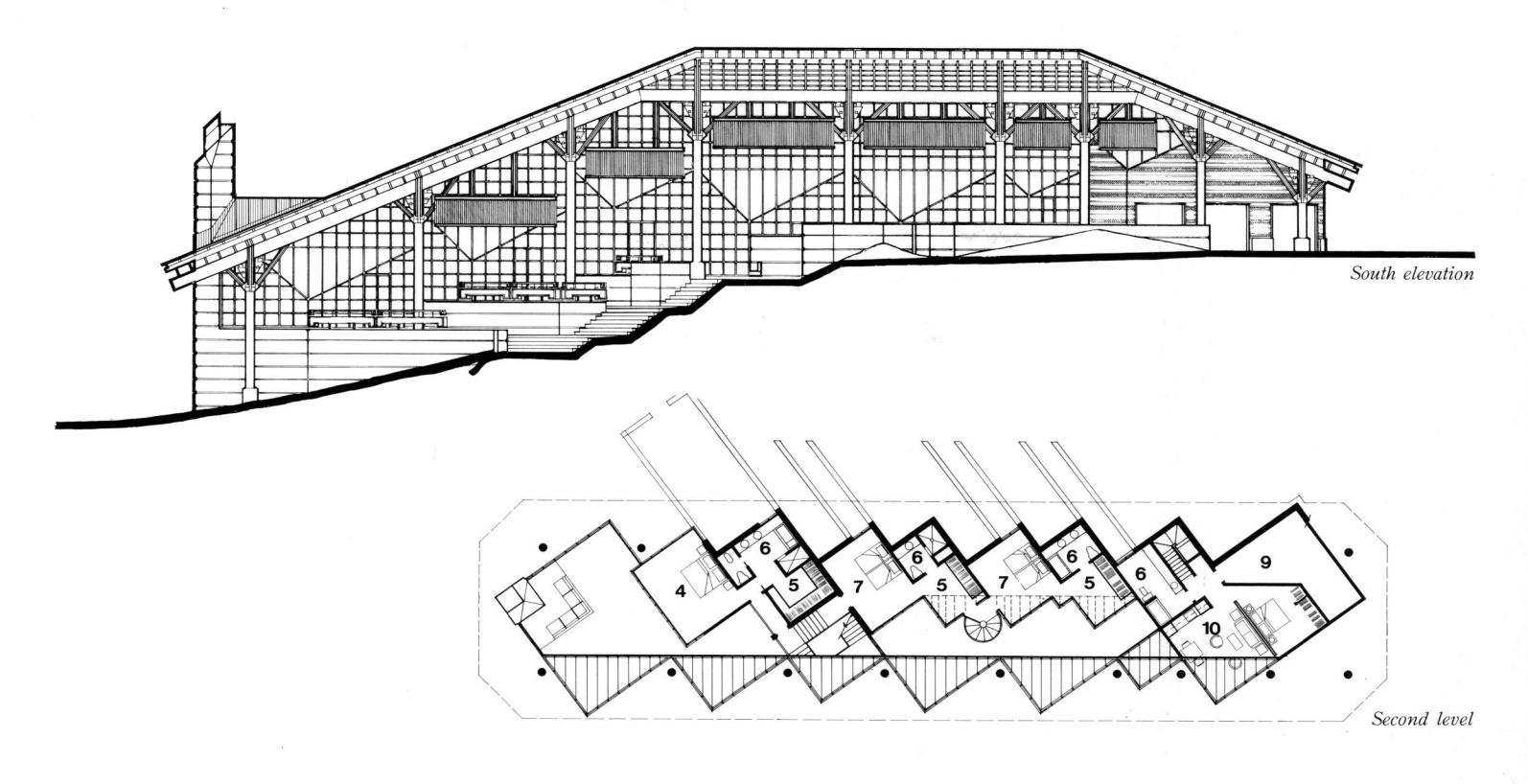

South elevation

Second level

1 LIVING ROOM
2 DINING ROOM
3 KITCHEN
4 MASTER BEDROOM
5 DRESSING ROOM
6 BATH
7 BEDROOM
8 SPA/GAME ROOM
9 STORAGE
10 STUDIO
11 GARAGE

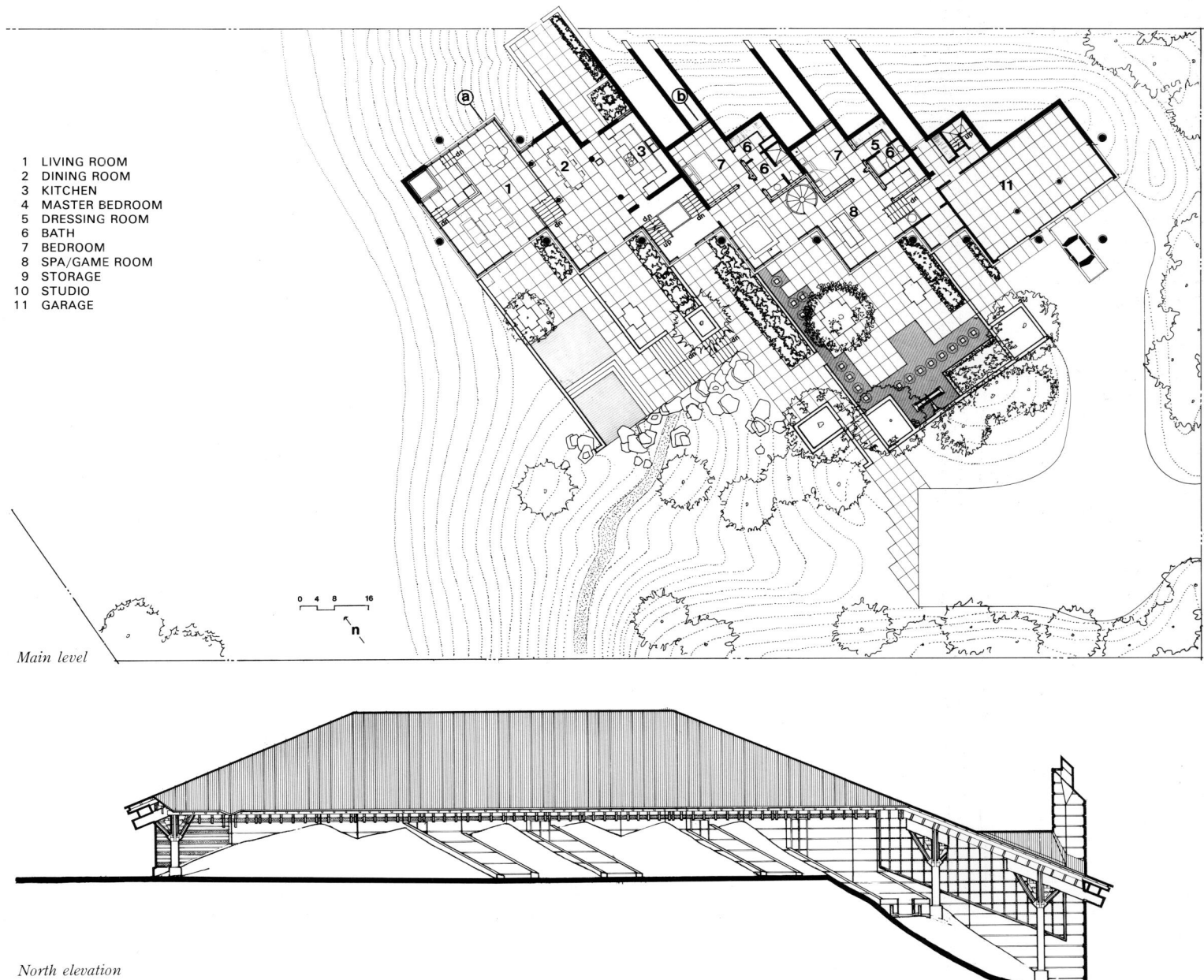

Main level

North elevation

Consultants: Darrold Bolton, P.E., structural;
Robert Murase, KM Associates, landscape;
ENSAR Group, Inc., energy
General contractor: Grabher Construction

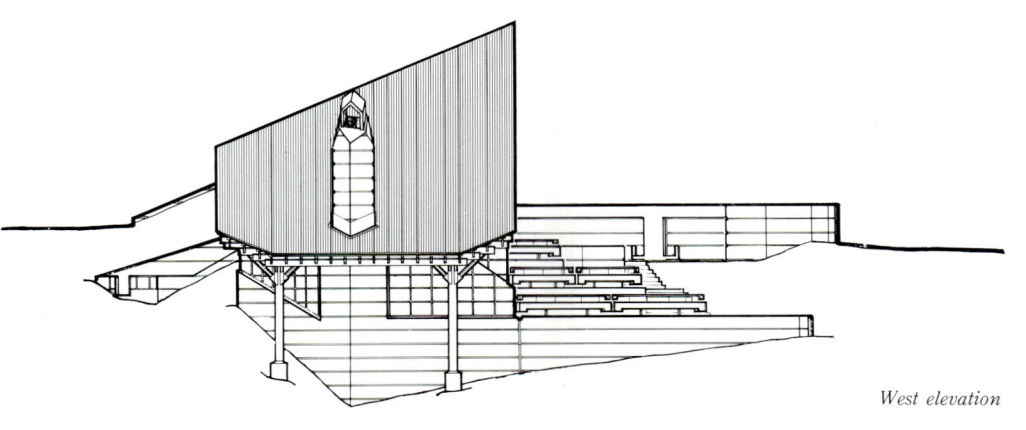

West elevation

East elevation

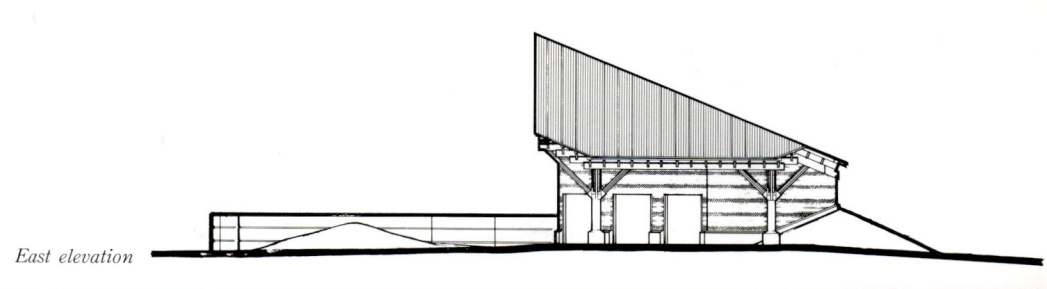

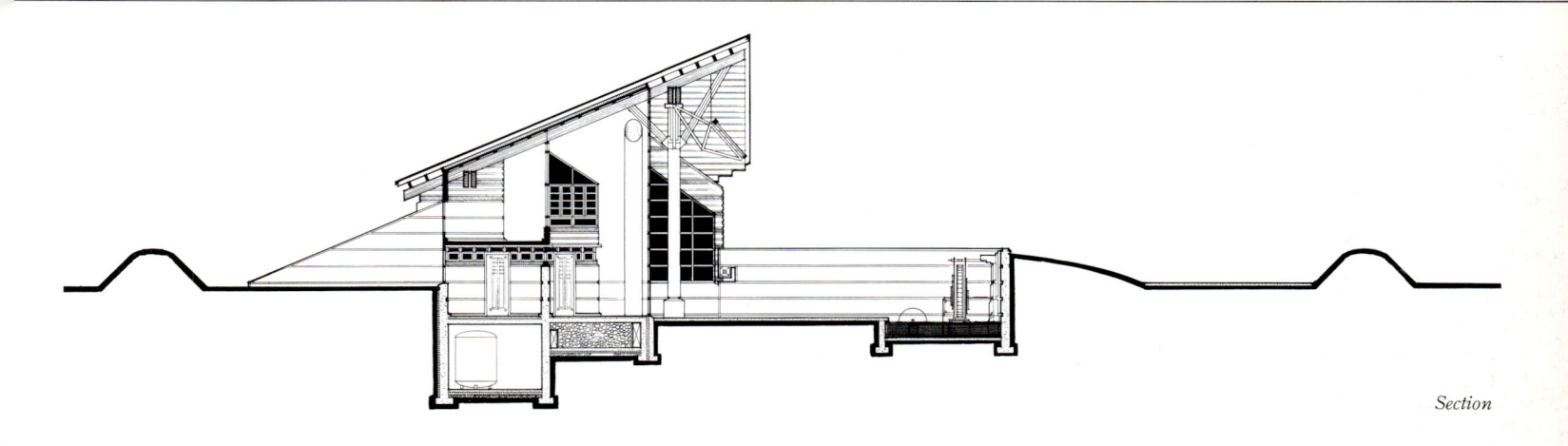

Section

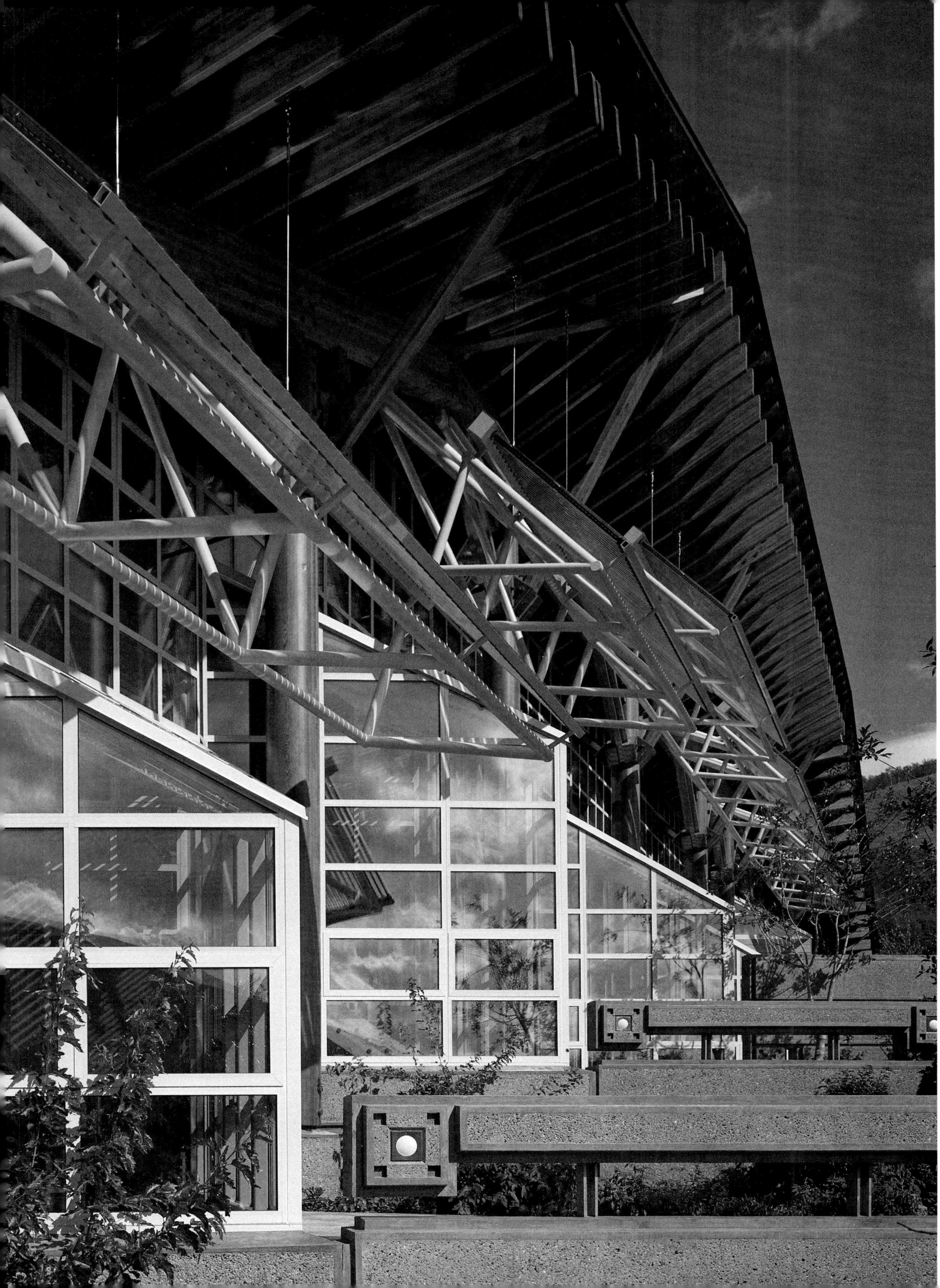

PASSIVE HEATING SYSTEM

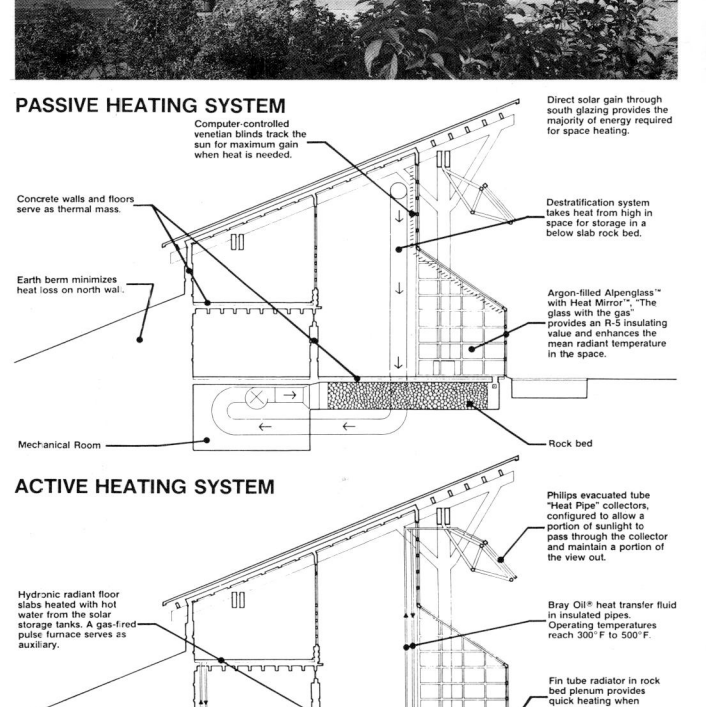

- Computer-controlled venetian blinds track the sun for maximum gain when heat is needed.
- Direct solar gain through south glazing provides the majority of energy required for space heating.
- Concrete walls and floors serve as thermal mass.
- Destratification system takes heat from high in space for storage in a below slab rock bed.
- Earth berm minimizes heat loss on north wall.
- Argon-filled Alpenglass™ with Heat Mirror™, "The glass with the gas" provides an R-5 insulating value and enhances the mean radiant temperature in the space.
- Mechanical Room
- Rock bed

ACTIVE HEATING SYSTEM

- Hydronic radiant floor slabs heated with hot water from the solar storage tanks. A gas-fired pulse furnace serves as auxiliary.
- Philips evacuated tube "Heat Pipe" collectors, configured to allow a portion of sunlight to pass through the collector and maintain a portion of the view out.
- Bray Oil® heat transfer fluid in insulated pipes. Operating temperatures reach 300°F to 500°F.
- Fin tube radiator in rock bed plenum provides quick heating when required.
- Low temperature solar storage tank (140°F±)
- High temperature solar storage tank (190°F±)
- Domestic hot water storage

ENSAR GROUP

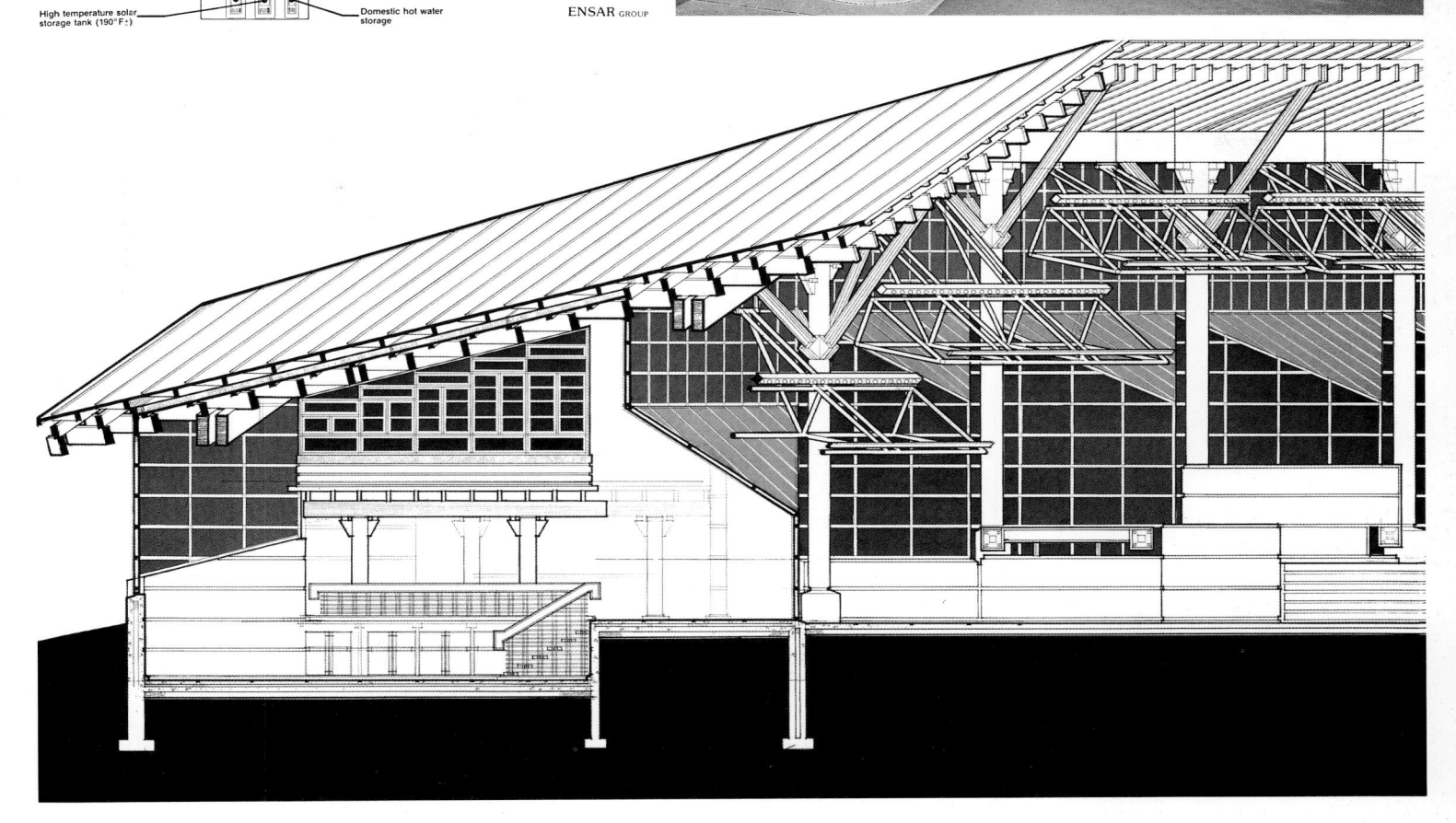

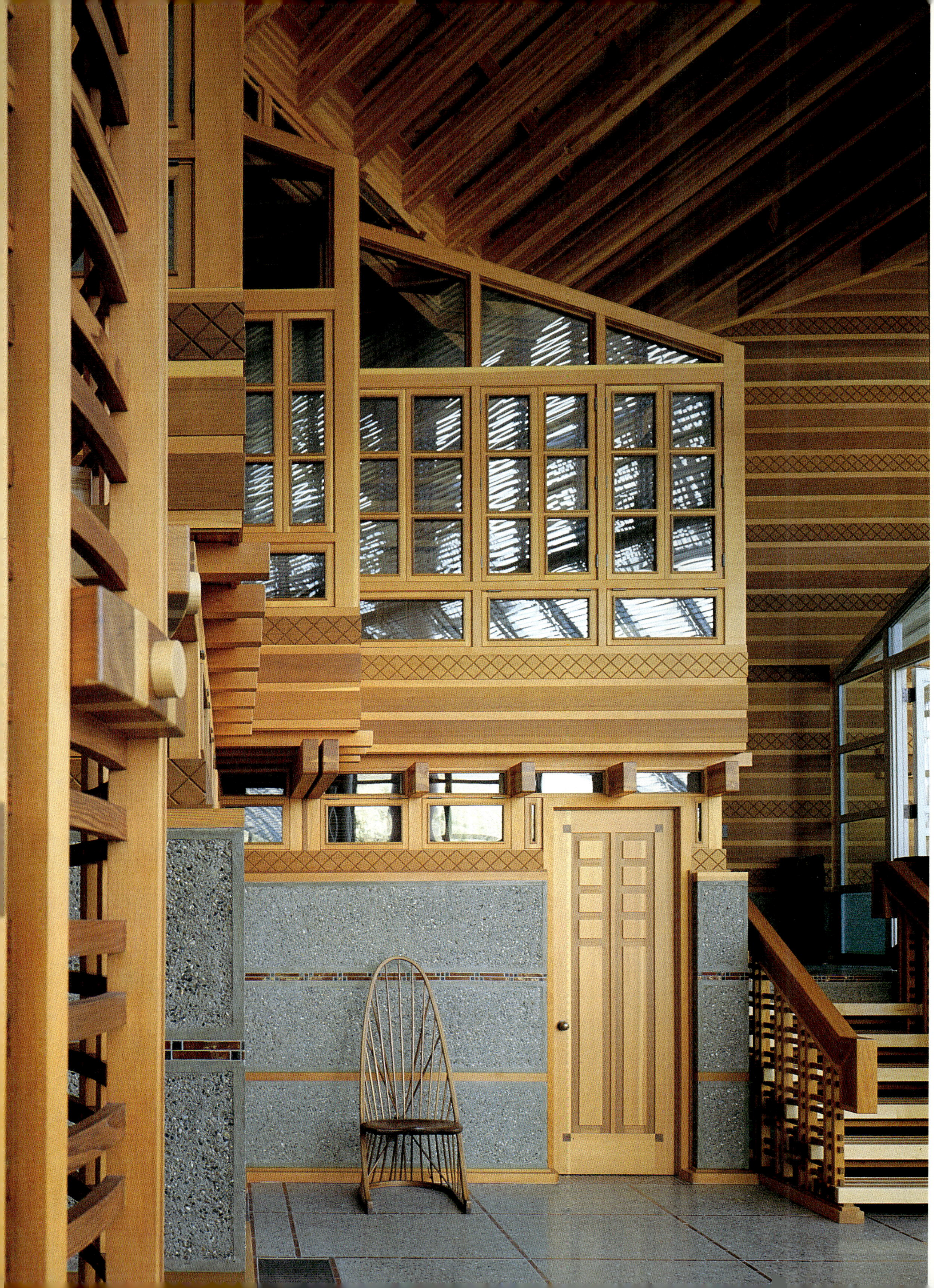

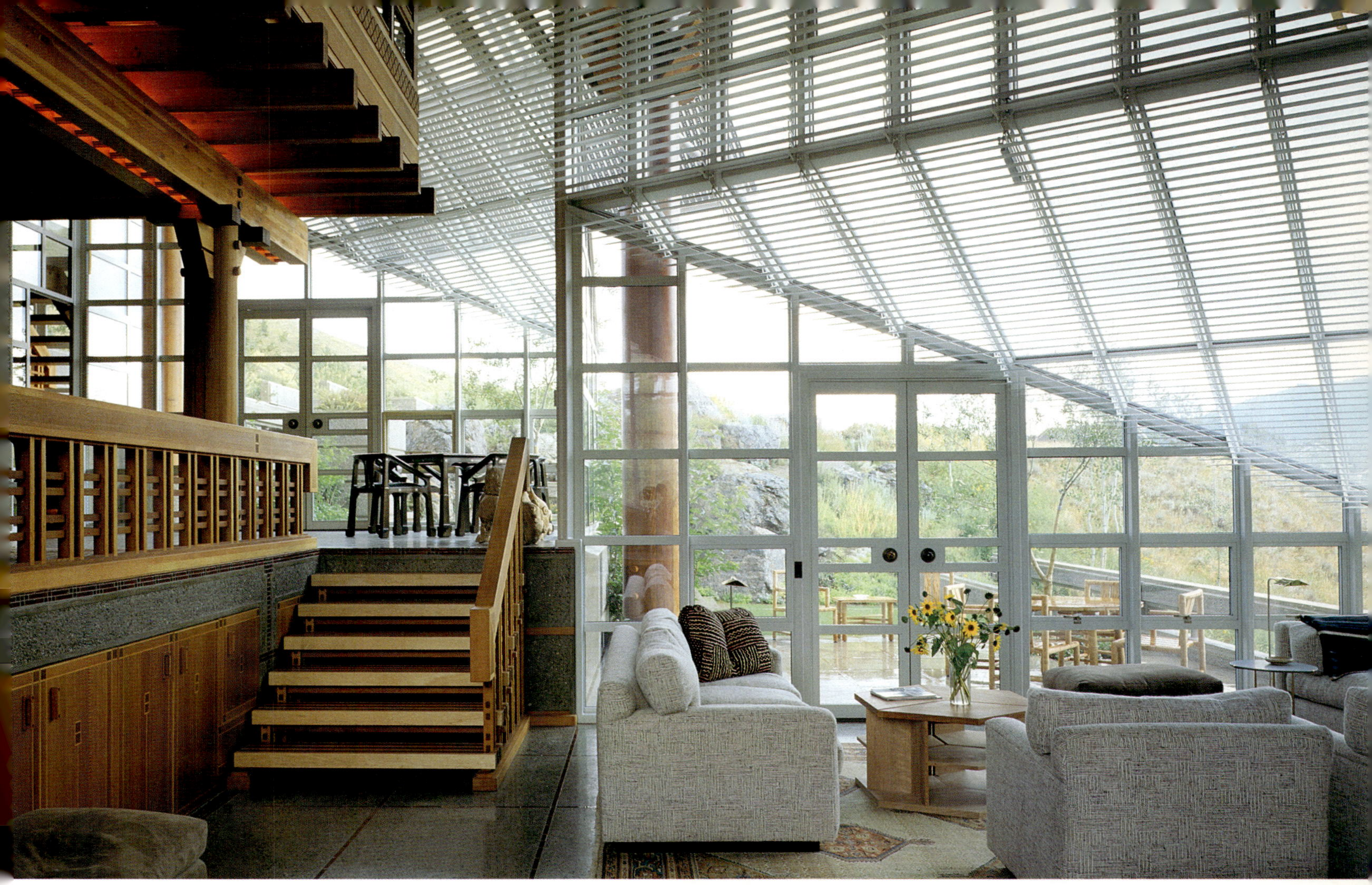

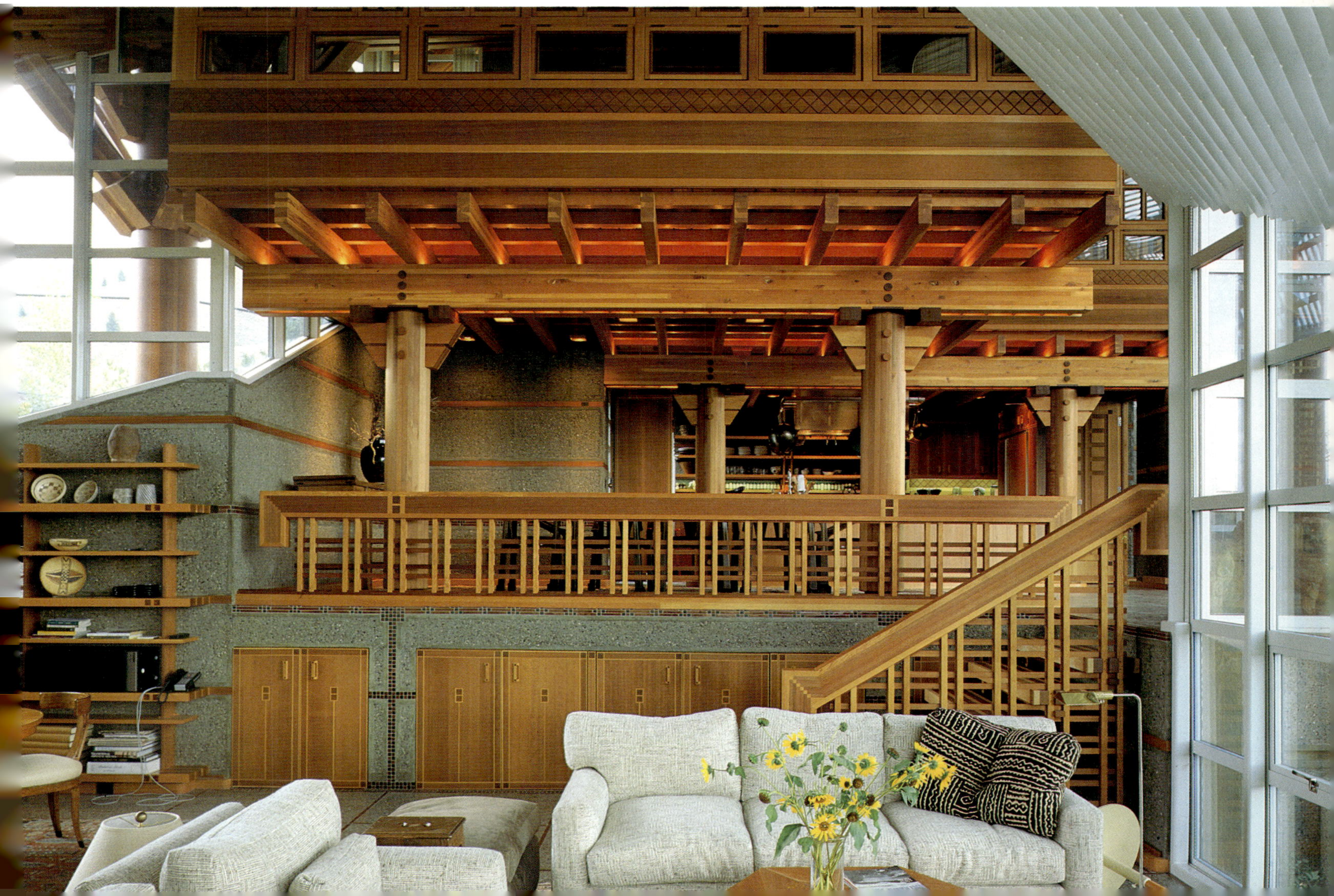

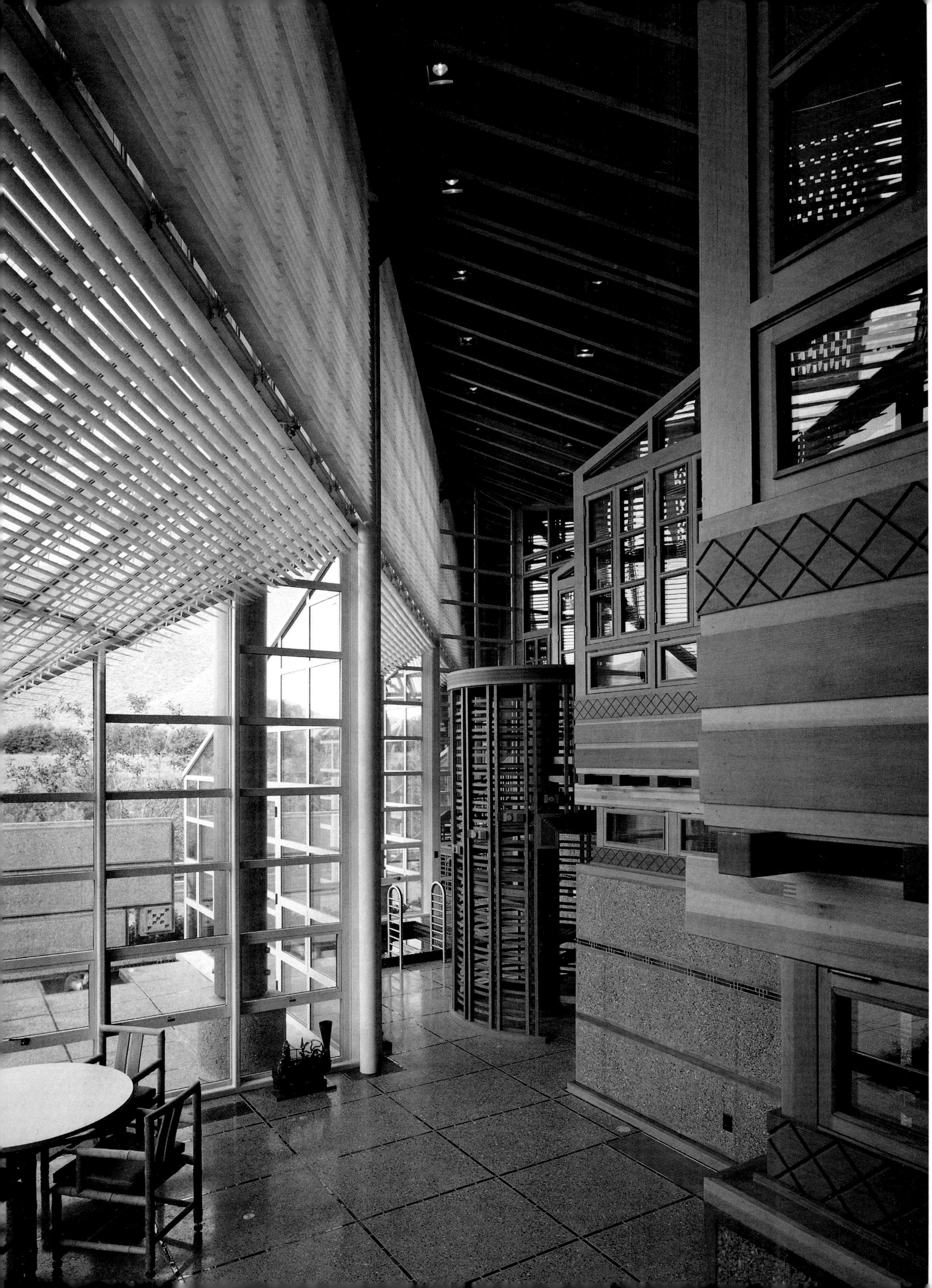

73

ANTOINE PREDOCK
Geoffrey Beebe, project architect
Rio Grande Valley House
Albuquerque, New Mexico
1983-85

Photos: W. Fujii

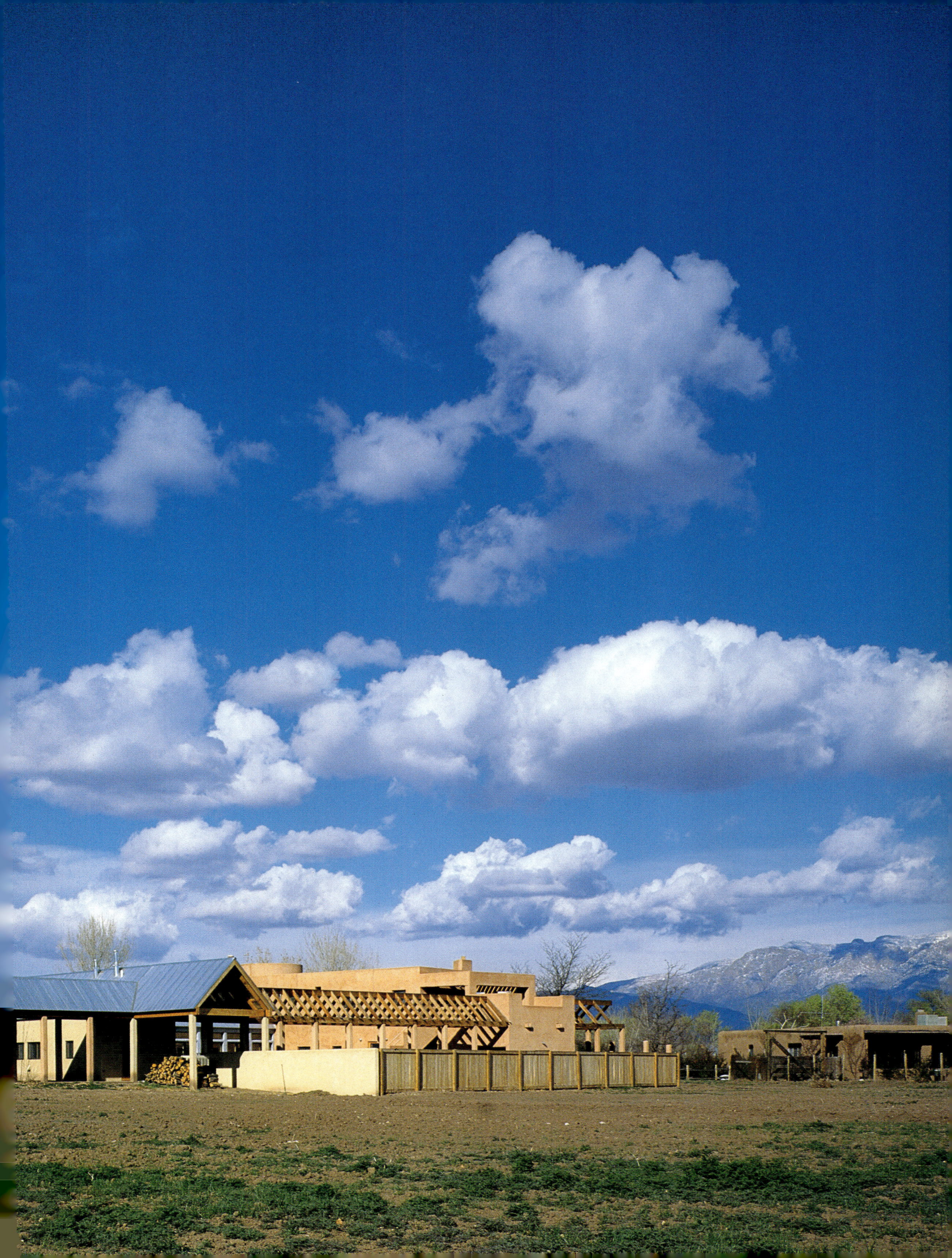

architecture derives from the elemental, spiritual, and human energy of a selected place. In my work in the American Southwest, for instance, I attempt to merge an image of a powerful, surreal landscape with an evocation of the area's cultural stratigraphy to produce an architecture that transcends both historicism and regionalism. Neither of these temporally and stylistically interpretive idioms results in an architecture sufficiently expressive of the richness and diversity which I see in the area.

The power of the Southwestern landscape emanates from the amalgamation of landform, climate, and light; that of the cultural stratigraphy, from a composite of physical artifacts and palpable spiritual forces. The elements of the landscape — the geology, violent diurnal and seasonal temperature extremes, and the highly variable quality of light — interact continually to suggest myriad architectural forms. The common denominator in the visual sequence of mesa, butte, gorge, desert, and mountain is a compelling starkness, a starkness modulated and dramatized by the intensity of climatic forces and light.

The cultures which have successively inhabited this region left behind fragments of their objects and traces of their rituals. Where no deposition of cultural sediment occurred, there are intangible remains, i.e. a noticeable gap in the historic, stratigraphic record and an echo of a habitation pattern. The layered memories in a cultural road cut of this region would range from the profoundly moving memory of the Anasazi and early Spanish settlements to the ephemera of the contemporary strip to the emanations of the UFO's. Popular images of the Southwest deriving from these echoes incorporate both the austerity of pre-Columbian sites and the extravagance of cowboy movie/Marlboro country scenography.

The architectural potential implicit in the imagery of specifically Southwestern settings is further enriched by other significant, indirectly related sources: concepts of transitions — de Chirico passages, the Taliesin West breezeway, Mark Rothko's dissolving color edges, and the Moorish sense of deep passage; the notion of layering — the Mosque upon the base of Luxor Temple signifying a secondary architecture astride a primary base, science fiction landscapes; and temporal notions — the telescoping of human, historical, and geological time at energy extraction sites.

From a variety of site-specific and thematically pertinent symbolic sources are conceived projects ranging from the following residential commissions to the Fine Arts Complex for Arizona State University. The selection of the images results not in a random assemblage of elements but rather in a poetic distillation. Each form, each pattern has multiple meanings reflecting and defining the overriding significance of the total work.

La Luz, Albuquerque, N.M., 1974

Photos: W. Fujii

Toy Villa for Susannah Rosenthal Antoine Predock Architect

Rosenthal Residence Manhattan Beach, Calif., 1985

建築は特定の場所がはらむ自然，精神，人間のエネルギーから生まれる。アメリカ南西部における私の仕事を例にとろう。そこでは，力強く超現実的なランドスケープのイメージを，地域がもつ文化的地層の中へ溶け込ませることで，歴史主義も地域主義も超越したひとつの建築を生み出すことが試みられている。つまり，歴史主義とか地域主義とかいった様式や世俗性を説明する用語から，私がその地域に見い出す豊かさや多様性を十全に表現する建築など導きようもないのだ。

南西部のランドスケープの力，それは地形と気候と光の混淆，人工的な実体と触知できる精神力の組合せ，すなわち文化的地層から醸成されている。地層，日ごと季節ごとのすさまじい気温，激変する光といったランドスケープの要素は，不断に，数限りない建築形態を暗示せんと作用するのだ。台地や孤丘，狭谷，砂漠，それに山などの視覚的シークェンスにおける共通分母はといえば，抑圧的なまでの断固さ，気候や光の強度によって変化し劇化する断固さなのである。

この地域に連綿と存在した文化は，独自の儀式性をもつ物象や形跡を断片的に残してきた。しかし文化上の沈殿が起こらないところでは，そこに残るものは漠然とせざるをえない。すなわち，そこでは由緒ある地層化された遺構と居住パターンへの反映といったもののあいだに明確な亀裂が存在する。件の地方の文化的断層に積層された記憶は，アナサジや初期スペインの開拓地がもつ深く感動的なそれから，現代都市のめまぐるしく変わる街路，さらにはUFOの放射物に至るまで広がっている。南西部のポピュラーなイメージは，プレ・コロンビアの土地がもつ厳格性と，法外なカウボーイ映画やマルボーロのカントリー的舞台性の合体した響きからもたらされているのである。

南西部という舞台に固有なイメージ，そこに潜む建築の潜在力は，源泉と非直接的に関連づいた他者的な意味作用によって，はるかに豊かなものにされている。たとえばトランジッションの諸コンセプト，デ・キリコの街路，タリアセン・ウエストのブリーズウェイ（被覆通路），マーク・ロットーの融解した色彩エッジ，ムーア的感覚の深いパッサージュ，といったものだ。あるいは多層化の観念，これはルクソール神殿上のモスクが示すような第1の基壇に重ねられた第2の建築といったサイエンス・フィクション的ランドスケープなどを考えればよい。また現世的な観念としては，エネルギーを得る敷地において立ち現われる人間的，歴史的，地層学的な時間の自在な伸縮などがあるだろう。

敷地に固有でかつテーマ的にも適切なシンボリックな源泉より，以下の住宅からアリゾナ州立大学の美術館コンプレックスに至るまでのプロジェクトが考えられている。イメージの選択は，諸エレメントのランダムなアッサンブラージュとしてではなく，むしろ詩的な蒸留として結実しているはずだ。それぞれの形，それぞれのパターンは，多様化した意味をもち，作品としての総体という意味作用を凌駕するものであることを規定し反映している。　　　　（AP）

Meet the Architect
ANTOINE PREDOCK

Citadel, Albuquerque, N.M., 1973

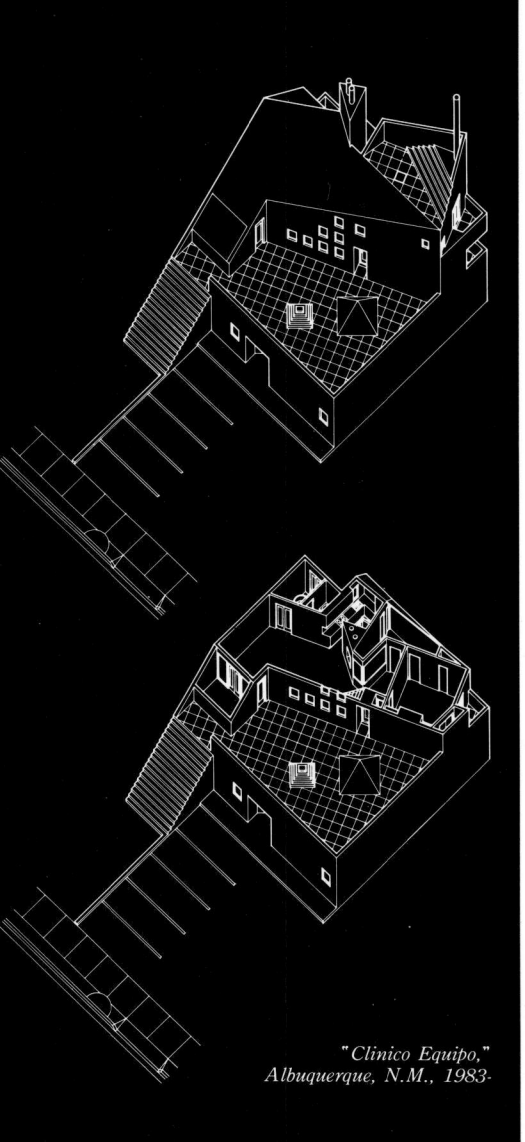

"Clinico Equipo," Albuquerque, N.M., 1983

アルバカーキの建築家
アントワーヌ・プレドック
作品論 ⑲

Albuquerque's north valley is charged with landscape memories. Over time, the widely meandering course of the now channeled Rio Grande left a rich residue of agricultural land. Present day irrigation of these lands has its engineering roots in Andalusia and Moorish North Africa. (The Spanish name for the ditches, Acequia, comes from the Arabic). The once abundant croplands on the Rio Grande's eastern banks have diminished with real estate development pressures.

Sited in this historic area, the Rio Grande Valley House responds gently to the valley ambiance. The house extends into the alfalfa covered site with a horizontality appropriate to the sweep of the valley and the wall of the Sandia mountains beyond. A rural North Valley feeling is projected through the pitched metal roofs, long, low massive walls and the promise of inner gardens.

A skewed grid of linear pavilion-like pieces align mountain views while maintaining the implication of the orthogonal pattern of surrounding fields. A pool/patio forms the centerpiece for the surrounding living/ dining/kitchen pavilions and a shady pergola. The double courtyard Pompeiian house comes to mind as does the early New Mexican hacienda with its figure-eight plan.

The intersecting pitched roof pavilions guide circulation, doubling on the east-west axis as a solar greenhouse. Retreating to the cool north side of the house, the sunken living area maintains winter southern exposure via the greenhouse pavilion.

Bedrooms are stacked in a 2 story "house" with the upper level Master Suite accessed by a circular stair, contained in a silo-like tower. A master bedroom terrace stair connects back to the central court level.

Retreat and respite from the two physician-owners busy professional lives is made possible by the inward turned, contemplative courtyard plan; and the restful image of the house rises softly from the irrigated fields of memory.

General contractor: Ron J. Romeo

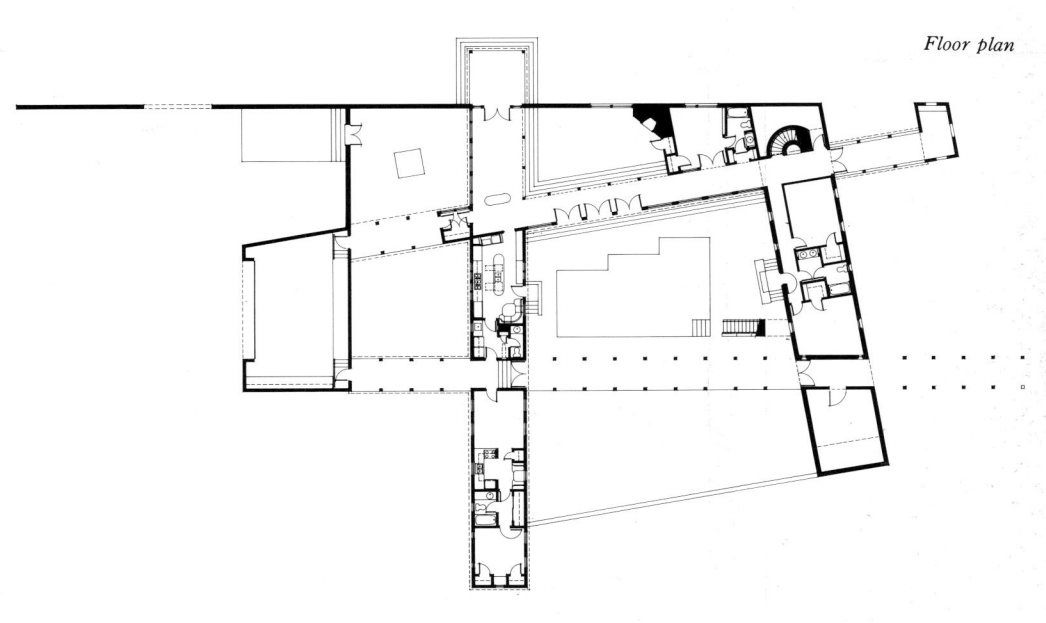

Floor plan

アルバカーキのノースヴァレーはランドスケープの記憶で充たされている。時代を超え今も，開削されたリオ・グランデの広く曲がりくねりながら流れる水筋は，農業地の豊かな残留価値を残していると言ってよい。今日，これらの土地の灌漑は，アンダルシアやムーア人の北アフリカにその技術上のルーツをもつ(掘割りのスペイン名アセキアAcequiaはアラビア語から由来している)。リオ・グランデの東河岸にある農作地帯は不動産開発からの抑圧によって減退してしまった。

このような歴史性をもった地域にある敷地で，この住宅は狭谷環境に穏やかな応答を見せている。アルファルファのおおい茂る敷地の中に，住宅は，狭谷一帯や背後のサンディア山脈の壁に合わせて水平に伸びている。田園的なノースヴァレーの気分は，金属の勾配屋根，長く低いマッシヴな壁面，中庭の気配などに反映されてゆく。

直線形をしたパビリオンの断面がつくる斜行するグリッドが山と一線をなす一方，周囲の原野がもつ直交パターンの意味を保全する。プール/パティオは，周りのリヴィング/ダイニング/キッチンをもつパビリオンと，日影を落とすパーゴラの中心部を形成している。2つの中庭をもつポンペイ式住宅は，初期のニューメキシコの農家に特徴的な8の字プランを彷彿させるだろう。

勾配屋根のパビリオンの交差は，ソーラー式の温室がつくる東西軸上で2重化されながら，サーキュレーションを導いてゆく。住宅の涼しい北面に引き込む形で沈み込んだリヴィングの領域が，温室パビリオンを経由して冬季の南面性を確保する．

ベッドルームは2層となった「住宅」内に積層される形で設けられ，上階にはサイロのようなタワーの中に設けられた円階段によってアクセスできる主人のスイートがある。マスターベッドルームのテラス階段は，中央の中庭レヴェルと背後で結ばれている。

忙しい職業生活をおくる2人の医師の隠遁と休息は，内側に向いた瞑想的な中庭式平面によって実現された。さらに，住宅のもつ安らかなイメージは，灌漑された原野という記憶から柔らかに立ち現われてゆくのだ。

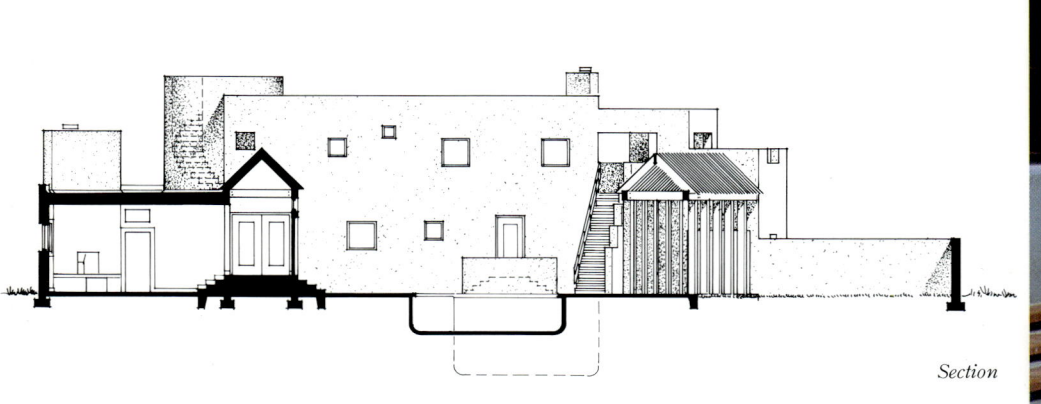

Section

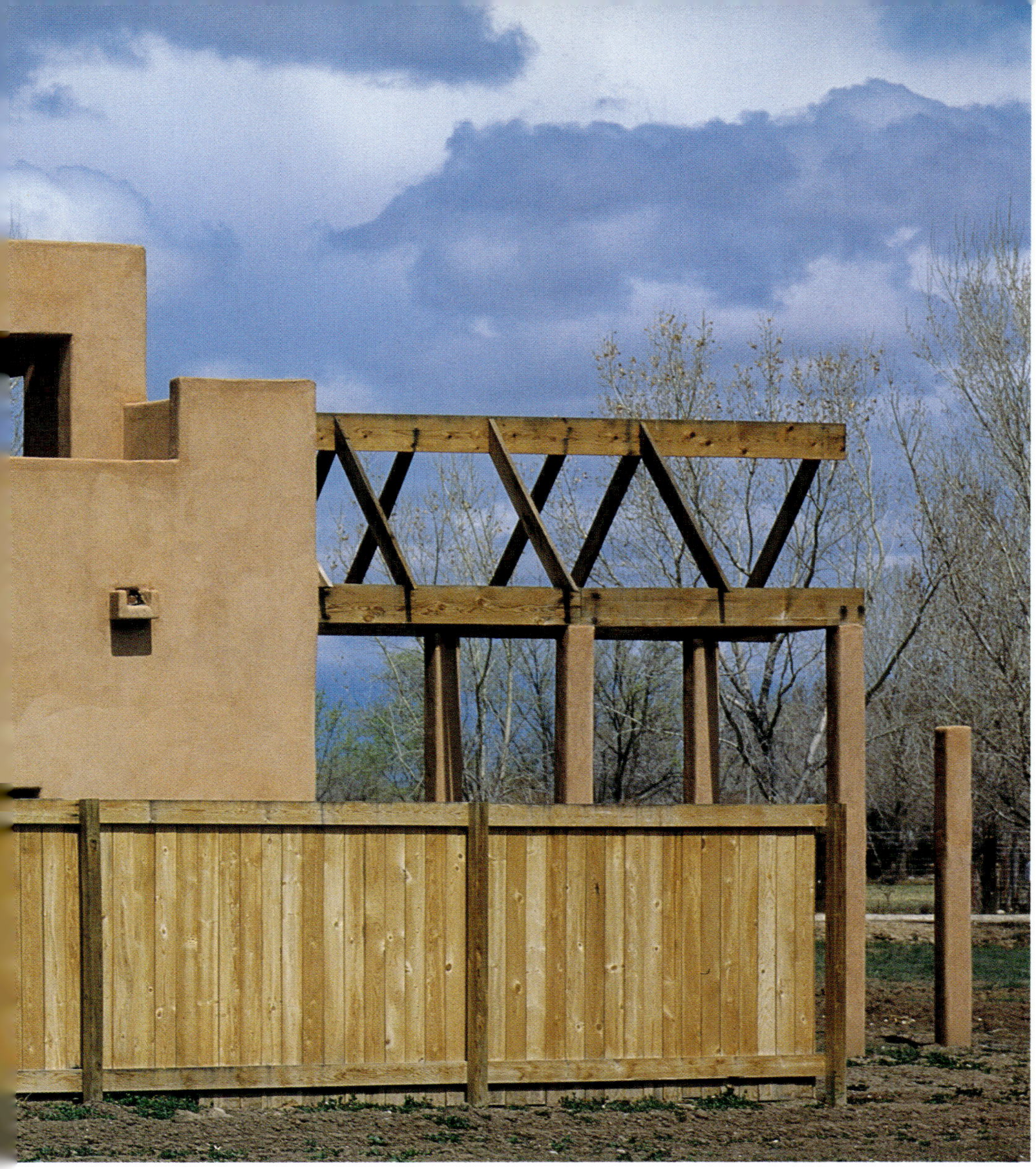

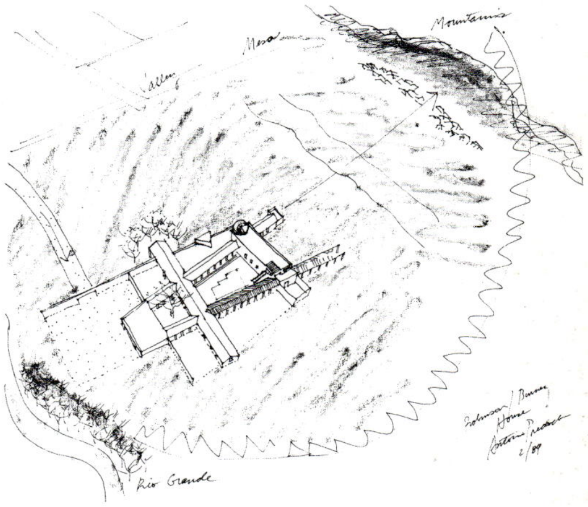
Mountains
Mesa
Valley
Rio Grande
2/89

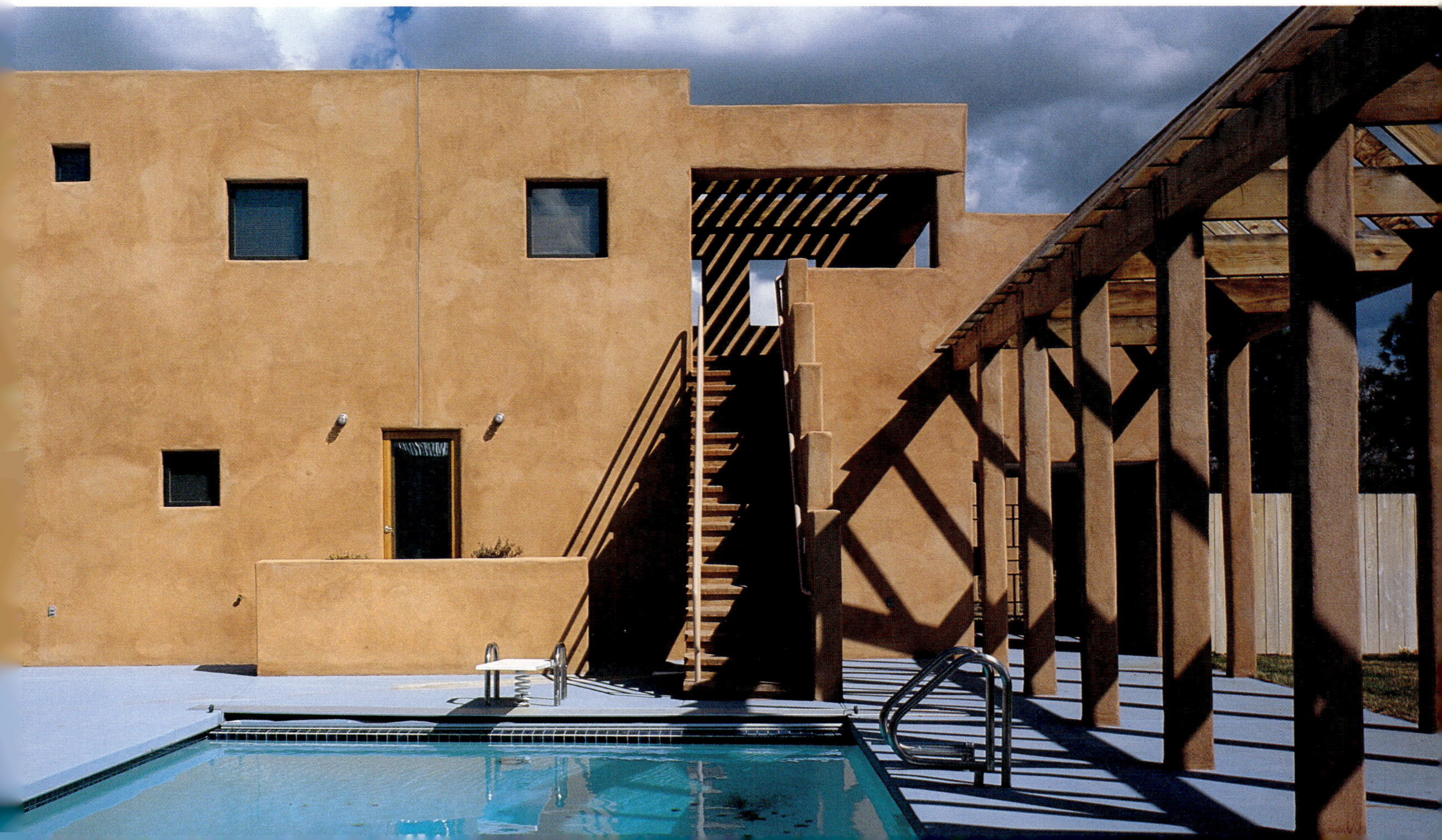

80

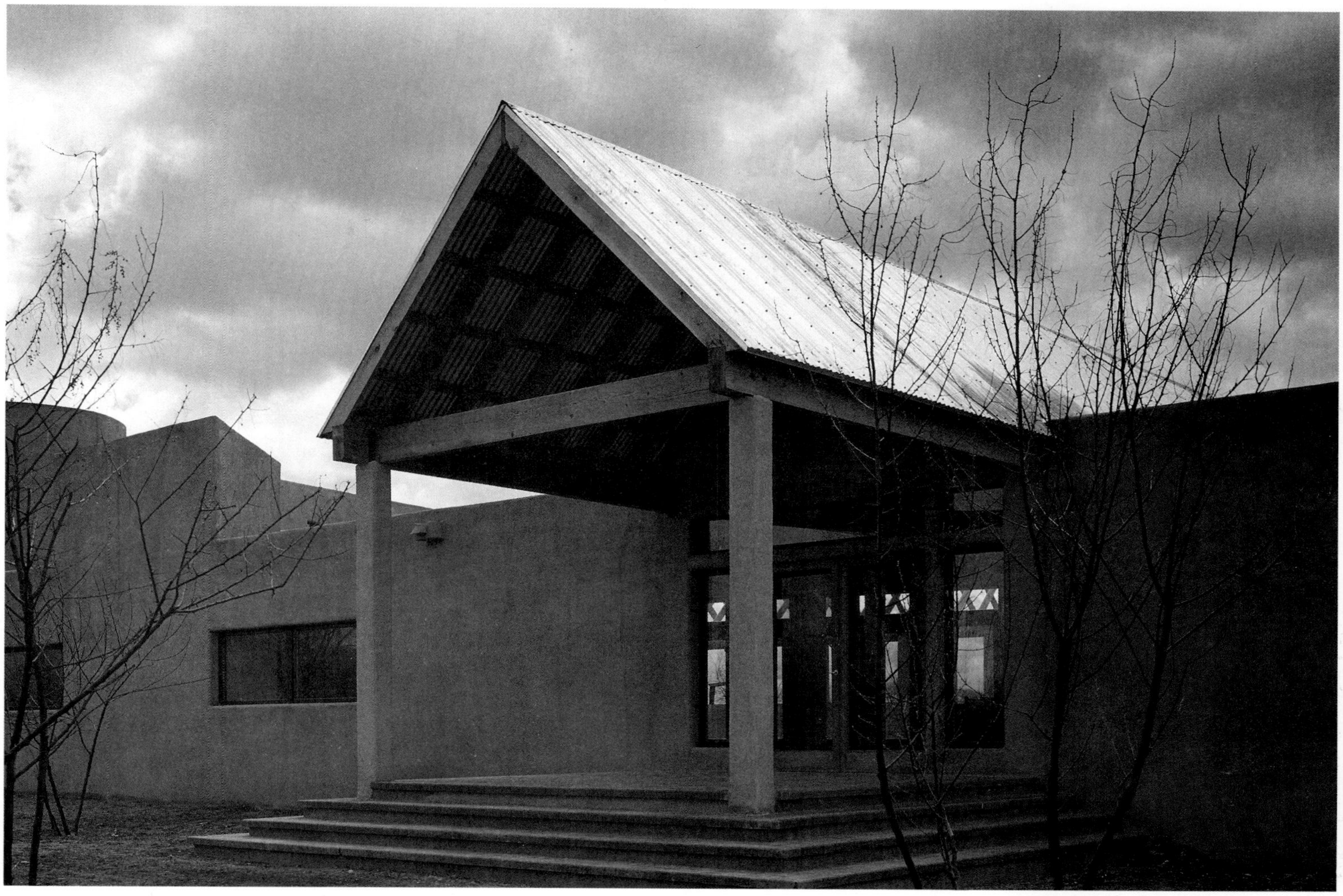

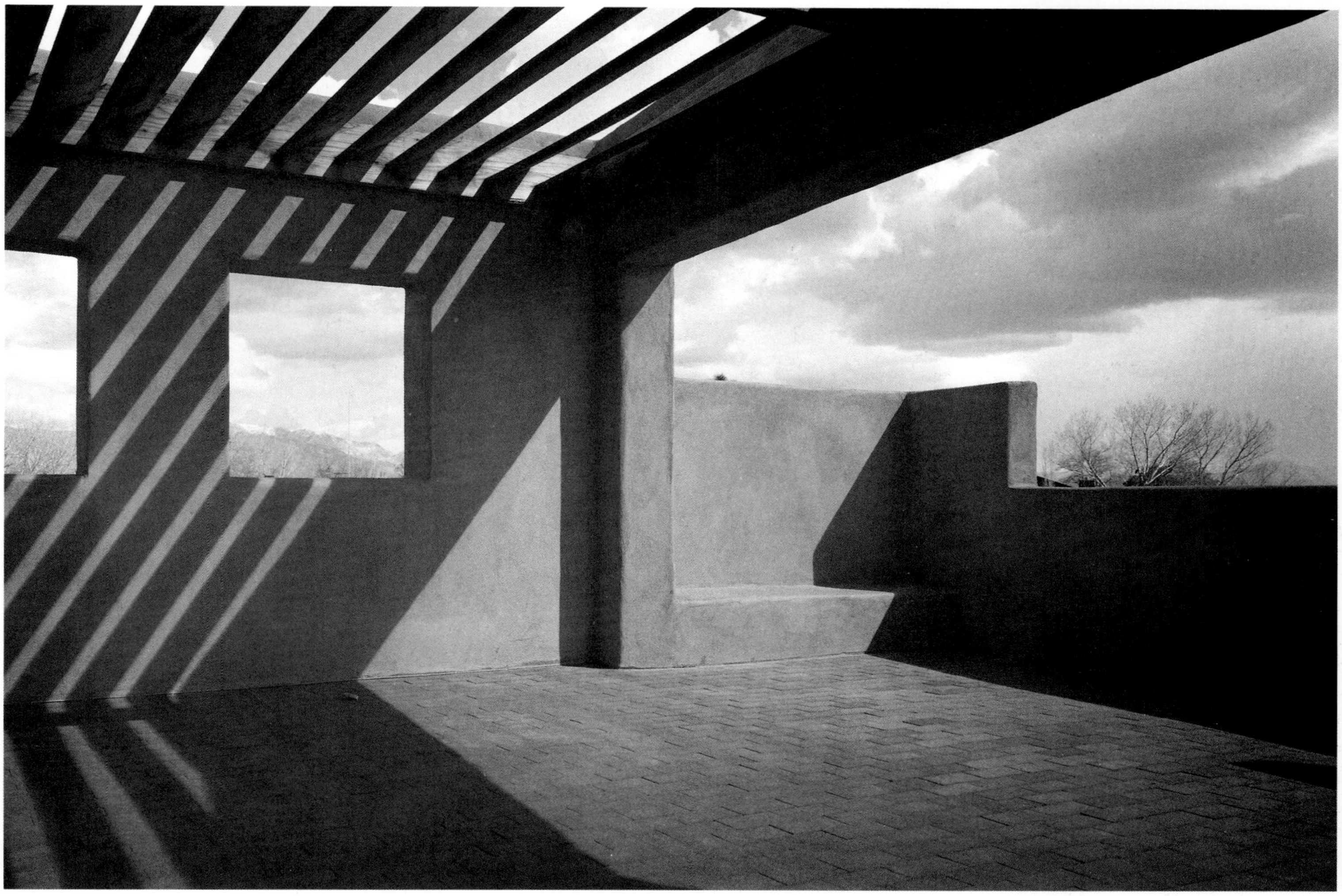

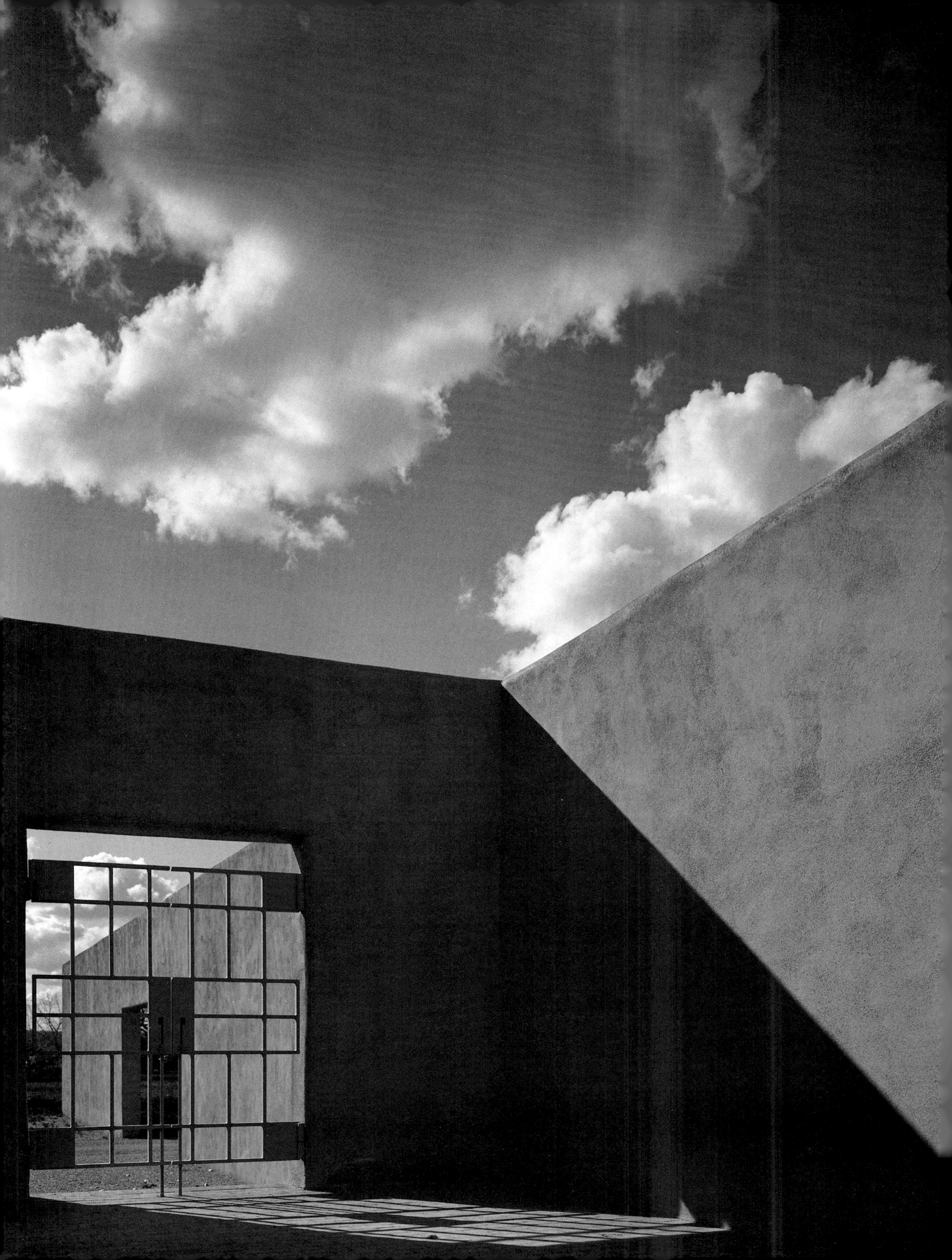

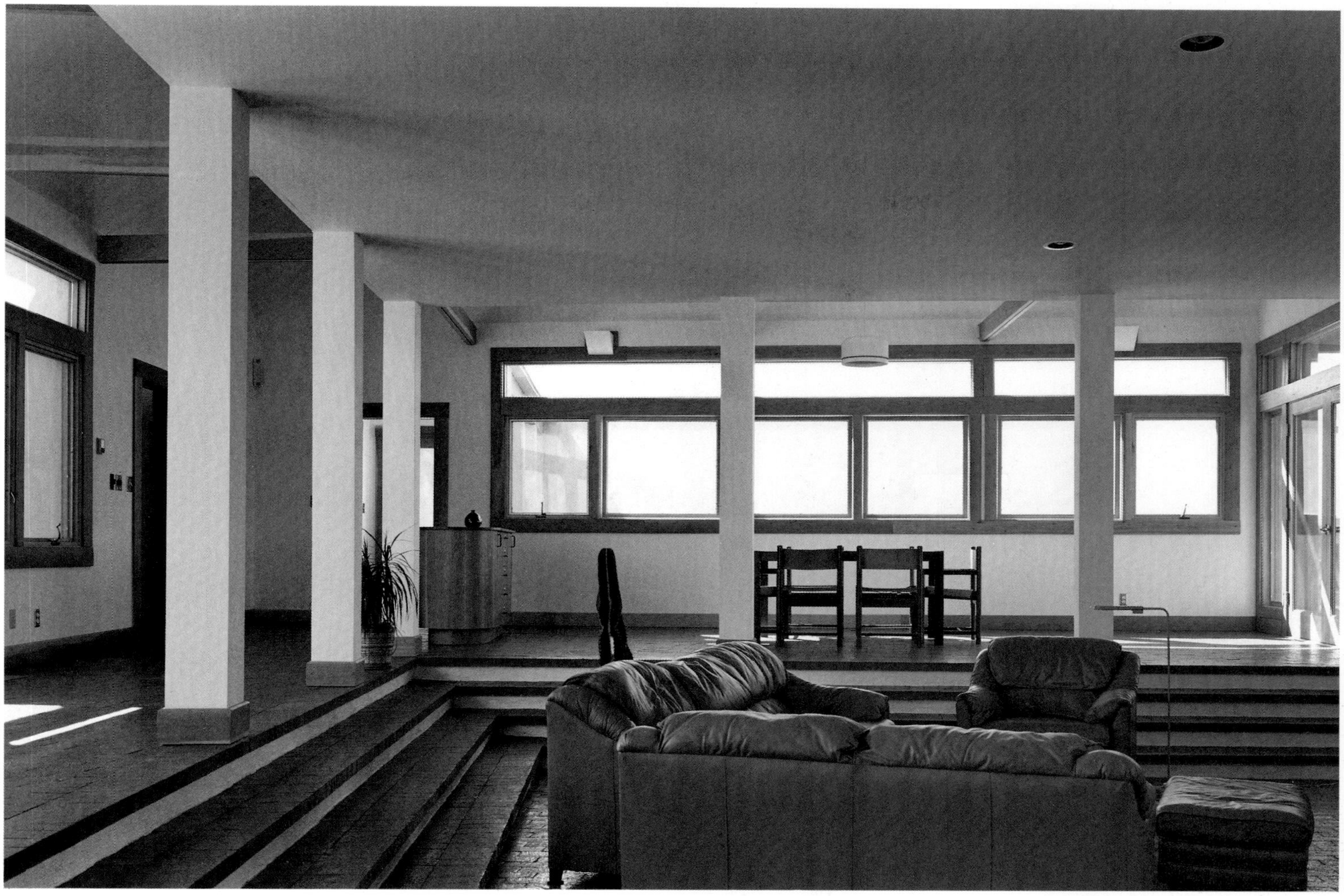

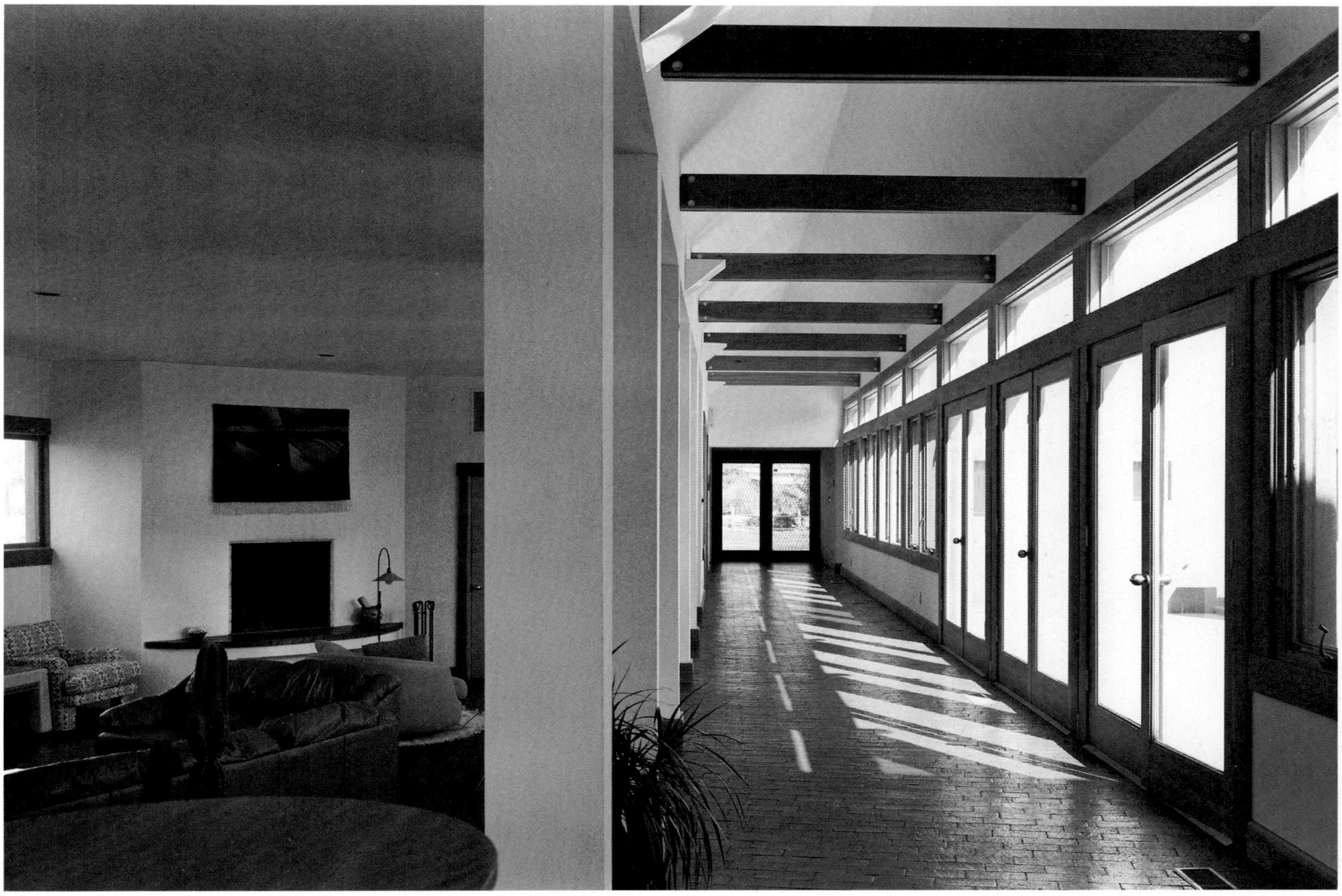

ANTOINE PREDOCK
Ronald Jacob, project manager
Fuller House
Pinnacle Peak, Arizona
1984-86

Photos: W. Fujii

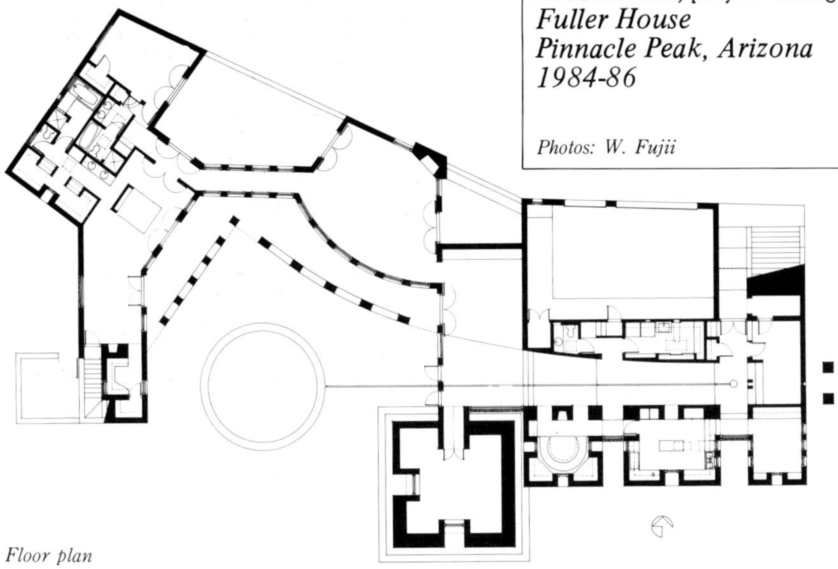

Floor plan

The Fuller house is centrally located in a single-family, detached-housing community north of Phoenix, Arizona. The high Sonoran desert site is enclosed by peaks and eroded, decomposed granite ridges. Saguaro, cholla, ocotillo, and prickly pear cacti are interspersed throughout the site with palo verde and ironwood trees and jojoba and creosote bushes.

In the harsh Arizona desert a cool retreat is created that physically and symbolically links house and landscape. A processional sequence across the building terrain from sunrise to sunset organizes elements of the plan: a sunrise – viewing pavilion is situated above the breakfast room; an interior 'canyon' (gallery with centered, sequential water system) leads past the abstracted kitchen and dining 'boulders'; the 'mountain' (pyramidal den) introduces the 'valley' (a central patio); across the 'valley' a trellised, sunset-viewing platform completes the sequence.

At each event in this sequence the building features vantage points for taking in the vistas. The stepped exterior of the pyramidal den provides seating for viewing the night lights of Phoenix. The living areas focus on the distant mountains beyond the city. The bedroom zone, set apart from the rest of the house, concentrates attention on its private patio and sunset viewing terrace.

The low weighty perimeter of the house connects in its massiveness to the powerful geologic context and in color to the olive-beige of the desert floor. Viewed from a distance this base becomes a mesa, and the pyramidal den, a mauve-purple abstraction of the surrounding sculptural peaks. Contrasting brittle shade structures create shadow patterns recalling the tracery cast on the site by the lacy branches of the ocotillo and palo verde.

Architecture as a defense system against a hostile environment is appropriate in the Sonoran desert. The potential claiming of architecture by the landscape sets into motion a dance between building and site. The gentle standoff between the two is expressed in the project as a poetic tension. Project edges are somewhat ambiguous – at times allowing the desert to enter, other times setting a tight line of defense. Refuge is created by the presence of water, shade, and enclosure. Looking out from this sequestered desert retreat, the vast landscape scale can be better comprehended.

General contractor: John Turner

フラー邸は、アリゾナ州フェニックス北にある一家族専用デタッチト・ハウジング・コミュニティの中心に位置する。ソノラン砂漠高地の敷地は山頂や峰や侵食され朽ちかけた花崗岩の尾根に囲まれている。ハシラサボテン、ウチワサボテン、オコティーロ、トゲのあるナシサボテンが、パロ・ヴェルデやアイアンウッド、それにホホバやクレオソート・ブッシュとともに敷地に散在している。

苛酷なアリゾナ砂漠では、涼しい避難所が物理的にも象徴的にも、住宅やランドスケープと結びついて創られている。建物が存在する土地を夜明けから日没まで横断する進行性のシークエンスがプランを組織化する。夜明けの眺望パビリオンが朝食堂の上部に据えられた。インテリアの「キャニオン」(集中式、連続式の水のシステムをもったギャラリー)が、洗練としたキッチンやダイニングの「ピラミッド型の密室へと導いてゆく。「マウンテン」(ピラミッド型の密室)は、「ヴァレー」(中央のパティオ)へと導き、「ヴァレー」を横切ると、格子棚の覆う日没の見晴台がシークエンスを完結させる。

このシークエンス上のそれぞれの場では、素晴らしい眺望を手にできる。ピラミッド型の密室の段状のエクステリアは、フェニックスの夜景を眺める各席ともなる。リヴィングの領域は、都市の彼方に存在するはるか遠くの山々に焦点が当てられつつ考えられた。住宅の他の部分とは分離されたベッドルーンを生み出してゆくのだ。

脅威の環境に対する保護システムとしての建築は、ソノラン砂漠では適切なものとされる。ランドスケープによってもたらされた建築の潜在化した意図は、建物と敷地のあいだに生まれる舞踏を胎動させてゆく。2つのあいだの穏やかなかけひき、このプロジェクトにおいては詩的な緊張として表現される。計画の境界はいくぶんか曖昧なものになっていて──すなわち、あるときは砂漠のにふるうな、別のときは堅固な防護線ともなる。水、陰影、囲いの引き込みによって、避難所は成立している。この引き込まれた砂漠の避難所から外界を見れば、広大なランドスケープのスケールがはるかによく理解できるようというものだ。

住宅がもっとも低く重い周界は、その量塊性は強靭な地質的コンテクストに、その色彩は砂漠面のオリーヴベージュ色に応答している。離れて眺めると、この基壇は台地となり、ピラミッド型の密室は周囲の彫刻的な山頂のマジェンタパープル色の抽象体として際立つ。

はかない影と構造物との対比は、オコティーロやパロ・ヴェルデのレースのような枝ぶりによって、トレーサリー細工のようなものが当てられつつ考えレーンを生み出してゆくのだ。

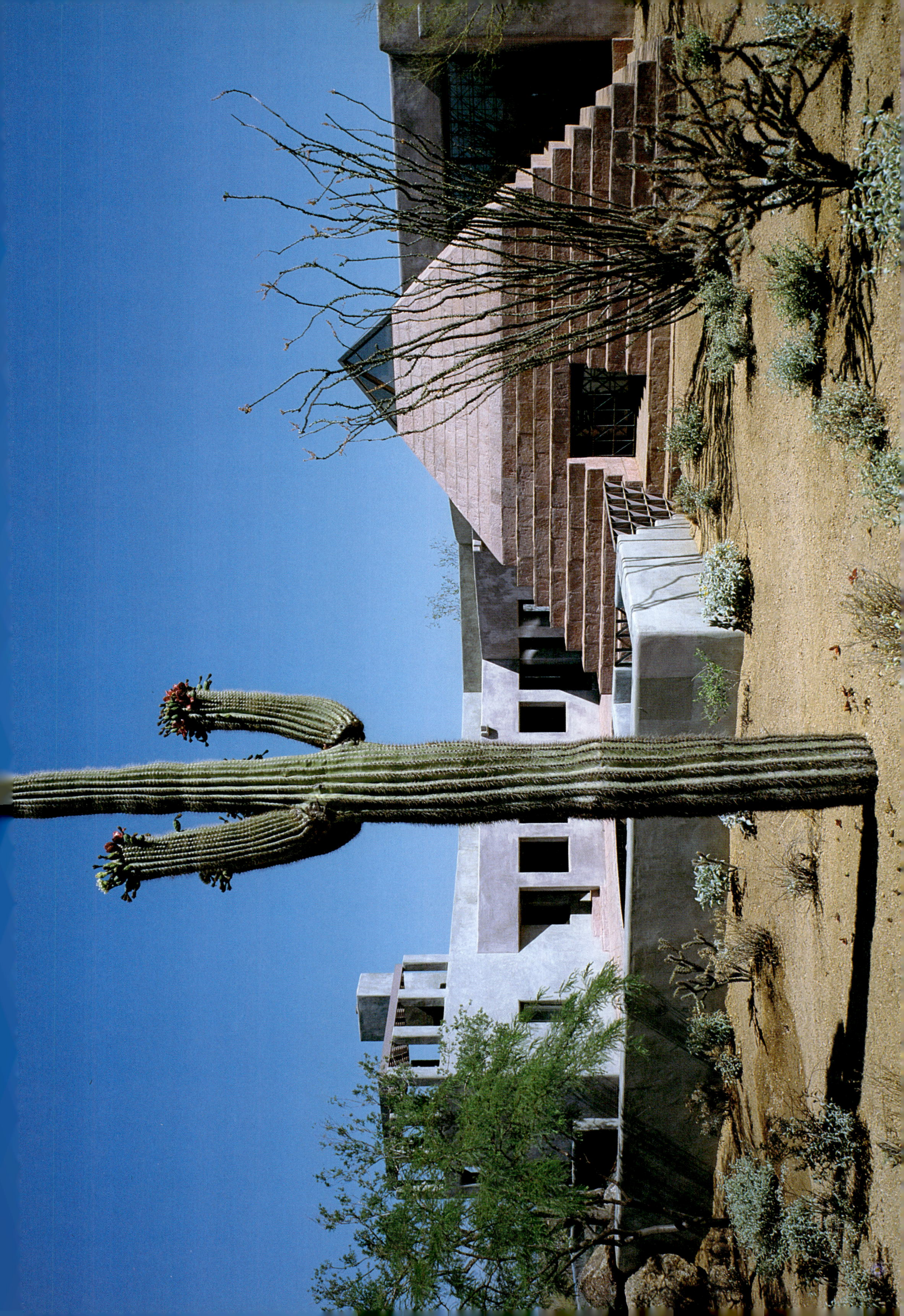

KITCHEN

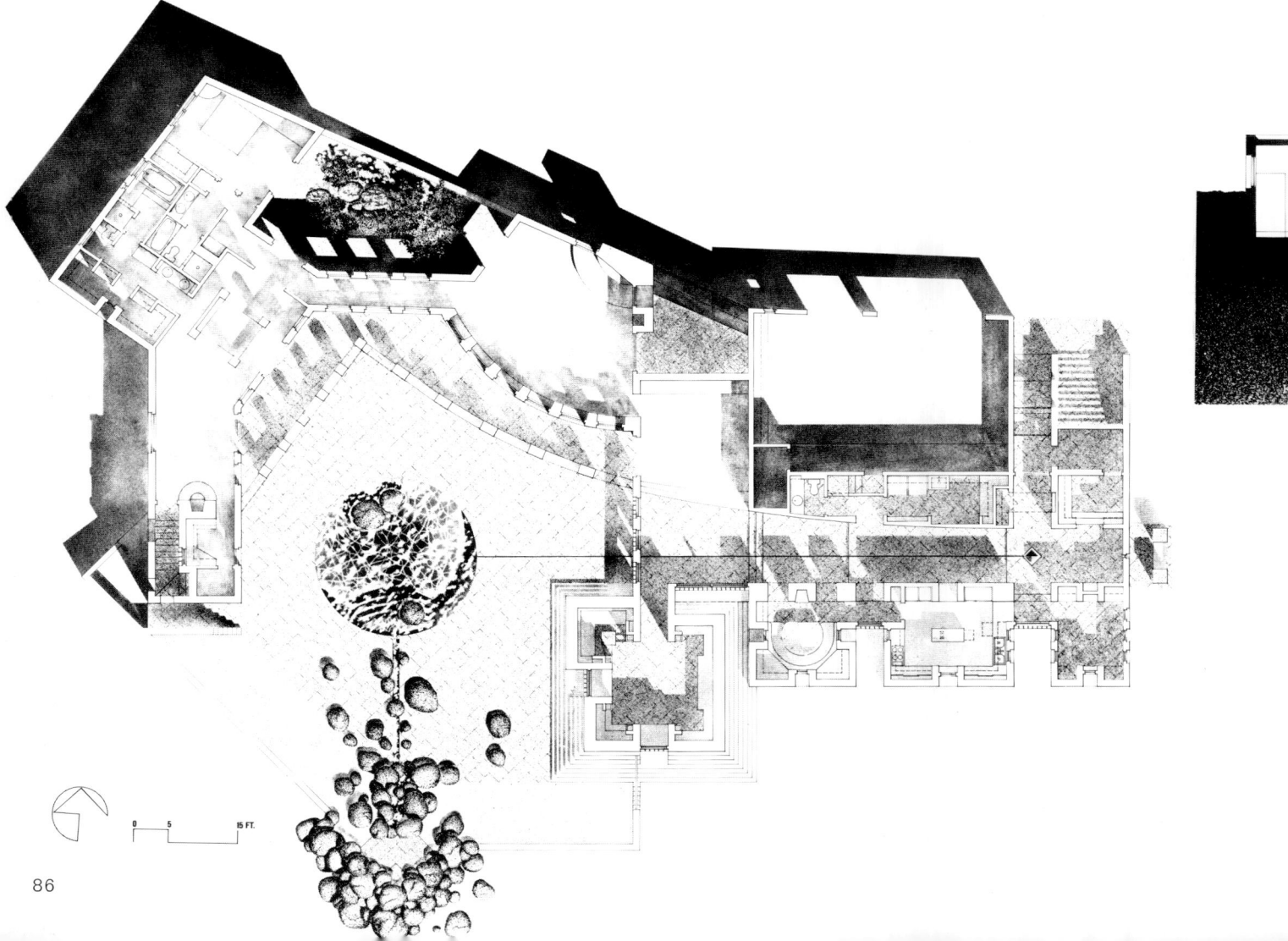

0 5 15 FT.

86

| BREAKFAST | DINING | DEN | POOL | STUDY |

| DEN | GALLERY | LIVING ROOM | PATIO |

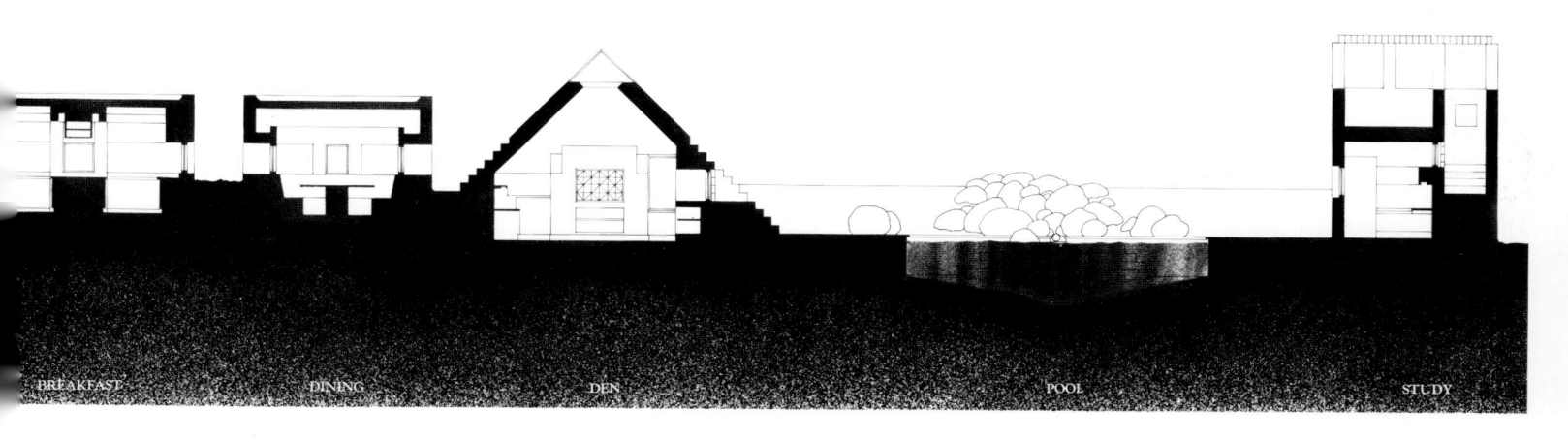

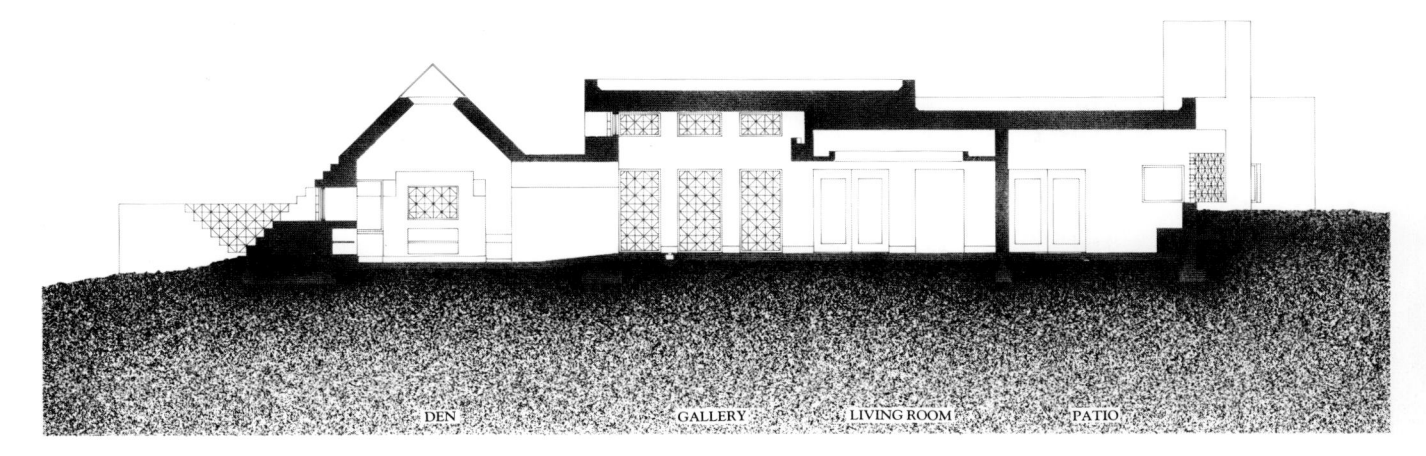

Sections

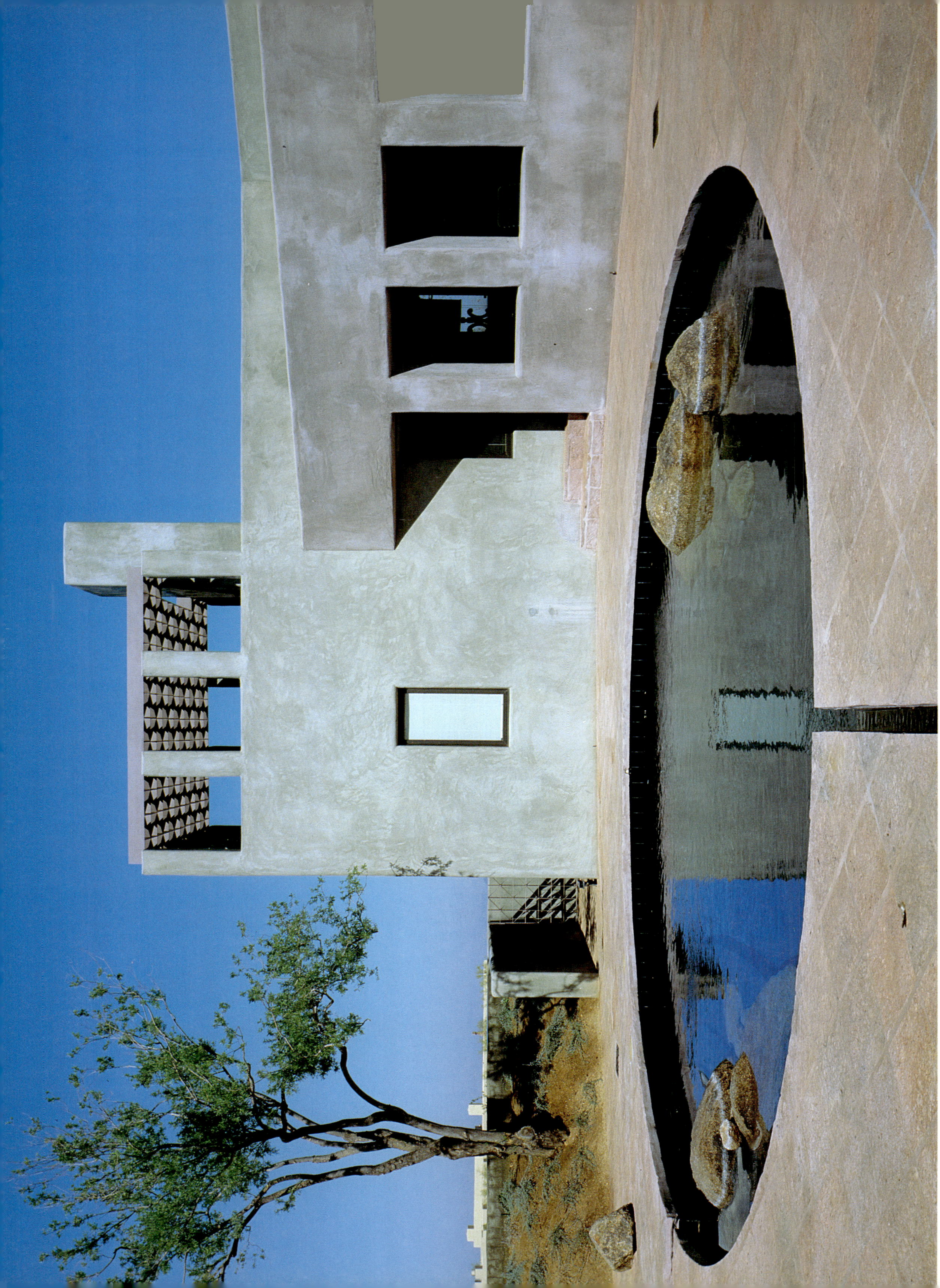

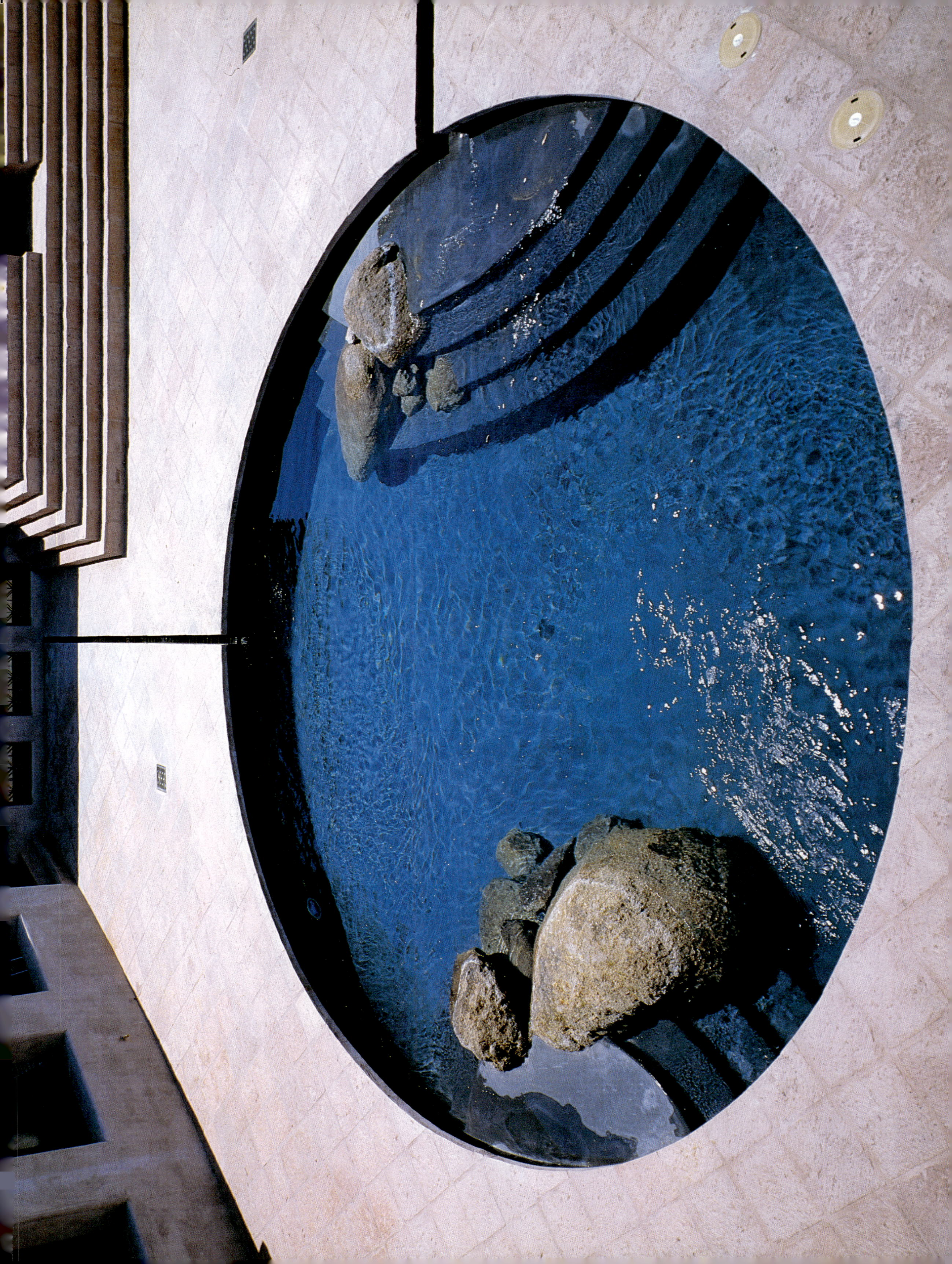

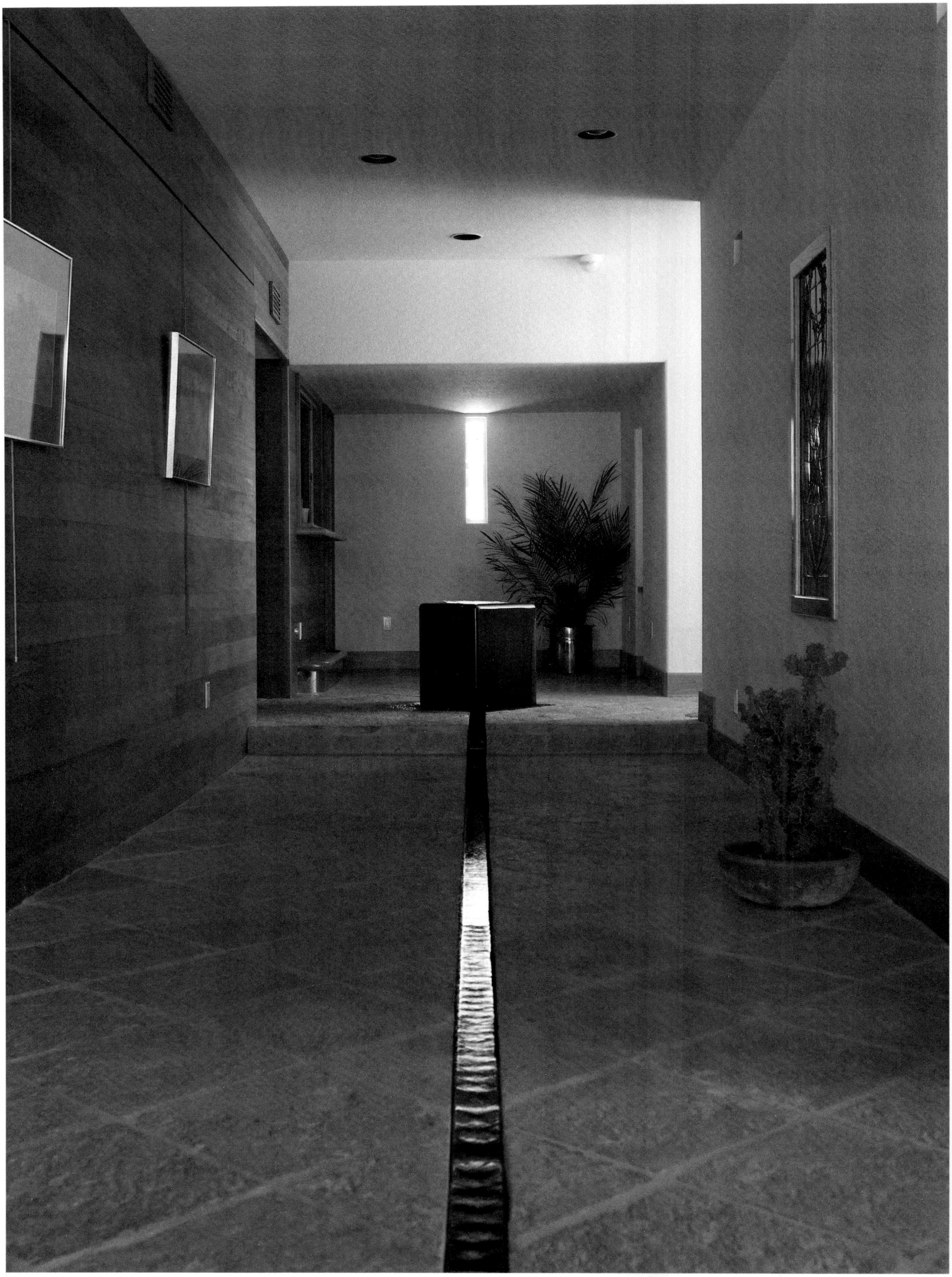

91

ANTOINE PREDOCK
Jon Anderson, project architect
Troy Residence
Taos, New Mexico
1984-85

Photos: W. Fujii

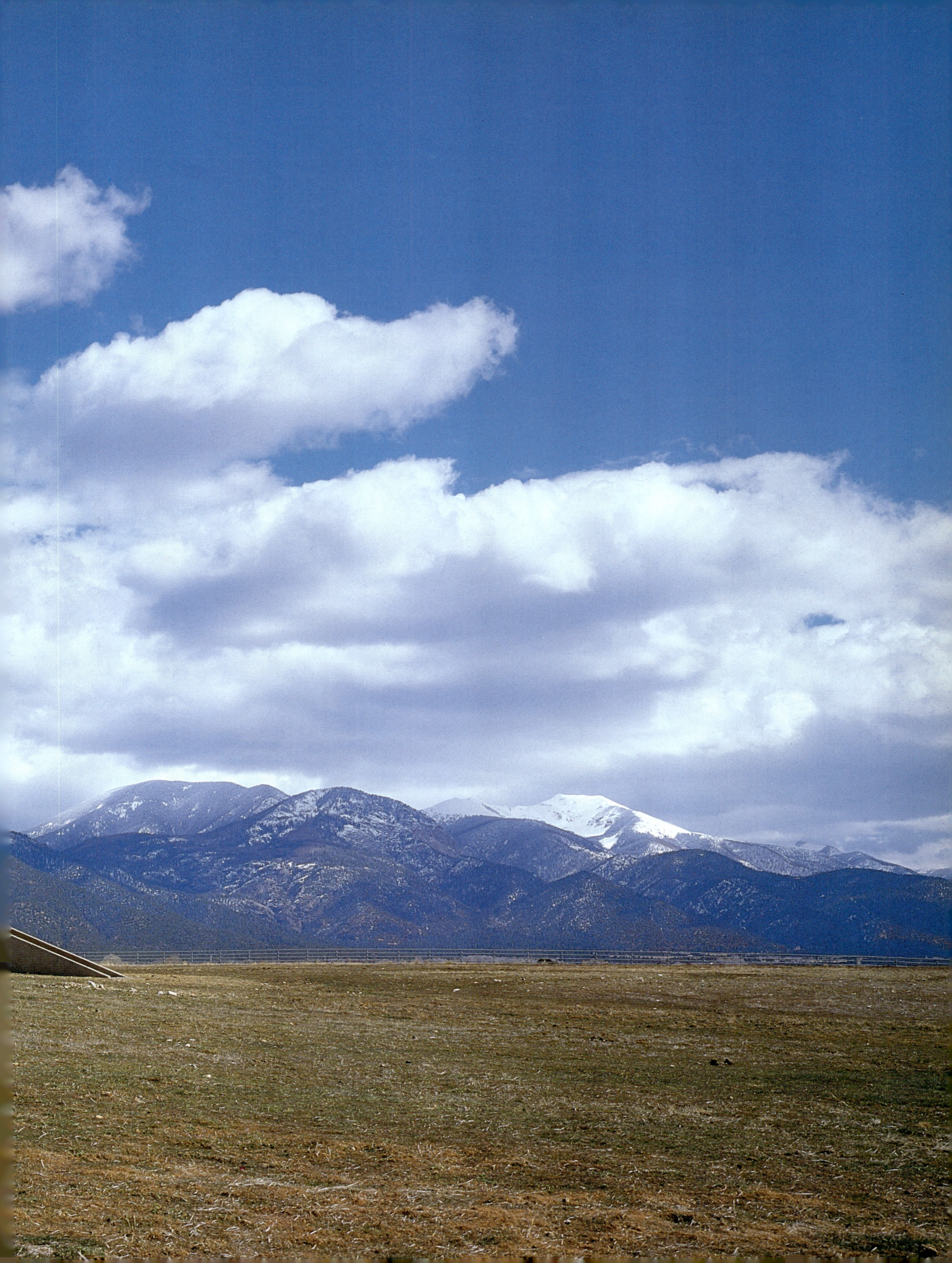

Near Taos, New Mexico a house rises like a mountain peak that is slowly emerging as the surrounding high plateau erodes. This new formation, the Troy residence, recalls literally the angles of mountains visible on the western horizon.

Both the coarse and fine grain of the neighboring, natural slopes find analogues in the man-made form. The dramatic profile of the house and the aggregation of lithic 'pieces' signal the interior arrangement of large volumes and ancillary spaces. The configuration of ceremonial stairs and interior and exterior balconies along the north-south axis provides a trail up the slopes and above interior and exterior 'canyons.' This trek reveals both the organization of the plan and the formal elements involved.

At the intersection of this north-south formal axis and the east-west entry axis occurs a decisive thematic intersection. The walled entry court, symbolic use of color around windows and along *portales*, and the building materials suggest the vocabulary of traditional, regional architecture. What was only intimated at a distance by building color becomes evident here at close range. The processional arrival at the entry hall introduces one to a cultural overlay which provides a counterpoint to the drama of the silhouette. The interplay continues throughout the interior where traditional detailing contrasts the upscaled spaces.

The hybrid result is both protective and gracious. It tempers summer and winter weather extremes, provides vantage points to surrounding views, and welcomes family and guests to its ample hearth. In eschewing a mere stylistic amalgamation the house achieves a creative, transcendent synthesis.

Site plan

Upper level

Lower level

Consultant: Don Felts & Associates, mechanical
General contractor: Colonias Builders

ニューメキシコのタオス近郊に，ひとつの住宅が山頂のように立ち上がり，周囲の高原を侵食しながらゆっくりとその姿を現わす。トロイ邸のこの新しい形態は，文字通り，西部の地平線に見ることのできる山の様相を呼び醒ましてゆく。

粗野であると同時にまた細かい肌理をもった周囲の自然のスロープは人工形態のアナログにもなっている。住宅のドラマティックな形象や石の「断片」集成が，インテリアの大きなヴォリュームと付属的空間の記号となる。南北軸に沿うインテリア，エクステリアのバルコニー群，そして儀式的な階段の配列によって，インテリアとエクステリアのつくる「キャニオン」上のスロープの軌跡が際立ってゆく。この行程によって，プランの組織化のみならず，そこに内包される形態エレメントをも露わにするのだ。

この南北のフォーマルな軸と東西の入口の軸の交差部に，断固としたテーマ性をもった交差が生起している。壁に囲われた入口中庭，窓回りおよび「玄関」に沿っての色彩のシンボリックな使い方，そして建物の素材は伝統的，地域的建築のヴォキャブラリーを暗示している。離れた観点から建物の色彩によって唯一暗示されているものは，近寄ってみるとそこで明らかなものとなる。入口ホールへ進行し，そこに辿り着いてみると，シルエットのドラマと対極をなす観点を提供する文化的重層性へと人を導いてゆく。この相互作用は，伝統的なディテーリングが巨大スケール化した空間と対比をなすインテリアを通して連続してゆく。

ハイブリッドは，保護的なもののみならず優雅さをももたらすものだ。それは夏と冬の極端な気候を調節しながら，周囲への眺望を有利なものとし，豊かな炉辺へと家族やゲストを迎える。たんなる様式上の化合を回避しつつ，住宅は創造的かつ超越的な統合を獲得するのである。

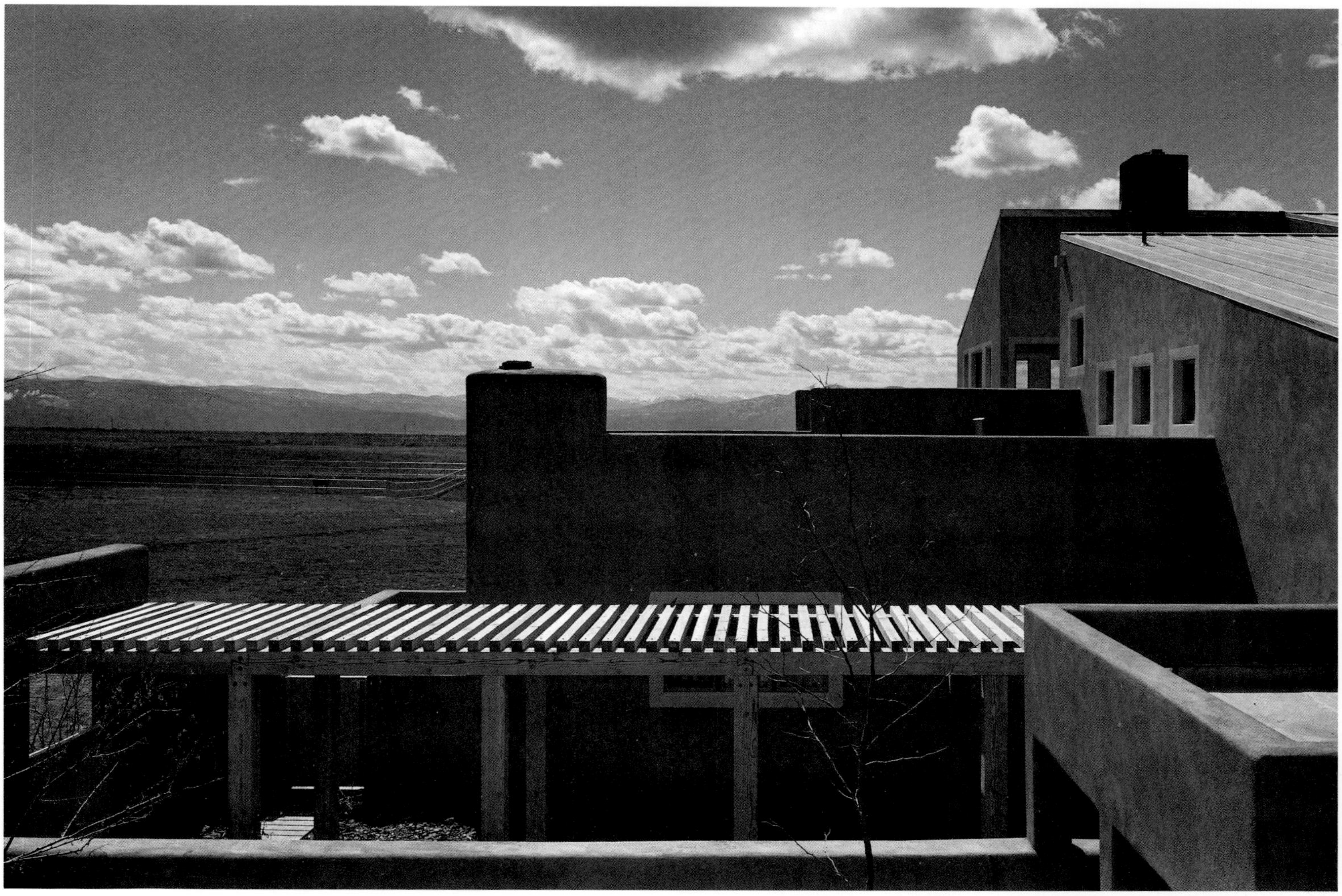

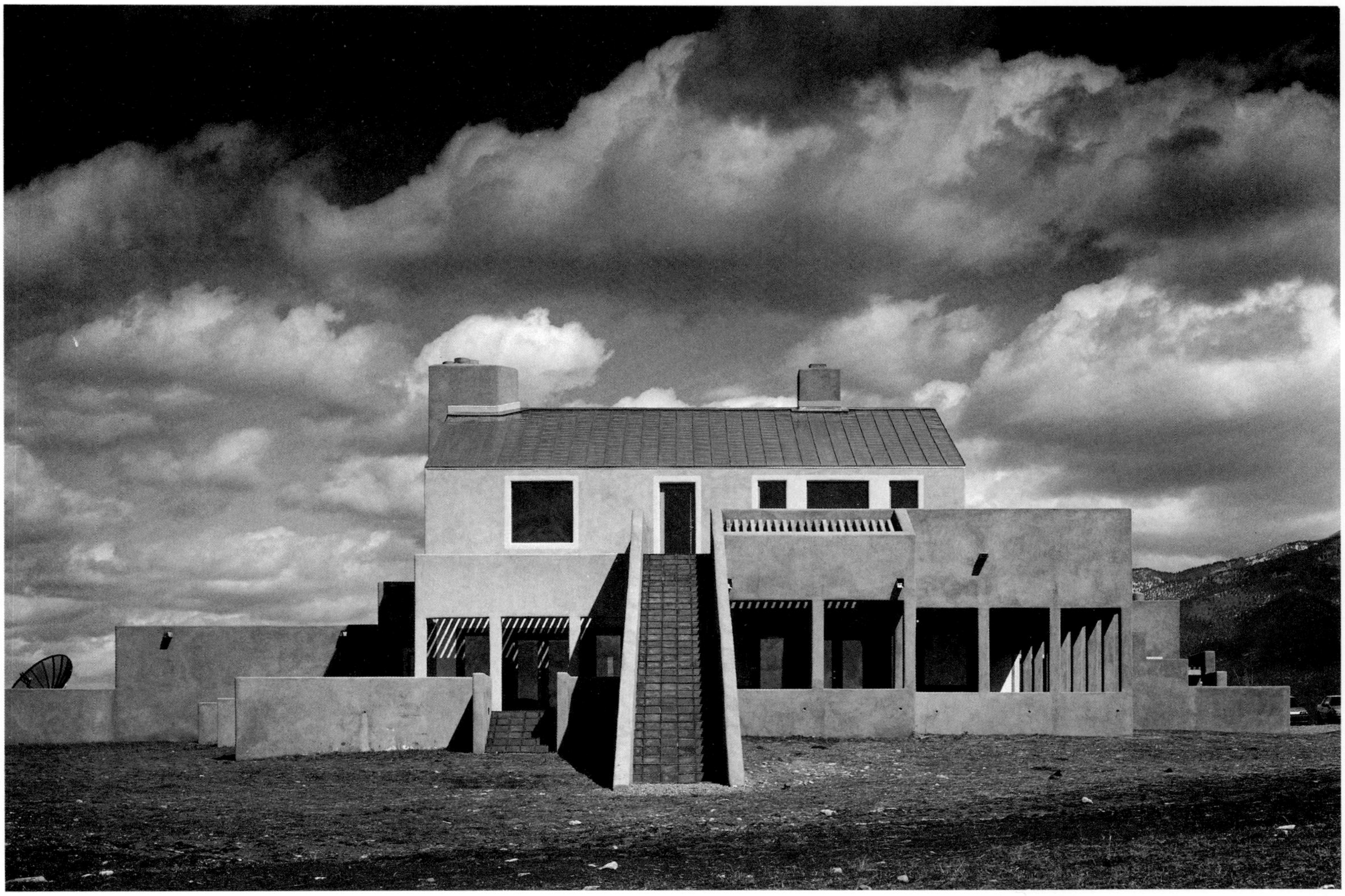

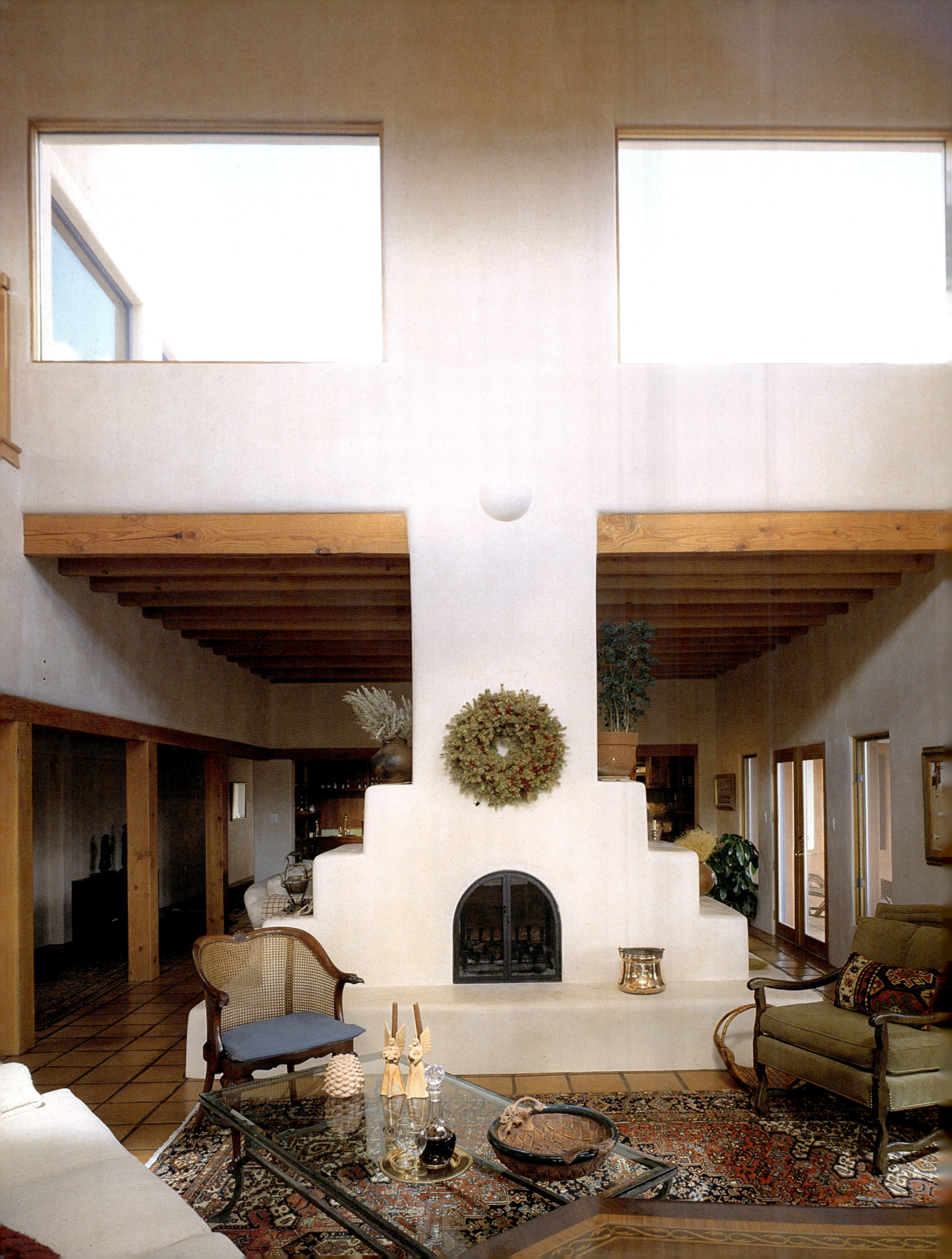

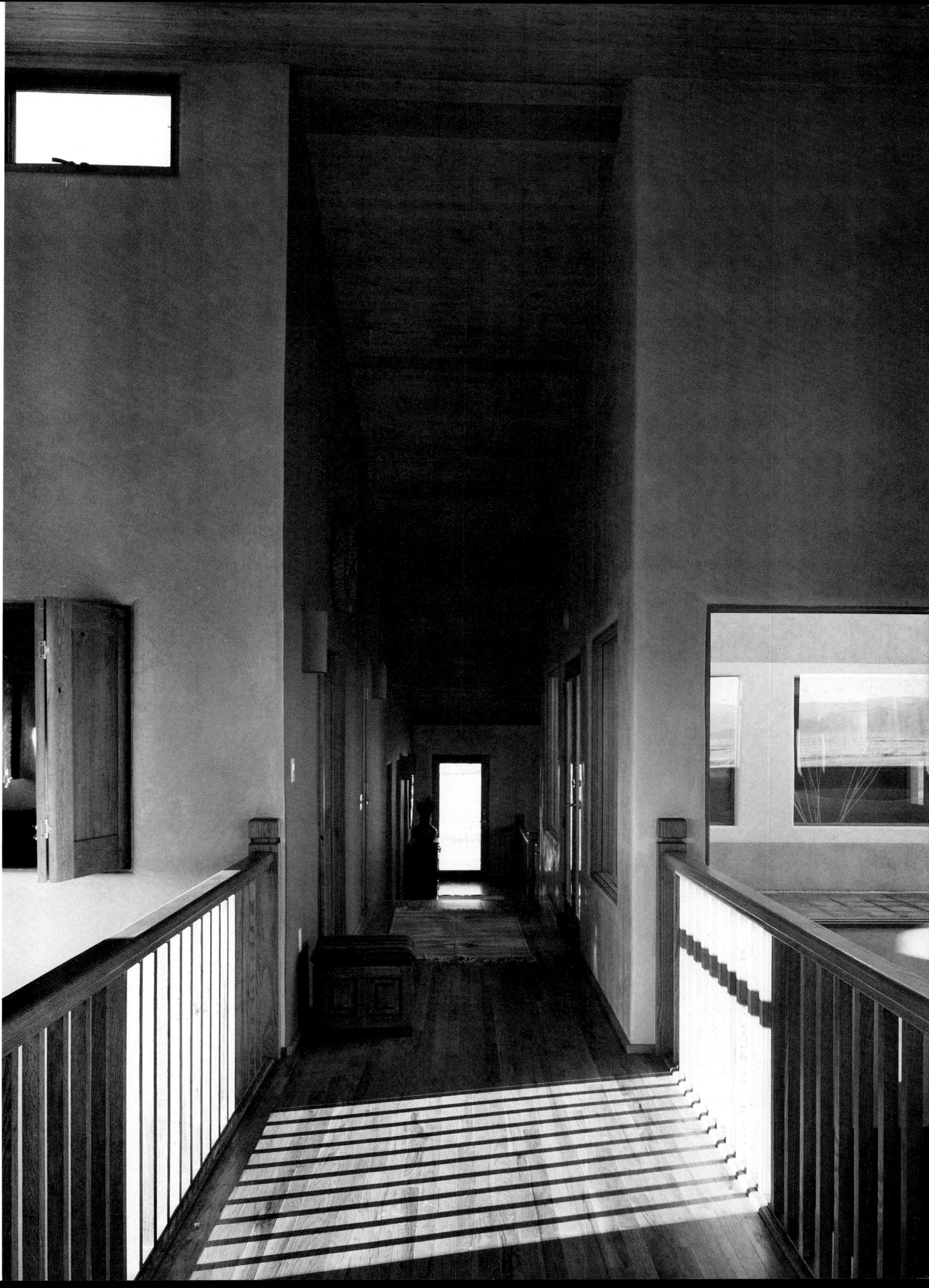

ANTOINE PREDOCK
Jon Anderson, project architect
Lazarus Residence
Tesuque, New Mexico
1985-86

Photos: W. Fujii

The Lazarus House stretches out in a clearing on the brink of a precipitous drop above a wooded slope north of Santa Fe, New Mexico. Arrayed like a necklace of varied pieces the house takes optimum advantage of both views and climate. The clients, a movie producer and a textile artist, share an interest in both the vernacular forms of the area and the world of computers and communication equipment. The site, the local design covenants, and the program suggested a hybrid form, a subtle synthesis of tradition and technology.

The historical, protective *hacienda* form of northern New Mexico is here broken open and unfurled. The soft, inner core faces south and is symbolically protected by its location on the precipice. A continuous 'defensive' wall is established along the north to guard against weather and to shield the entry. Only small openings perforate the wall, except the auto court entry which recalls the *zaguan*, the primary access into the *hacienda*. Arrival into the auto court presents to view dazzling vistas which are then selectively framed and revealed over and over as one progresses through the interior.

The small, serial views are given a broader framework when one diverges from the linking circulation path to the outdoor areas. These patio are warm, sunlit, socializing areas which contrast with the cool, shaded public face. The dichotomy established between shell and core, between north and south, between formal entry and informal gathering spaces reflects the tensions inherent in the design problem. Resolution is achieved through invention and adaptation. Hard, smooth finishes and soft massive forms agree syntactically in an idiom which acknowledges, extends, and ultimately escapes the regional, vernacular language of forms.

Consultant: Claude L. Lyon, mechanical
General contractor: Blue Raven Construction Works

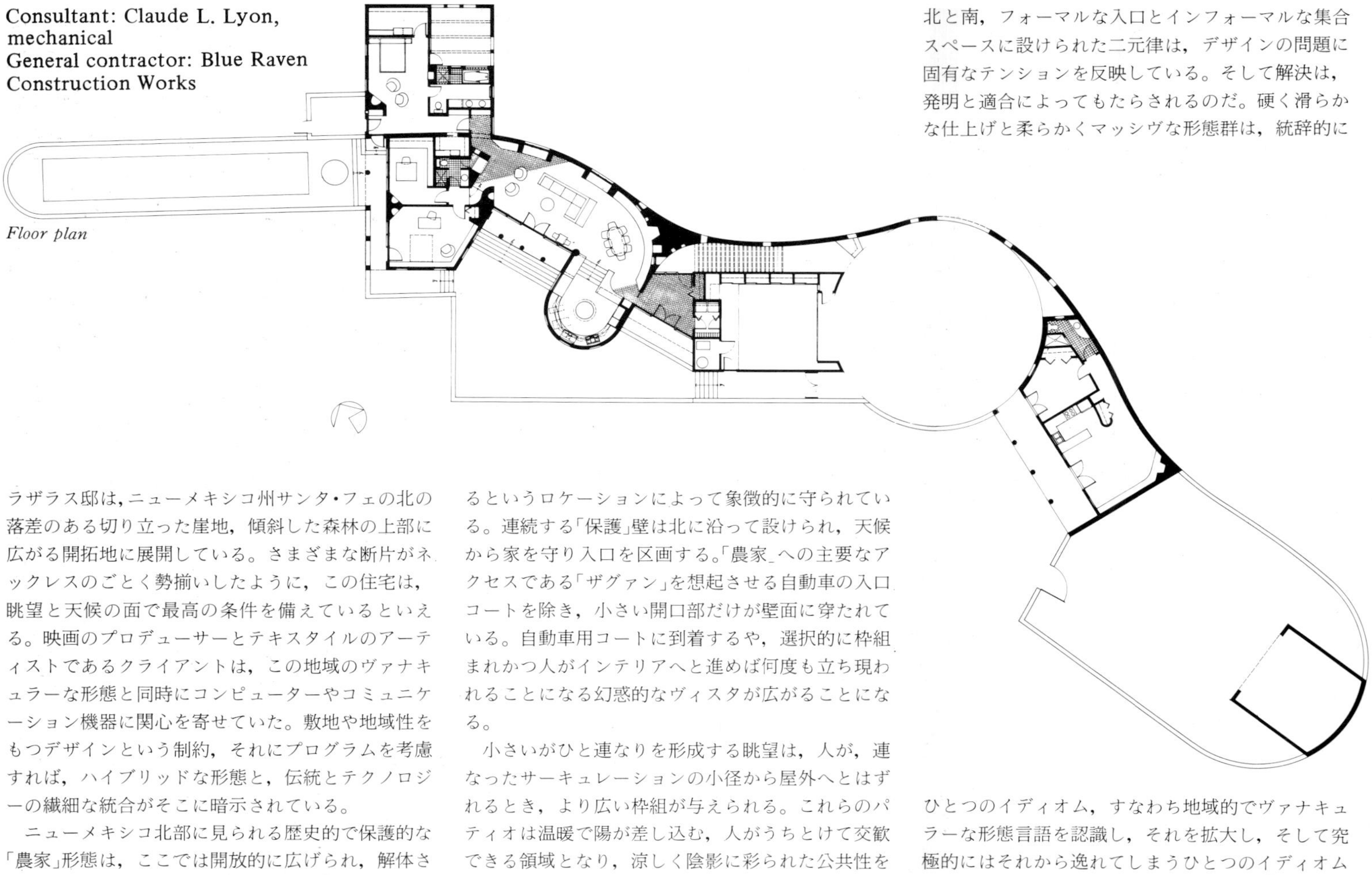

Floor plan

北と南、フォーマルな入口とインフォーマルな集合スペースに設けられた二元律は、デザインの問題に固有なテンションを反映している。そして解決は、発明と適合によってもたらされるのだ。硬く滑らかな仕上げと柔らかくマッシヴな形態群は、統辞的に

ラザラス邸は、ニューメキシコ州サンタ・フェの北の落差のある切り立った崖地、傾斜した森林の上部に広がる開拓地に展開している。さまざまな断片がネックレスのごとく勢揃いしたように、この住宅は、眺望と天候の面で最高の条件を備えているといえる。映画のプロデューサーとテキスタイルのアーティストであるクライアントは、この地域のヴァナキュラーな形態と同時にコンピューターやコミュニケーション機器に関心を寄せていた。敷地や地域性をもつデザインという制約、それにプログラムを考慮すれば、ハイブリッドな形態と、伝統とテクノロジーの繊細な統合がそこに暗示されている。

ニューメキシコ北部に見られる歴史的で保護的な「農家」形態は、ここでは開放的に広げられ、解体された。柔らかい内部のコアは南を向き、絶壁上にあるというロケーションによって象徴的に守られている。連続する「保護」壁は北に沿って設けられ、天候から家を守り入口を区画する。「農家」への主要なアクセスである「ザグァン」を想起させる自動車の入口コートを除き、小さい開口部だけが壁面に穿たれている。自動車用コートに到着するや、選択的に枠組まれかつ人がインテリアへと進めば何度も立ち現われることになる幻惑的なヴィスタが広がることになる。

小さいがひと連なりを形成する眺望は、人が、連なったサーキュレーションの小径から屋外へとはずれるとき、より広い枠組が与えられる。これらのパティオは温暖で陽が差し込む、人がうちとけて交歓できる領域となり、涼しく陰影に彩られた公共性をもつ正面と対照をなすといってよい。シェルとコア、ひとつのイディオム、すなわち地域的でヴァナキュラーな形態言語を認識し、それを拡大し、そして究極的にはそれから逸れてしまうひとつのイディオムのうちに符号するのである。

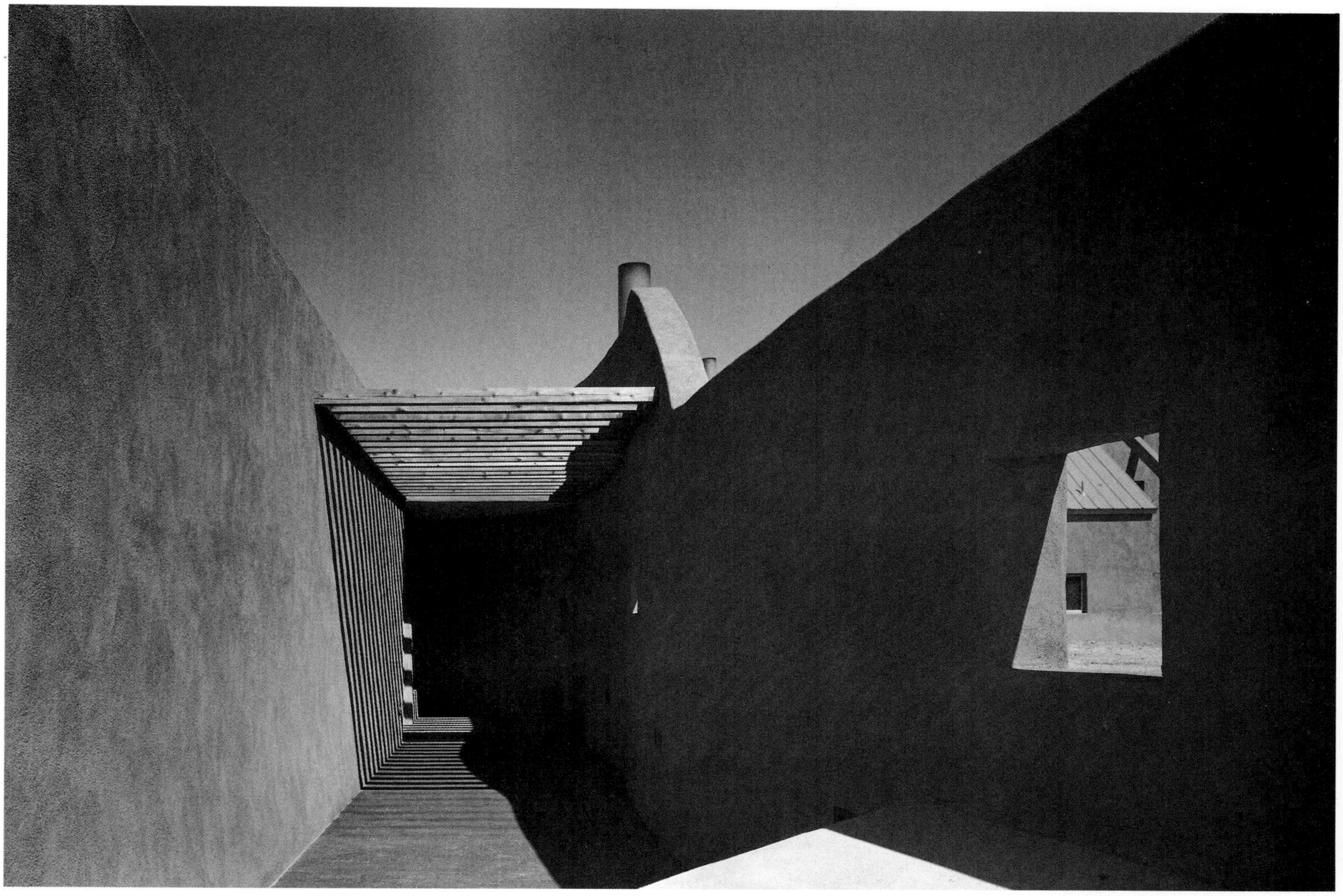

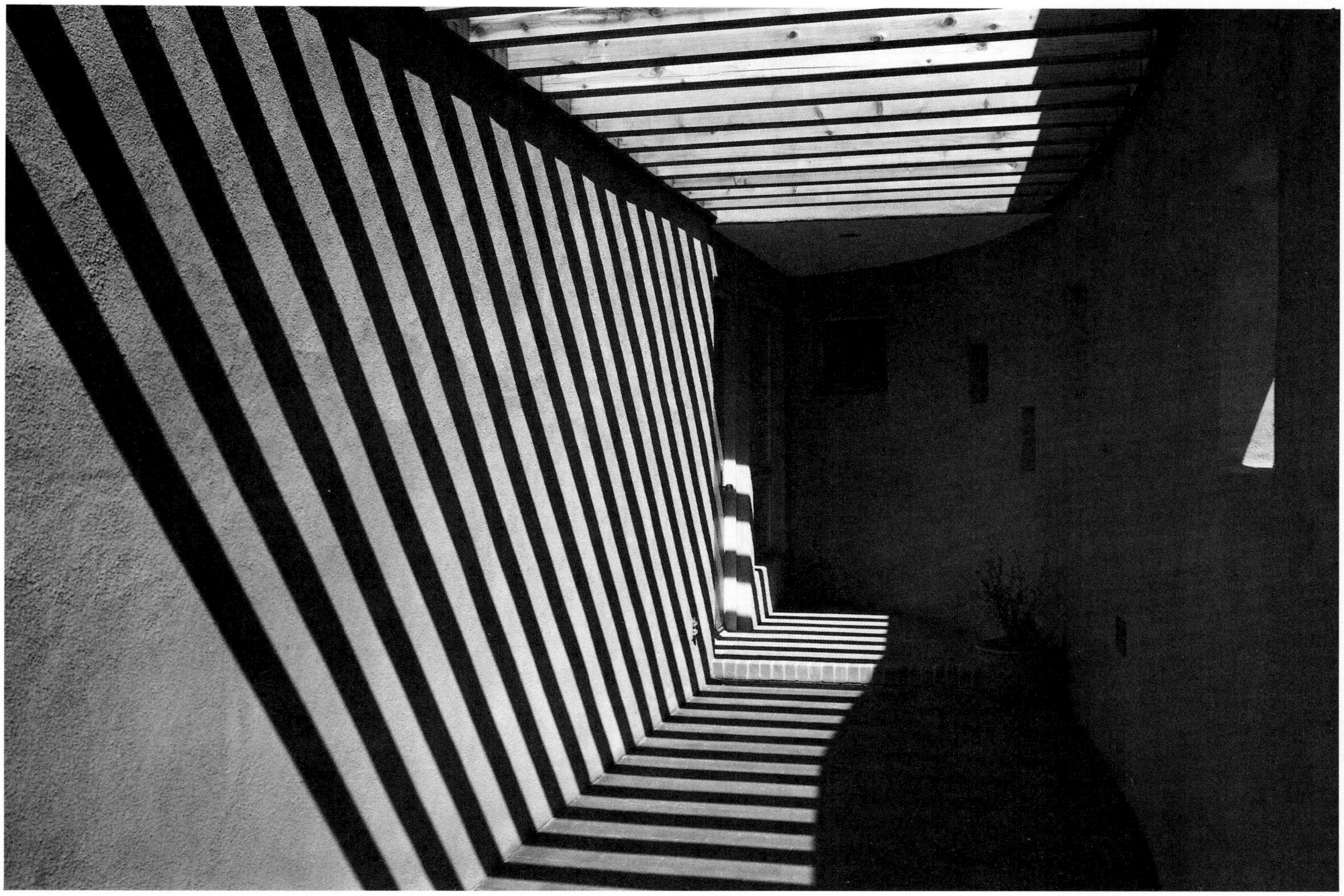

Elevations

103

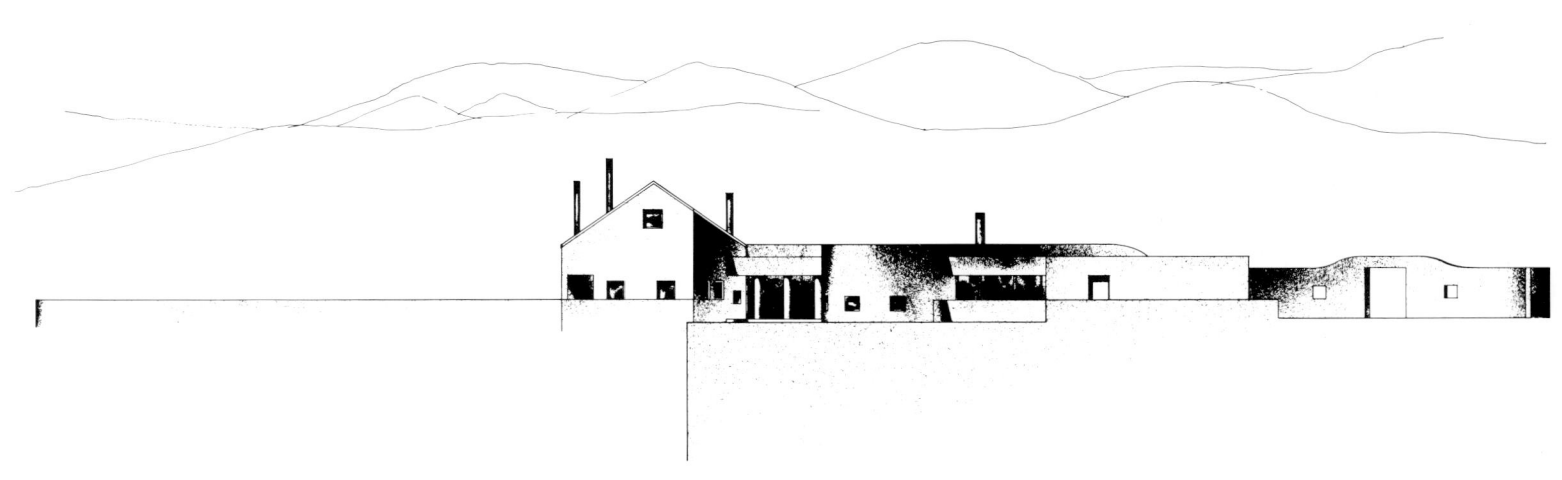

ANTOINE PREDOCK
Jon Anderson, project architect
Treaster Gray Residence
Tesuque, New Mexico
1983-85

Photos: W. Fujii

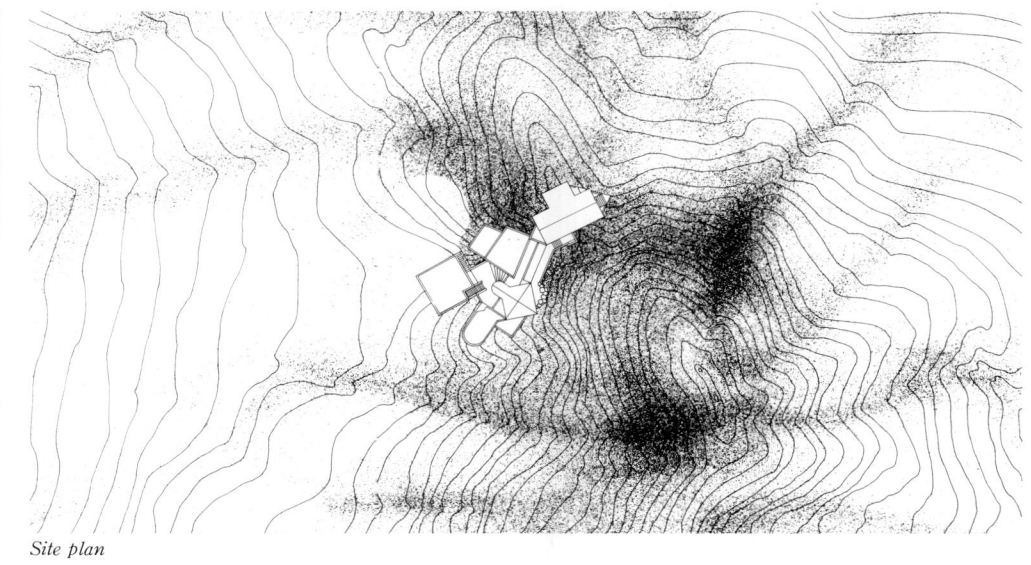

The Treaster/Gray House unfolds as a fragmented village of rooms as it climbs the flank of a ridge.

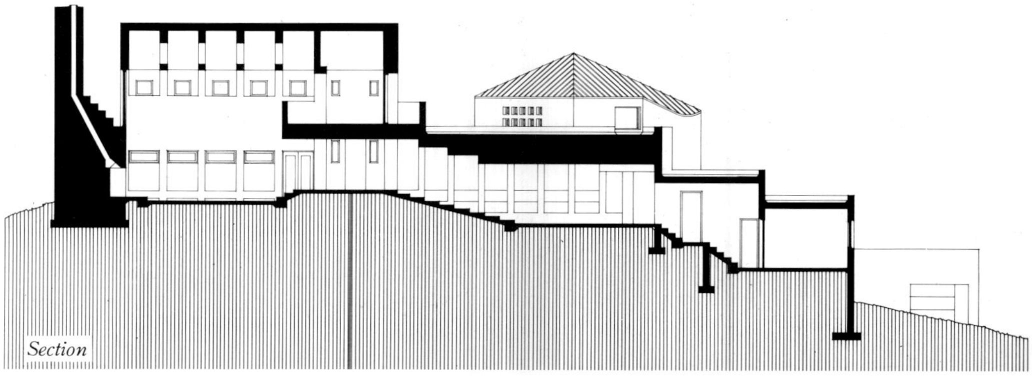

The ceremonial approach to the house from a distance — circuitous dirt road amidst aromatic pinon/juniper trees; distant views of the vernacular metal roofed bedroom tower rising above huddled pieces of the house— each piece a different frozen sunset color — sets the stage for this "house as theater" for the musician/owners.

The processional, sequential, places then experienced on ascending the site through the house culminate in the living room (performance space) breaking like a wave over the ridge, high above the Tesuque Valley.

The simple, archetypal pieces of the house resemble the accreted villages of Northern New Mexico. Colliding shifting axes of the six fragments result from relationships to topography, views and the preconceived ceremonial path up the hillside.

Imagining an evening gathering, the visitor arrives in a parking placita then climbs a series of steps on axis with the Stair Tower, enters into a space with views channeled toward the Jemez Mountains and the lights of Los Alamos, passes along a gallery/greenhouse, ascends through a stage-like proscenium opening, then emerges as an "actor" on the living room stairs at the same time witnessing a musical performance below joined by the audience on the balcony/loft above.

The theater-diagram aspect of the house must of course simultaneously address pragmatic issues of the owners' day to day lives. But the romance of the site overlayed by the artistic persuasion of the Treaster/Gray's produces an experiential sequence going hand in hand with, and at the same time transcendent of program.

Consultant: Don Felts, mecanical
General contractor: Blue Raven Construction Works

Site plan

Floor plan

Section

トリースター／グレー邸は，山の側面を登るように複数の部屋の断片化した村落として展開している。

住宅への儀式的なアプローチは，芳香性のある西洋ネズの松林のあいだを縫う舗装していない回り道からなされる。離れたところから，ヴァナキュラーな金属屋根をもつベッドルーム群が，ひしめきあった住宅の空間的部位の上部に立ち上がるのが遠望でき，それぞれの部位は，異なったフローズン・サンセット色に染まり，音楽家であるオーナーのための「劇場としての住宅」の舞台装置となる。

進行性をはらんだ連続する場所は，住宅を通して敷地を登る体験を誘い，テスク・ヴァレーのはるか上部，尾根を越えて砕けようとする波頭のようなリヴィングルーム（パフォーマンス空間）で最高点に達している。

単純で原型的な住宅の部位は，ニューメキシコ北部の村に似ている。6つの断片の軸をシフトし衝突させる。それはトポグラフィーや眺望，そしてあらかじめ考えられたヒルサイドを上がる儀式的な小径との関係性によって導かれた。

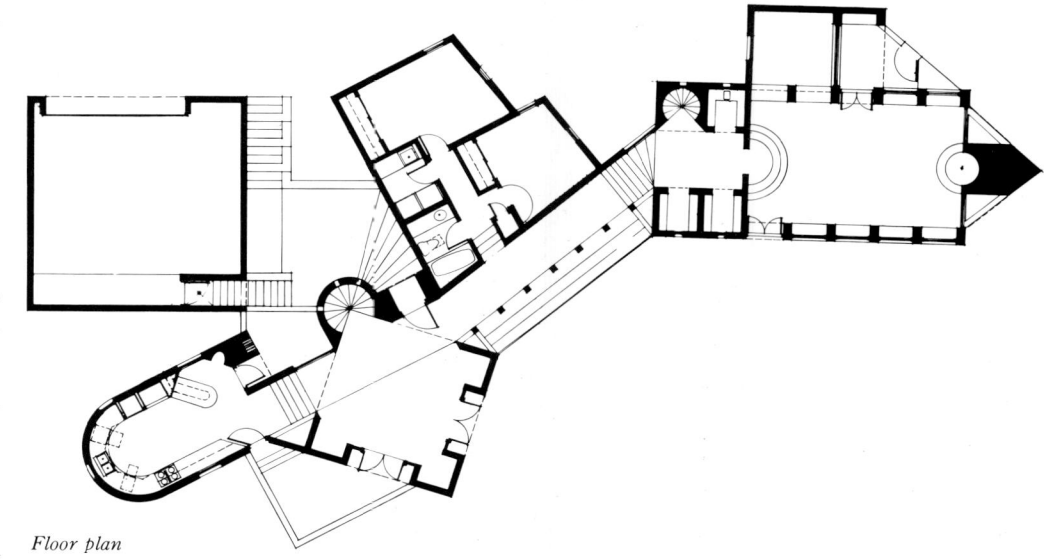

夜会を想像してみよう。訪問者たちは駐車場の「プラシータ」に到着し，その後，階段タフーをその内部にもつ軸上のひと続きのステップをのぼる。ジュメズ山脈やロス・アラモスの夜景へと向けられた眺望をもつスペースに入り，ギャラリー／温室に沿って横切ると，ステージのようなプロセニアム型の開口部を通って上がることになる。そして，リヴィングルーム階段上で，「俳優」として登場し，同時に上部のバルコニーロフトの観客たちと一体になって，下部の音楽パフォーマンスを観ることになる，というわけである。

もちろん，住宅の劇場的図式には，同時に，オーナーの日々の生活における実際的な問題をも提示されていなければならない。しかし，トリースター／グレー邸のアーティスティックな信念によって重合された敷地のロマンスは，経験的なシークェンスと合体され，また同時にプログラムを超越するなにものかを生み出しているのである。

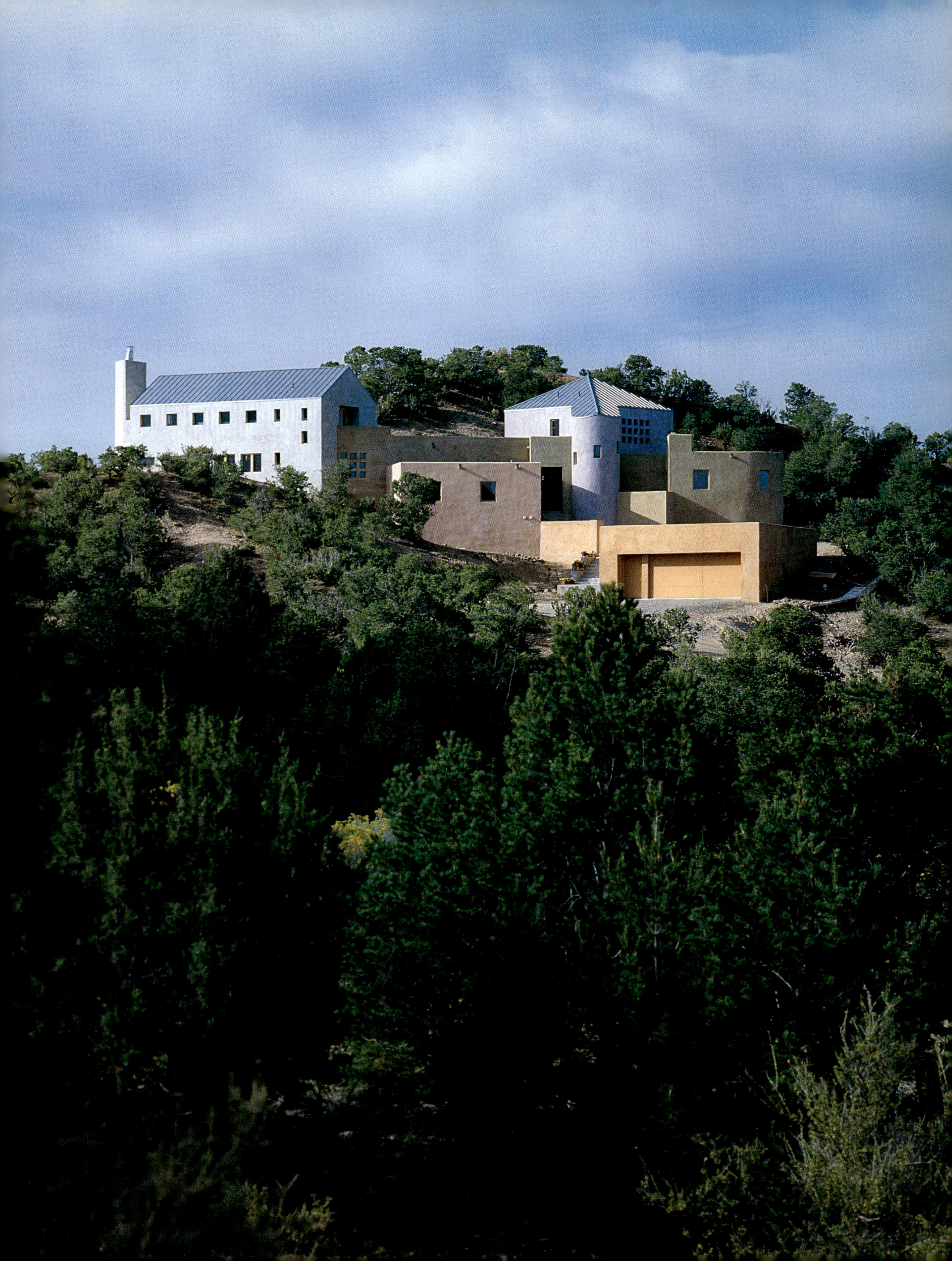

106

107

ANTOINE PREDOCK
Ronald Jacob, project manager
The Beach
Albuquerque, New Mexico
1984-86

Photos: W. Fujii

Consultants: Randy Holt and Associates, structural; 4 Seasons Engineering, mechanical; Chavez and Grieves, civil engineering
General manager: Bradbury and Stamm Construction

The Beach is a big 74-unit low-rider parked on the historic mainstream of our country—Highway 66. Highway 66—the name alone evokes a thrilling bombardment of images for anyone who has traveled that special route. The poignant motels and cafes that remain along 66 in West Albuquerque are vestiges of what should have long ago been recognized as a linear National Historic Place. The Beach site straddles a cultural fault line— the habitat of the West Central Cruiser meeting the white belts and white shoes of the Albuquerque Country Club.

Architecturally, the existing context is so poetically loaded that one must selectively edit the stream of consciousness of images— from the Grapes of Wrath voyagers to the San Gabriel Park wheeled version of the evening paseo around any Plaza Mayor in Spain. The 66 frontage of the Beach addresses the cacophony of images and multiple scales of the highway. The opposite Country Club elevation is subdued quasi-Mediterranean averaging out of that neighborhood's stylistic drift. The resultant hybrid Apartment on the historic Beach Motel site represents an abstraction of Highway 66 iconography. The accreted atmospheres of the site are expressed through feelings of the historic place that avoid copping easy nostalgic references. Advancing and receding patterned portal frontispieces reduce the 750 feet long behemoth to familiar 66 scale parking courts. The graphic facade patterning has a Navajo blanket terraced grid implication but is articulated by neon tubes as are stepping balustrades and parapets which are three dimensional analogs to the two dimensional colored patterns.

Four peaks of penthouse sky plazas rise above the intermediate parking court valleys, the whole arrayed in an architecture cum landscape fashion against the Sandia Mountain backdrop of the site. Views from within the Apartment units, terraces and courts are toward the Sandias across the Country Club Golf Course with secondary views toward the West Mesa volcanoes and sunsets. Faintly glowing neon emanating from recessed courtyards rekindles the intrigue of Old Highway 66.

Site plan

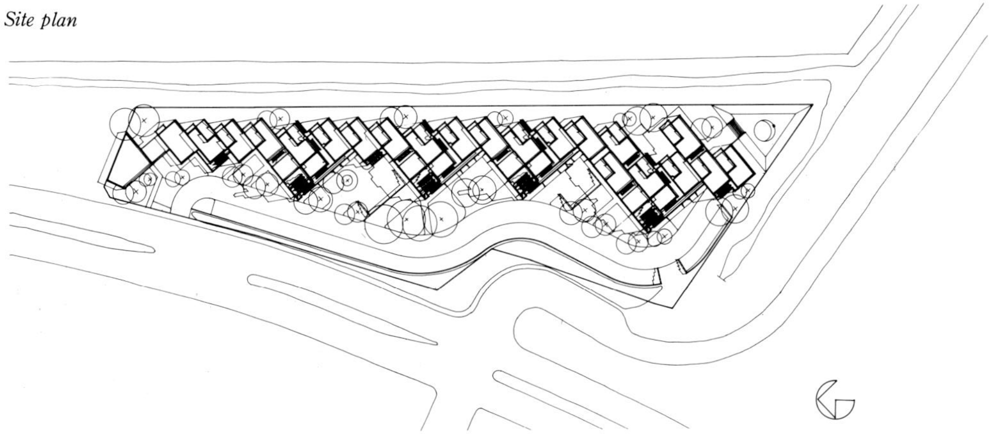

ザ・ビーチは、我が国における歴史的な幹線道路であるハイウェイ66に駐車した巨大な74戸の低層住棟である。ハイウェイ66——この名前だけで、この道路を旅した者なら誰でもスリリングなイメージの衝撃を呼び醒ます。ウェスト・アルバカーキのハイウェイ66沿いに今も残る痛快なモーテルやカフェは、昔、いわば直線化した国立歴史広場として認識されていたハイウェイの痕跡とでも言えるものだ。ザ・ビーチの敷地は、ウェスト・セントラル・クルーザーの住民がアルバカーキの白いベルトに白い靴をはいた連中と出会うといった文化的断層線をまたいでいる。

建築的に言えば、所与のコンテクストは潜在的にたいへん混濁の流れを選択的に編集させざるを得なくなる——それは怒りの葡萄の漂流者から、スペインのあらゆる市長広場まわりに見い出せる夜の散歩道の変形版でもあるサン・ガブリエル・パークにまで至っているのだ。ザ・ビーチのハイウェイ66側正面には、諸イメージの不協和音とハイウェイのもつ多層化されたスケールが覗く。対面するカントリークラブの立面は、付近に見られる擬似地中海的なものへの平均化を伴った、抑制されたビーチモーテル式近隣のスタイル的なドリフトと言えよう。ザ・ビーチモーテルの敷地に生じたハイブリッドなアパートメントは、結果としてハイウェイ66のイコノグラフィーを抽象化して生じたものだ。敷地に付着した雰囲気は、ノスタルジックな参照対象を簡単にコピーすることを拒絶して歴史的な場所の感覚によって醸し出されている。凹凸のパターンとなった表側正面は、750フィートのドでかいモスのような巨大さをハイウェイ66の親密なスケールのもつ駐車場コートへと還元する。グラフィックなファサードのパターンは、ナヴァホ族の格子縞の毛布を想起させるものであり、平面の色彩パターン

を立体的にアナログ化した段状の手摺とパラペット同様、ネオンチューブによって分節されている。4つの頂部を形成するペントハウス・スカイプラザは、中間階の駐車場コートの谷間に立ち上がり、敷地の背景を形成するサンディア山に抗するようにとても建築の背景を形成するサンディア山に抗するようにとても建築の背景を形成するランドスケープをもったようにある。アパートメントの住戸内から眺めれば、テラスと中庭はひとつはカントリークラブのゴルフコースを超えてサンディア山脈へと向かう。引っ込んだ中庭から発するほのかなネオンの光は、旧ハイウェイ66の密やかな企みをふたたび燃え上がらせるものである。

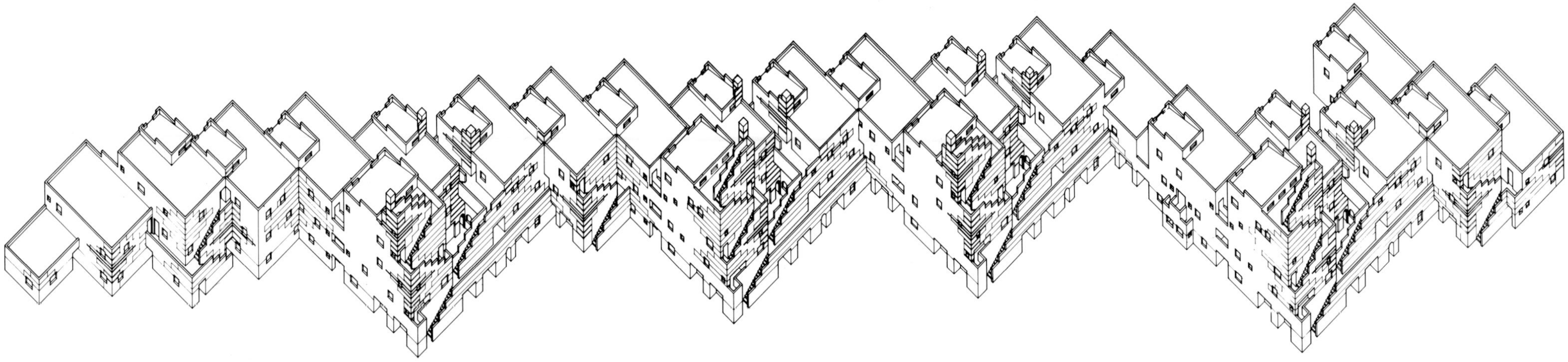

Elevations and plans

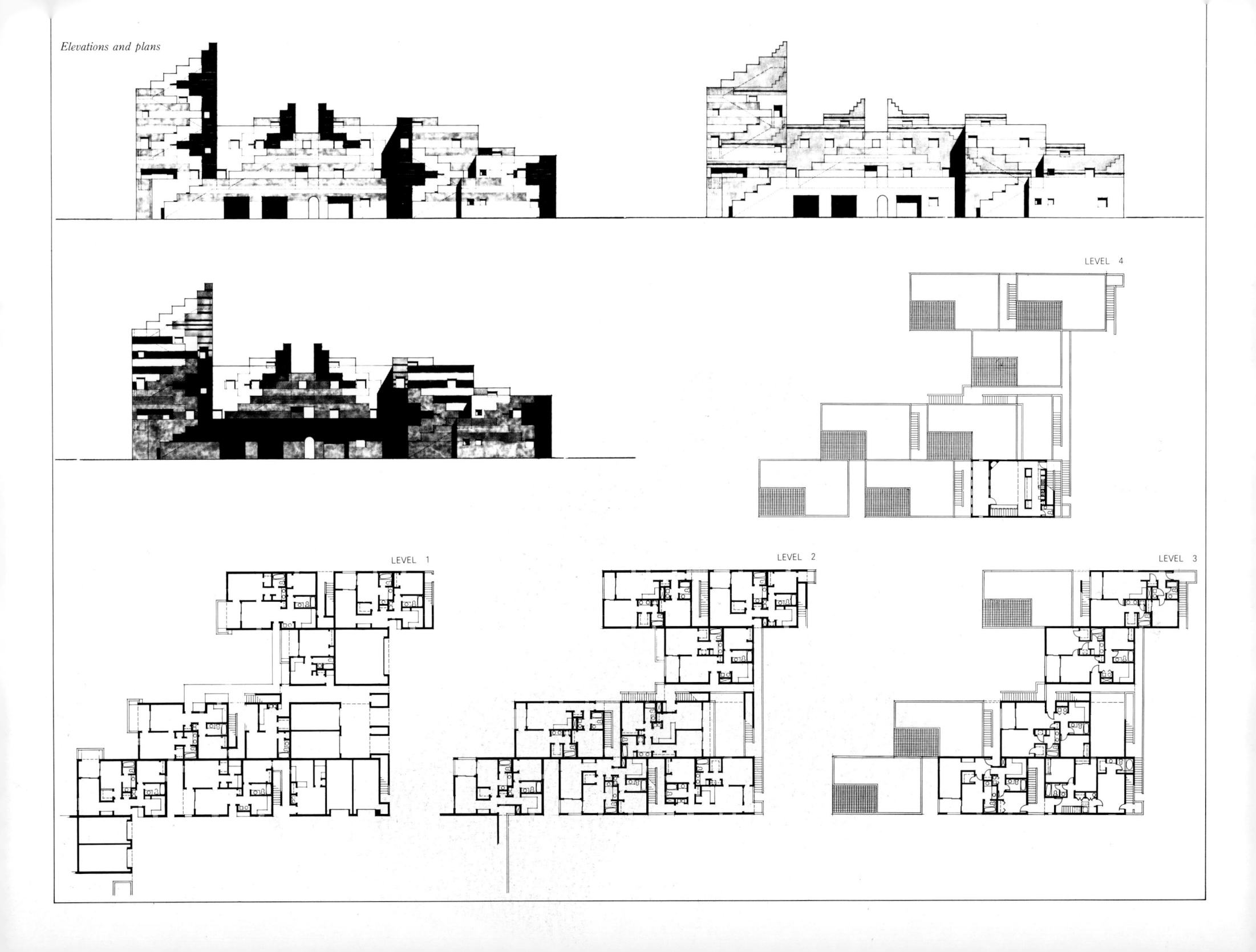

LEVEL 4

LEVEL 3

LEVEL 2

LEVEL 1

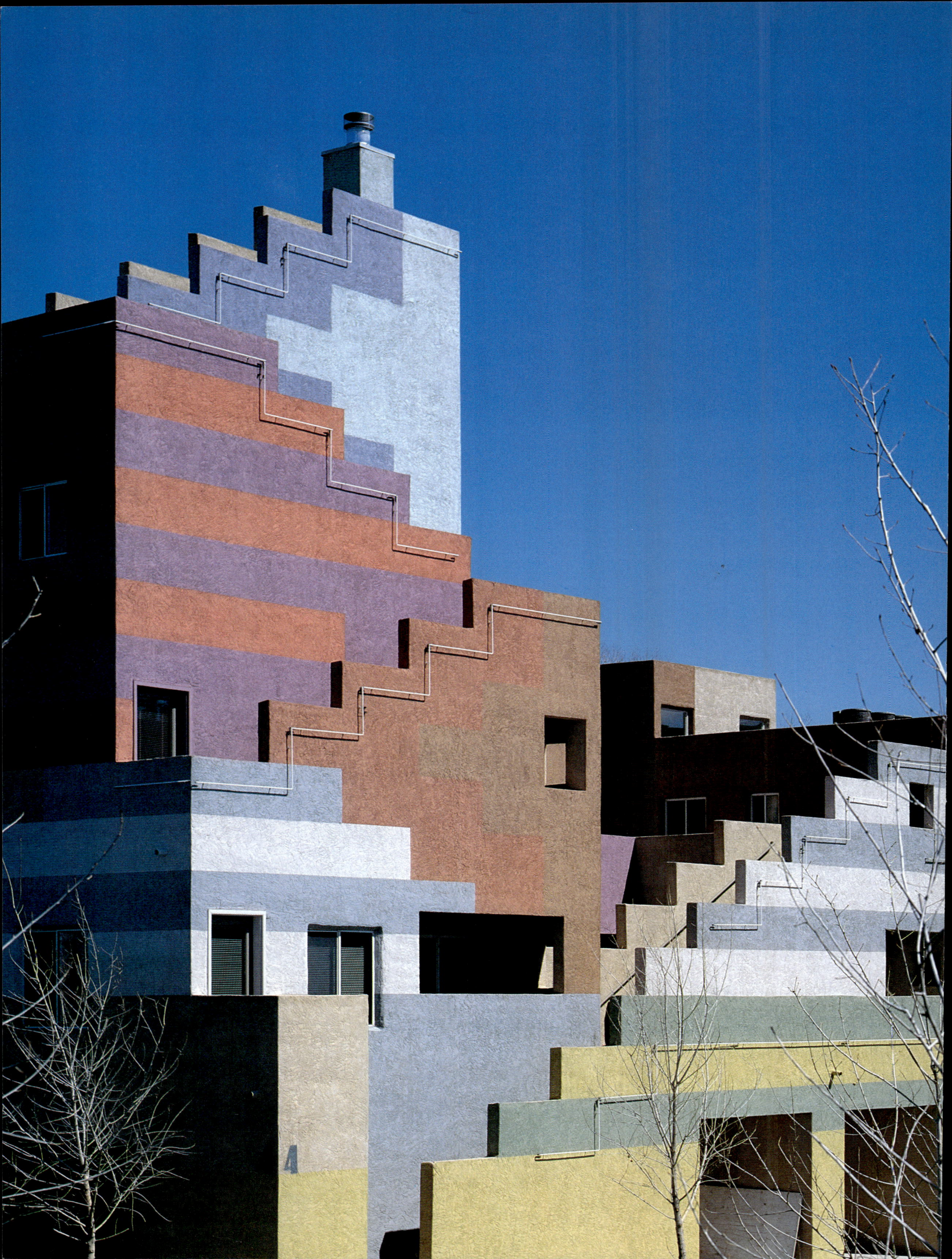

ANTOINE PREDOCK
with Jon Anderson, Geoffrey Beebe, and Ron Jacob
Desert Highlands Golf Cottages
Pinnacle Peak, Arizona
1982-83 (construction not applicable)

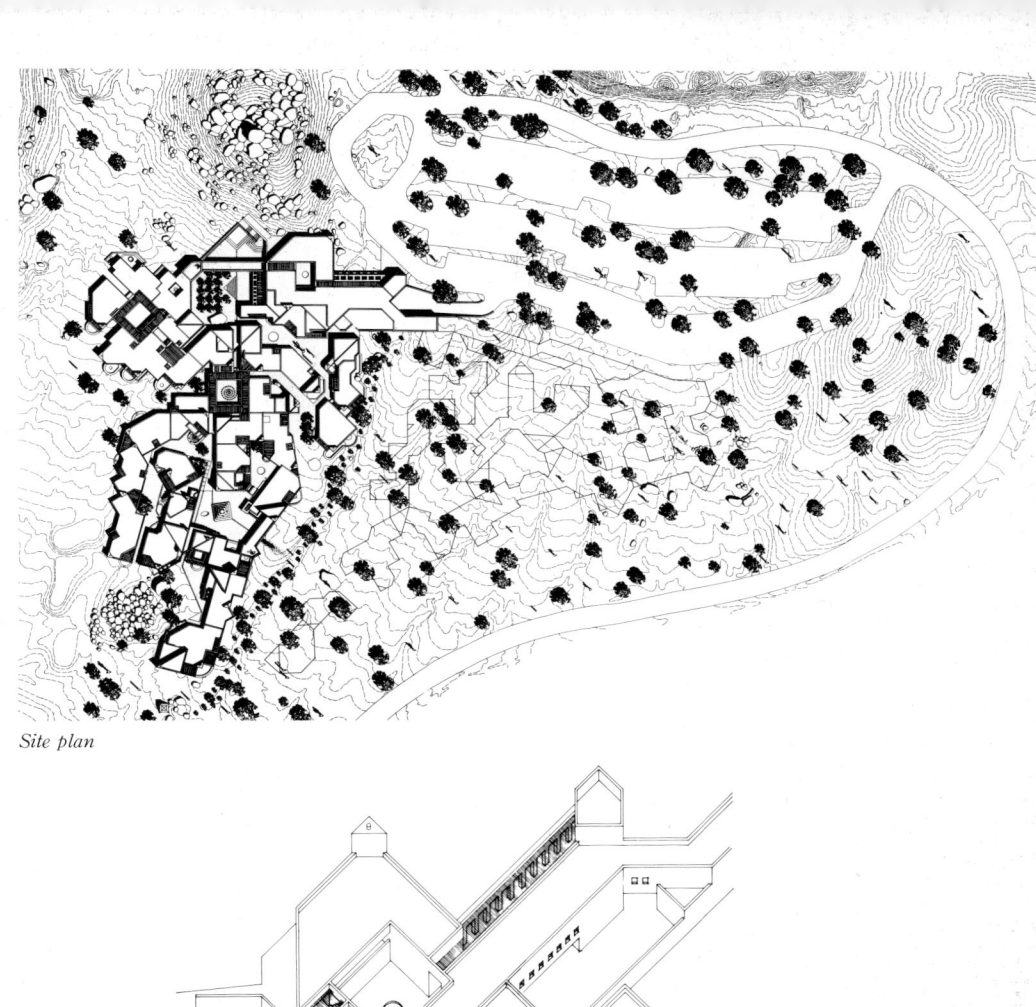

The 29-unit attached-housing complex sited on 17 acres of high Sonoran desert will be occupied continuously by owners during a portion of the year, but will be used primarily on a transient basis.

At a distance, at night, small fires glow on the rooftops. During the day, mauve, burnt orange, and pink abstractions of the background ridges jut above the olive-beige perimeter of the desert floor. The linking of the attached housing units suggests thick walls (the width of the units themselves) entrapping outdoor rooms open to the sky (*placitas*, courts, natural features) and yields one large 'house' in the desert.

These courts and *placitas* inform the housing precinct with rituals of the desert such as sunset viewing (Sunset Rock), camp fires (Circle of Stones), sun worhip, and night sky viewing (hollow, stepped pyramid of the sun containing stargazing view ports). Natural features themselves, entrapped within courts, become foci of power (Flat Rock, Passage Rock, Tree Rock, triple saguaro icon, torii saguaros). The *placitas* and courts are sequentially linked together with a water 'score,' a recirculating linear system of water that changes from mist to spray to sheet to audible-but-unseen as it gradually traverses the project. The low and massive desert-floor perimeter of the housing precinct has triangular, 'barbed,' second-level multi-use rooms and chimneys that emerge from the low silhouette, appearing as abstractions of the surrounding natural ridges — as though softer, higher strata had eroded away to expose the 'barbs.' These upper rooms function as wind catchers, inductive air-release points, and high vantage points for view and breezes. In pairs they form links between courts. Common upper-level pedestrian vantage points are sandwiched between the 'barbs'; the sheltered passages below form tunnels for heightened summer breezes.

The haunting, surreal, science-fiction presence of the desert opens a further dimension for exploration. Edge conditions where buildings meet desert can have a mirage-like, ruinous romance about them. Imagined forays into future lives of a particular building can usefully loop back to the design of the straight, present day project. The future can inform the present.

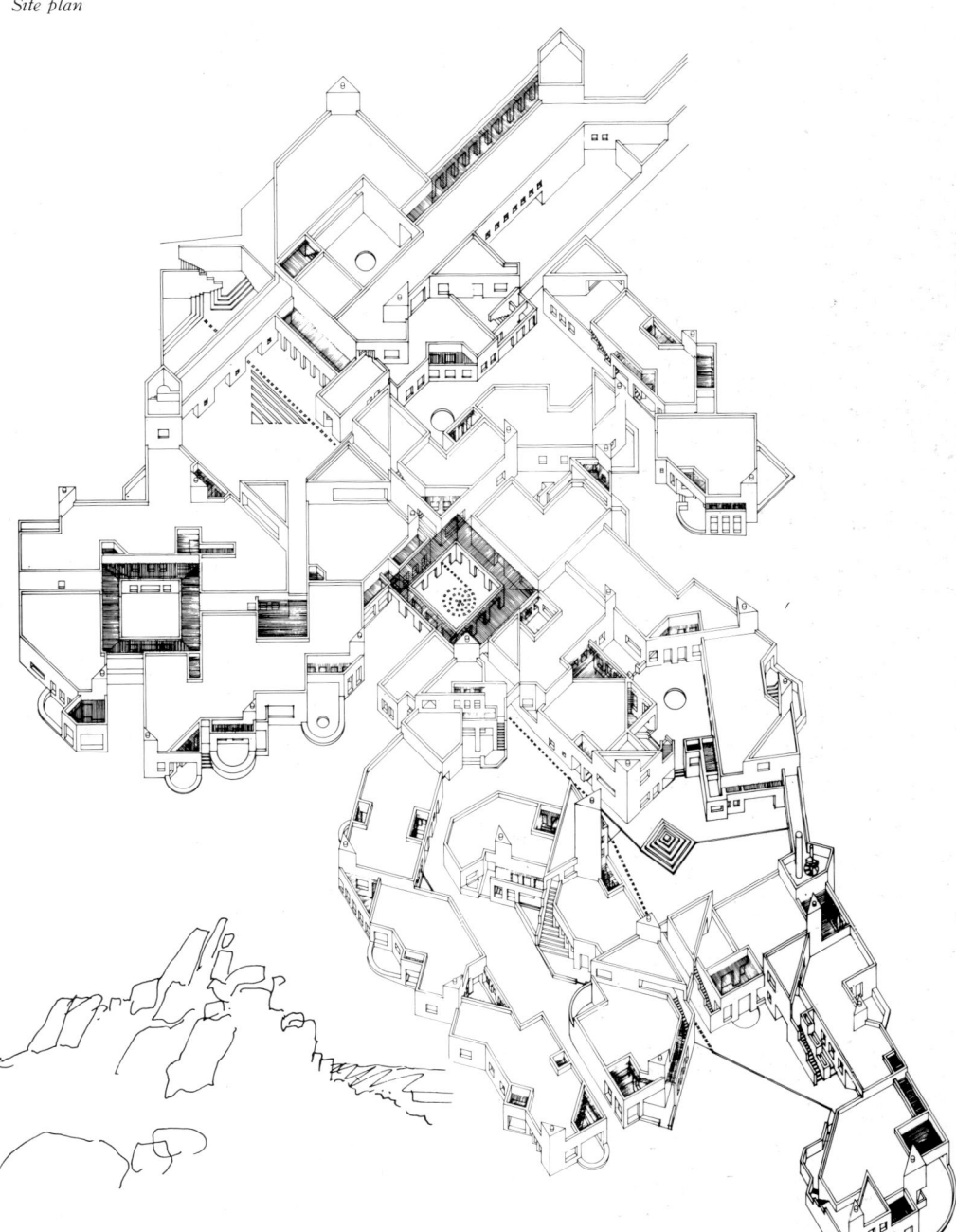

Site plan

Floor plan

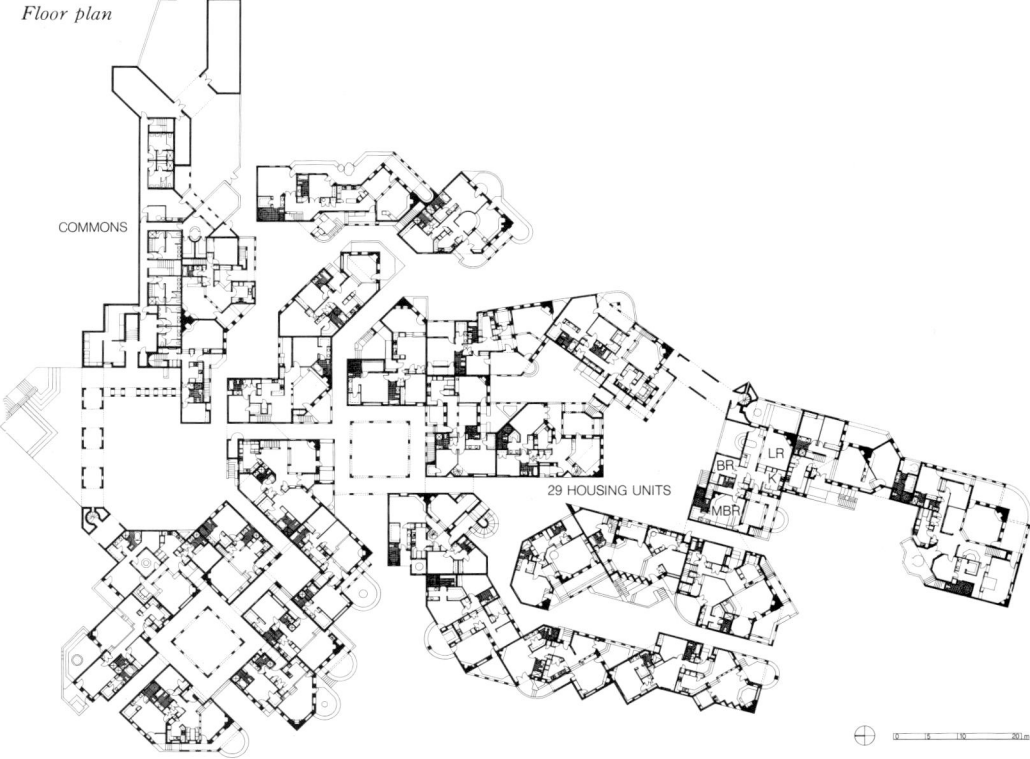

COMMONS

29 HOUSING UNITS

　ソノラン砂漠高地，17エーカーの敷地に建つ29戸のハウジング・コンプレックスは，オーナーたちによって1年のある期間連続的に使われるが，基本的には一時的な宿泊基地として使用されることが予想されている。

　夜，少し離れた地点から眺めると，その屋上頂部に小さな炎が上がるのを目撃することができる。昼間は，背景の山々がフジ色，燃えるようなオレンジ，そしてピンクの抽象画となり，砂漠面のオリーヴベージュの周界上に突出する。隣接する住戸のつながりによって，分厚い壁(住戸群それ自身の幅)が空へ開いた屋外の諸室(「プラシータ」，中庭，自然造作)を囲い込み，砂漠の中のひとつの大きな「家」を具現化した。

　これらの「プラシータ」や中庭は，日没景(サンセット・ロック)，キャンプファイアー(石の環)，太陽崇拝，そして夜の天空景(占星術的な視点も含んだ太陽の段状ピラミッドと中空)といった砂漠の儀式性をもつハウジング環境を伝えている。中庭に陥入した自然造作それ自身は，力の焦点群を結んでゆく(フラット・ロック，パッサージュ・ロック，ツリーロック，3種のサボテンの図像，鳥居サボテン)。「プラシータ」と中庭は，「水溝」とシークェンシャルに結びつけられる。計画地を漸次的に横切ってゆくこの「水溝」

は，霧吹きから音は聞こえるが見えない広がりまで変化する水を直線的システムに再流通化させるものにほかならない。砂漠に面する，ハウジング下層のマッシヴな周界は，三角形で「とげ」のある形をしている一方，2階では多目的室と低いシルエットから立ち上がる煙突があり，周囲の自然の山脈を抽象化するとともに，より柔らかく高い地層が「とげ」を露わにするような侵食がなされたように映っている。これら上階の部屋は，風を採り入れ空気を吐き出す道ともなり，見晴らしと風通しの点で地の利を得ている。それらは一組となって中庭をめぐる連結を形成してゆくのだ。共有の上階ペデストリアンは「とげ」にはさまれたところで通風や眺望に有利な場を形成し，下部の被覆されたパッサージュは夏の微風のトンネルとなる。

　砂漠という幻視的，超現実的，SF的存在が，より拡大した次元の探究路を開いてゆくのだ。建物が砂漠と出会う境界性は，奇跡にも似た荒廃的なロマンスだと言ってよい。固有な建物が未来生活へ想像上の侵略をなすことは，まさに，現在のプロジェクトのデザインと円環を結ぶ。未来は，現在を告知し得るのである。

TORU MURAKAMI & ASSOCIATES
House in Hongo-cho
Toyota, Hiroshima
1984-86

Photos: T. Kobayashi

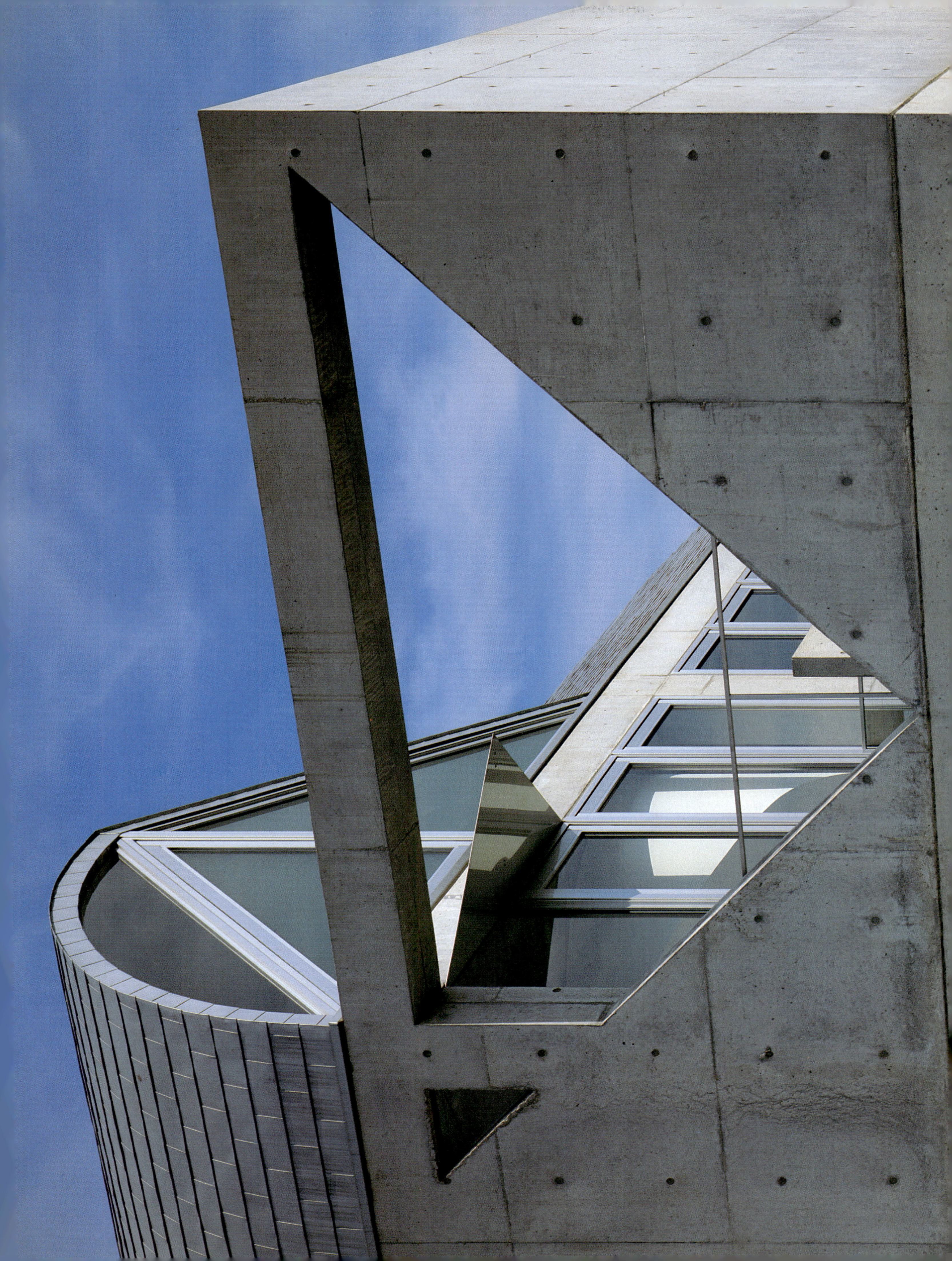

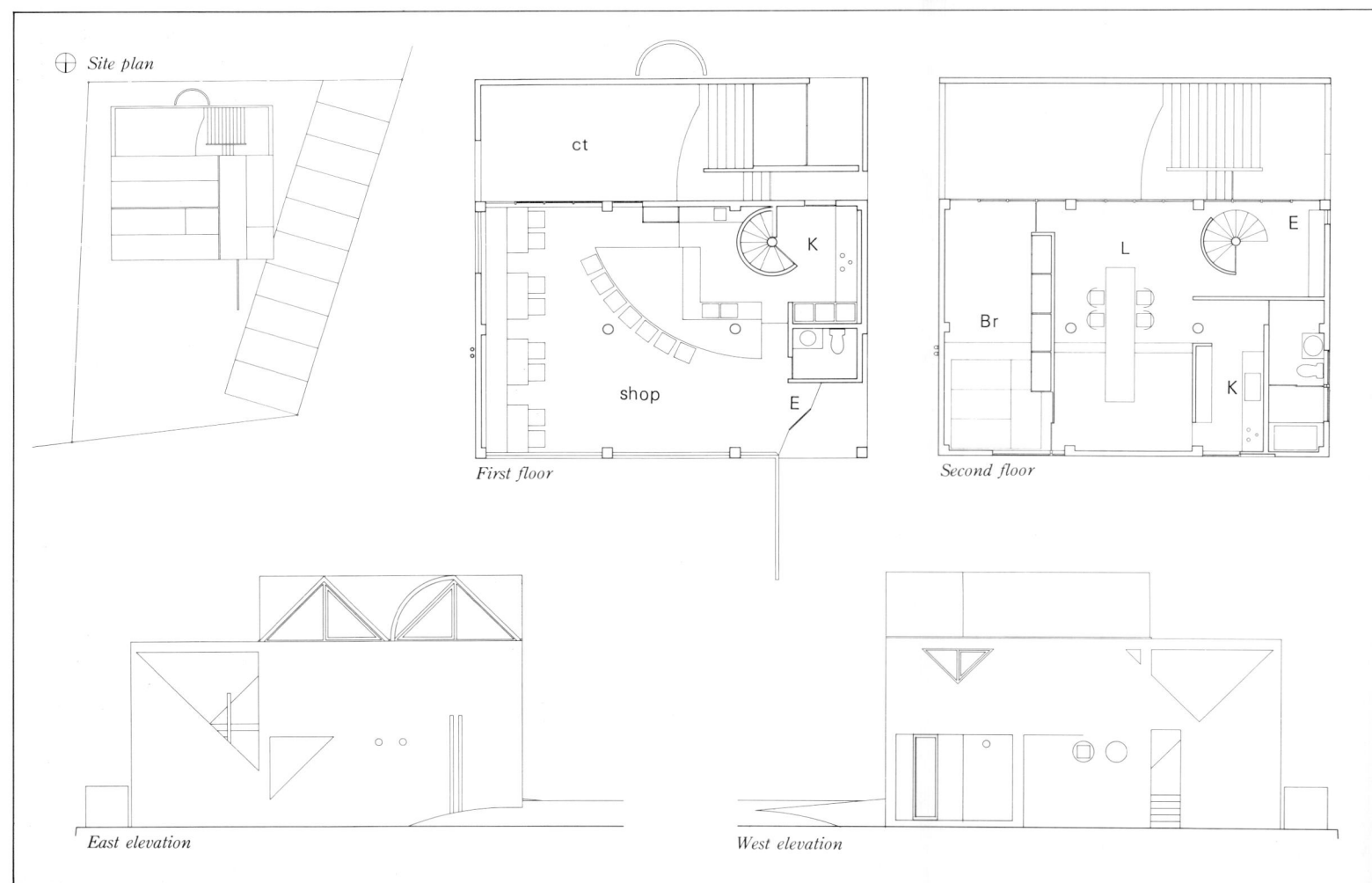

Site plan

ct

K

shop

E

First floor

L

Br

E

K

Second floor

East elevation

West elevation

Third floor

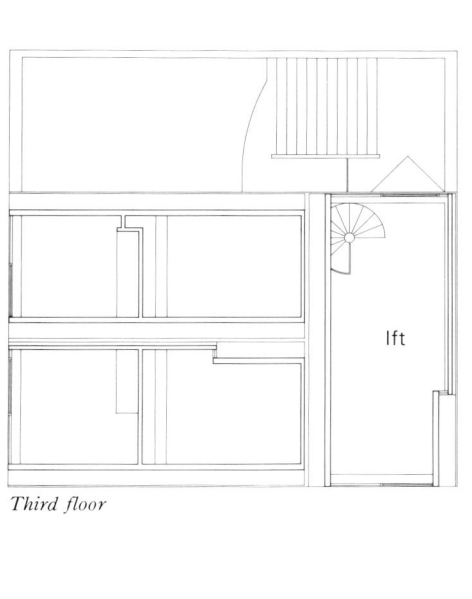

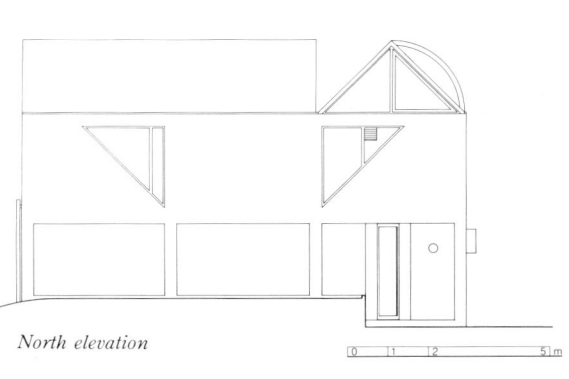

North elevation

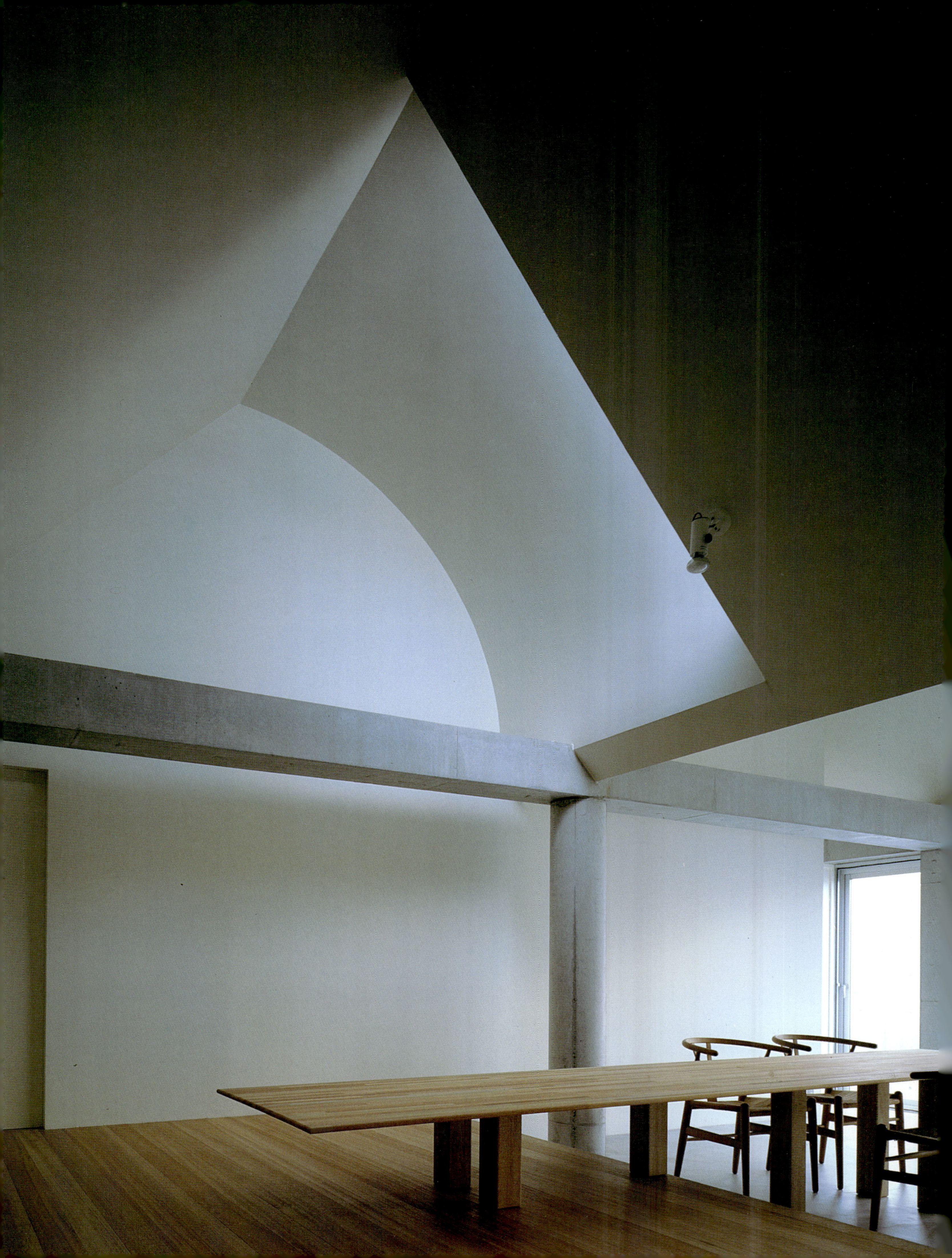

The site for this building is at the intersection of a national road and a prefectural road. The roads were built strictly for thru-traffic and are the source of much vehicular noise. All around are paddy fields, land covered with trees and plants, and wooded hills, with scattered buildings standing in their midst—in short, a landscape typical of the suburb of a provincial city. A small store is on the first floor and an apartment for the storeowner is on the second floor.

To give order and form to the living spaces, a structure of reinforced concrete columns and beams (with cross-sections measuring 300 millimeters × 300 millimeters or 300 millimeters in diameter) on a 3.6 meter grid was provided. The intention was to make concrete a human, weightless material by reducing the sections of the columns and beams as much as possible. The structure here is a cross between a framed structure and a walled structure; the two systems cancel out each other's apparent forcefulness, resulting in an ambiguous yet anti-seismic design.

The rectangular prism on the outside is packaging intended to provide the architecture with an autonomous landscape of its own amid the incoherent landscape of the surrounding environment. The windows have been given unusual forms inspired by the sections of the gabled roofs that suggest a light shelter. The rectangular prism and the roofs thus have equal presence and exist as part of a single shelter. The conventional means of providing continuity between inside and outside is here interrupted by a diagonal and the windows take on the character of apparatuses. The intention was to make the regular structure ordinary and sympathetic to natural factors through the addition of parts and openings that were apparatus-like or ornamental and to create simple, unadorned, living spaces with a staged quality and having a garden, a *doma* (earthen-floored working area), and an *itanoma* (a room with a wooden floor).
Toru Murakami

計画：本郷町の家／広島県豊田郡
主要用途：店舗＋住宅
建築設計：村上徹建築設計事務所（村上徹，西宮善幸）
構造設計：S.A.P.建築構造設計室
設備設計：森木設計事務所
施工：村田組
主体構造：RCラーメン構造＋S造
主な仕上：合板型枠コンクリート打放し
敷地面積：453.65m²
建築面積：94.29m²
延床面積：196.44m²

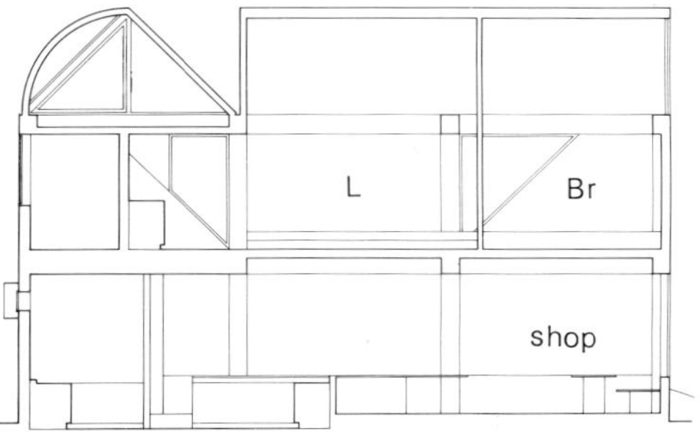

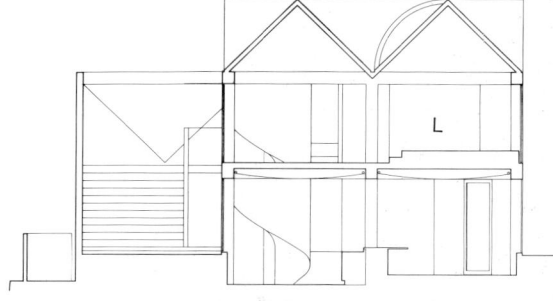

国道と県道との交差点にこの建築の敷地は接している。単なる通過交通のためにつくられた幅の広い道路は騒音を撒き散らし，周辺は，水田・草木地・山林等が拡がり，その中に建物が点在するという地方都市の郊外としてごく一般的な環境風景である。平面構成は1階が小店舗，2階は店主の住宅である。

生活空間に秩序を与え，求める空間形成のために，鉄筋コンクリート造の300×300（あるいは300φ）の柱・梁による3.6mグリッドの柱梁構造を採用した。柱梁断面を最小限にし，コンクリートという素材をヒューマンに，非重力的に用いたい。ここでの構造は柱梁構造と壁構造の中間的なものとし，相互の力強さを互いに打ち消しあい，曖昧に見せながら耐震設計している。

外周を取り囲んだ直方体は，この周辺環境のとりとめのない風景の中で，建築自身が自立した固有の風景を演出することをめざしたパッケージである。軽いシェルター的切妻屋根の幾何学断面を直方体に異形の窓として発生させた。直方体と屋根とを一体のシェルターとして同等に存在させ，内外の通常の連続の仕方を斜線で切断し，開口に装置的意味を持たせたかった。均質な架構に装置的あるいは装飾的な部品・開口を付加することで日常化し，自然要因のみに呼応させ，庭・土間・板の間と段階性のある簡素で素朴な生活空間を意図している。
（村上徹）

Floor plans

Sixth floor

Fifth floor

KUNIHIKO HAYAKAWA
& ASSOCIATES
NW House
Shinjuku, Tokyo
1985-86

Photos: T. Kobayashi

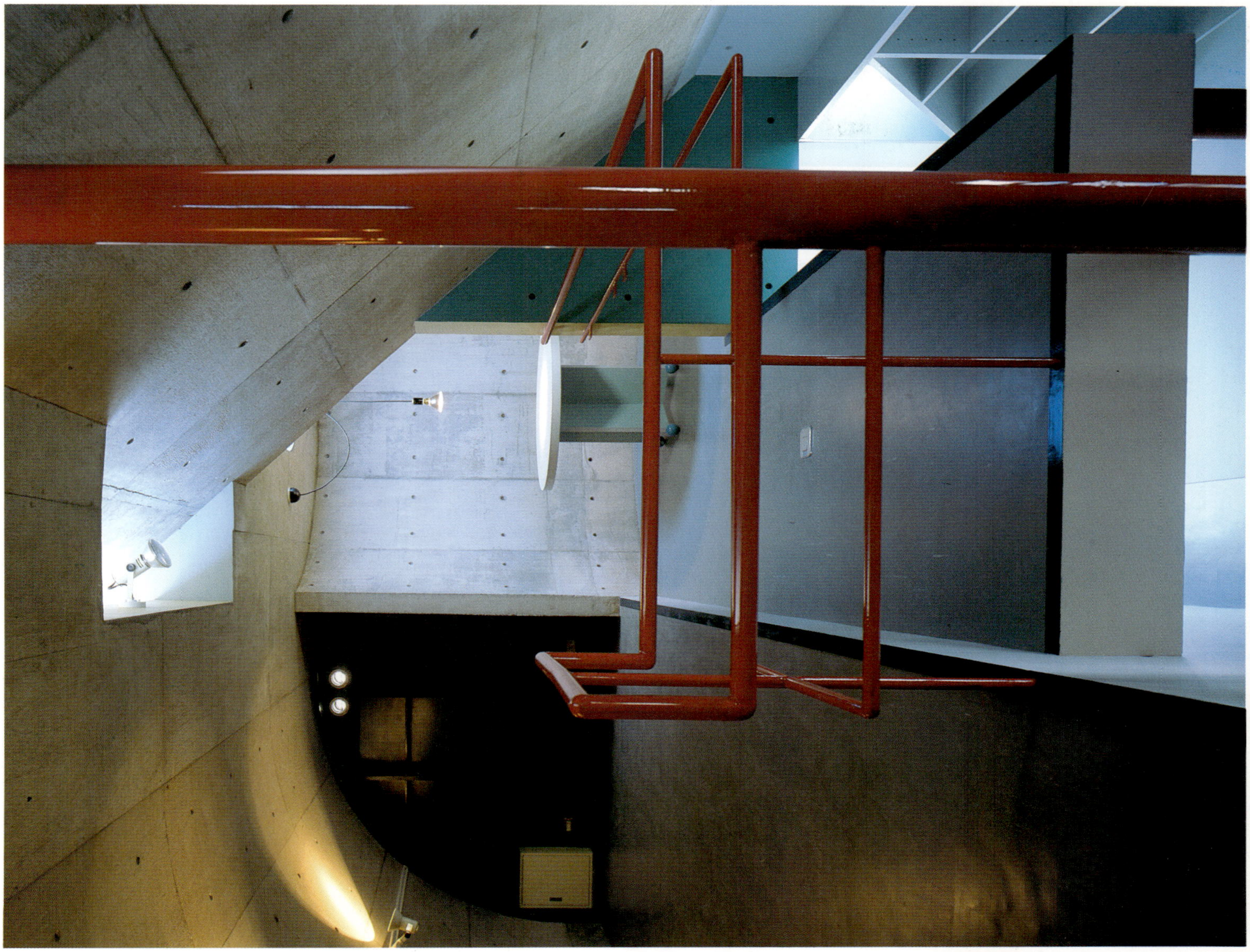
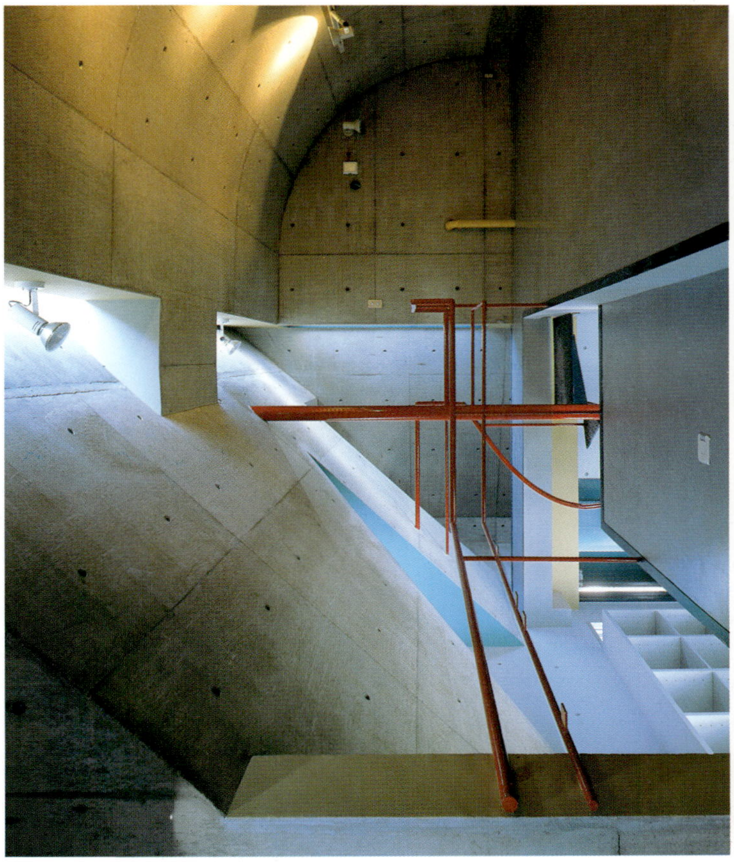
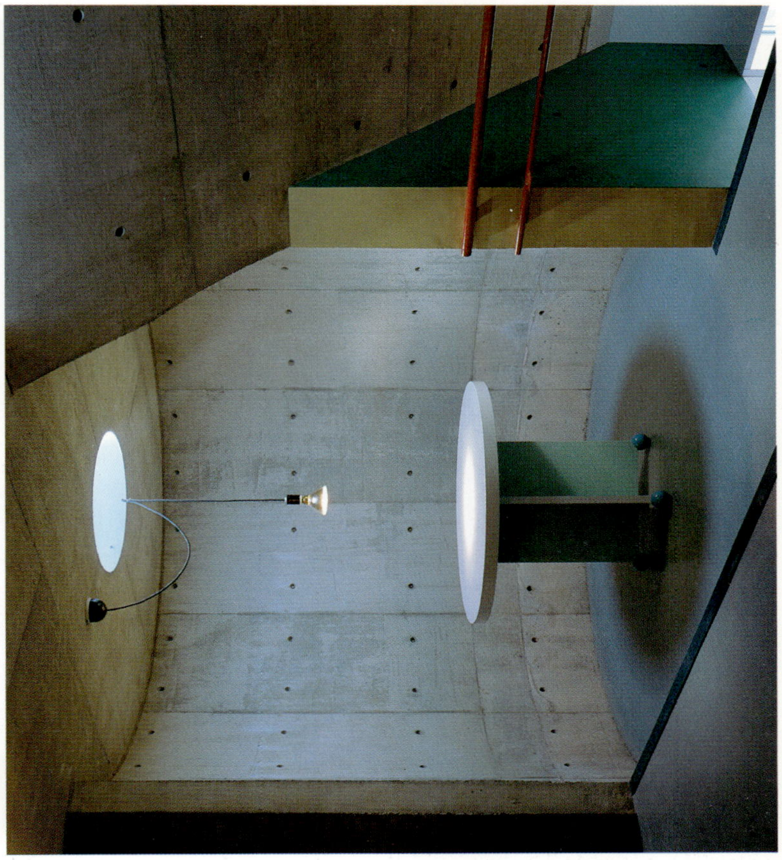

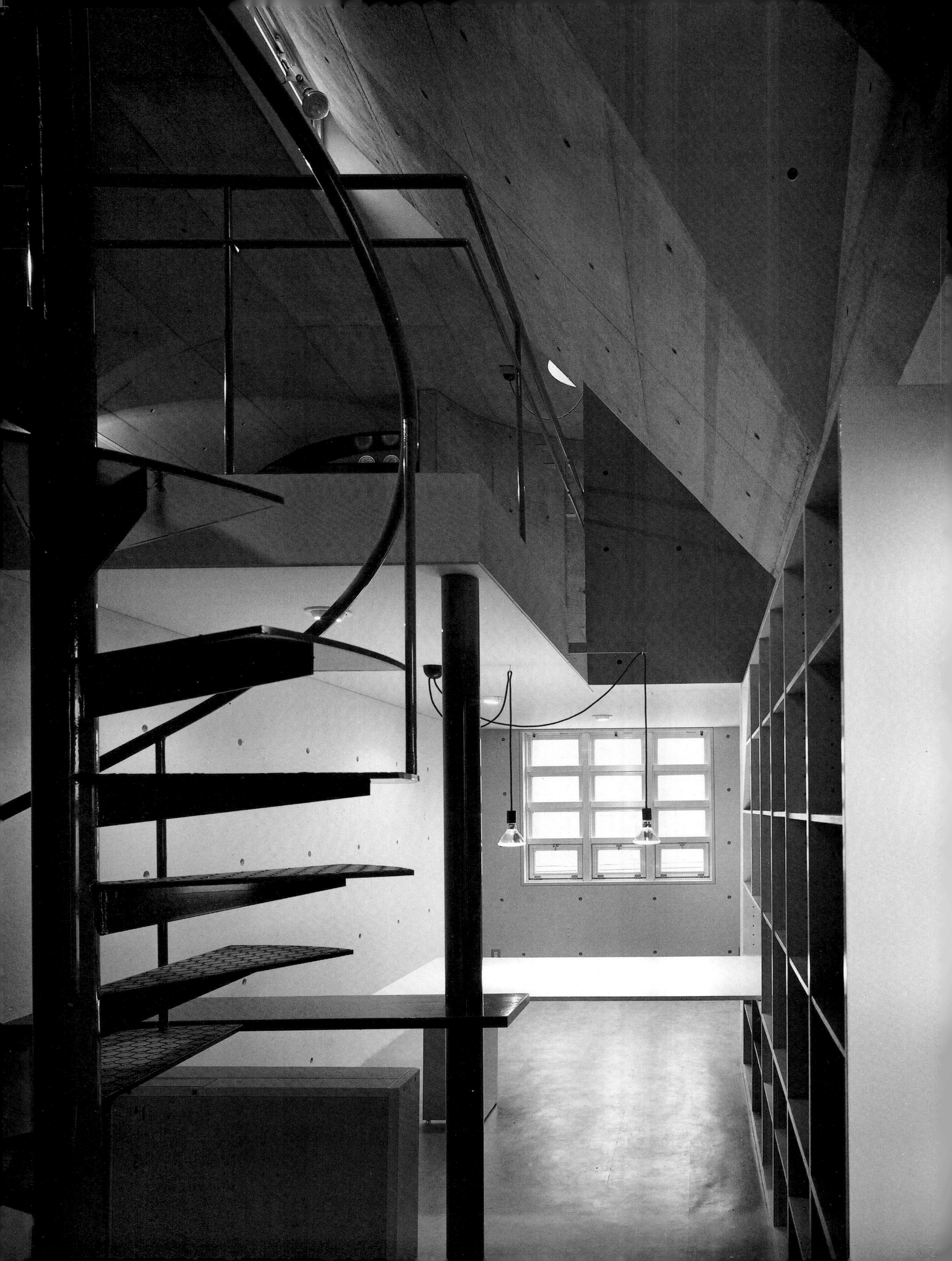

計画：NWハウス／東京都新宿区
主要用途：ギャラリー＋アパート＋アトリエ
建築設計：早川邦彦建築研究室
構造設計：百田構造設計
施工：門脇建設
主体構造：RCラーメン構造
主な仕上：コンクリート打放し
敷地面積：50.12m²
建築面積：43.10m²
延床面積：246.04m²

NW House stands near the Waseda University campus on a corner of the intersection of Waseda Dohri and a 4-meter wide street. Unlike previous works that were predominantly compositions of horizontally-extended walls that were static in character, this design, since it was located in a commercial district, was intended to be very much a part of the surface composition of the city. Although 6- and 7-story office buildings and condominiums stand on the opposite side of the street, there are two-story buildings of various exterior finishes for two to three hundred meters to the left and right of this building, including wood buildings with tiled roofs that must be 50-years old. The area has been passed by as far as urban development is concerned, and there are no large volumes nearby. Consequently, a multitude of fragmentary elements floating in the urban landscape—sign boards, advertisements, water tanks and cooling towers on rooftops, vending machines on the street, twisted trees and numerous utility poles, transformers and various traffic signs, electricity lines that are hung in anarchic fashion overhead and the countless antennas on roofs — enter one's vision as elements of equal weight. This is a shifting landscape typical of Tokyo. NW House has a number of different functions (a gallery, an apartment, an atelier and an office) piled one on top of another. Its various formal elements (half a vault, half a gabled roof, a cylinder, a cube, a triangle, etc.) and various materials (stainless steel, stucco, exposed concrete, etc.) will no doubt join the floating fragments that are parts of the urban landscape, that is, the surface composition of the city. If NW House stands out for the moment, it is probably only because its group of floating fragments are deployed vertically instead of horizontally as is the case with its neighbors. *Kunihiko Hayakawa*

早稲田大学のキャンパスに近い，早稲田通りとそれに直行する４ｍ道路の角地に建つNWハウスは，水平にのびる静的な壁の構成が支配的であった従来までの仕事と異なり，商業地域に建つという立地条件により，都市の表層構成に，より密着して参加するものとして意識された。向かい側の通りには，６～７階の事務所ビルやマンションが立ち並ぶのに，この建物側の通りには，築後50数年は経つ古い瓦屋根の木造建築をはじめとし，さまざまな外装の２階建の建物が左右２～300m連なっている。都市開発という点でいえば，いわばエア・ポケットのようなところである。したがって，大きなヴォリュームをもつものはないだけに，周辺の看板，広告塔，屋根の上の給水塔やクーリング・タワー，道路に置かれた自動販売機，曲がりくねった街路樹と林立する電信柱，その上のトランスやさまざまな交通標識，さらに空中を無秩序に飛びかう電線と，それに競うように直行する屋根面に立ち並ぶアンテナ群，といったように，都市の風景のなかに浮遊する断片ともいうべきものが，等価値で視覚のなかに飛びこんでくる。東京のどこにでもありそうな，移行的な風景といっていいだろう。いくつかの異なった機能（ギャラリー，住宅，アトリエ・オフィス）が垂直に積層されたNWハウスのさまざまな形態要素（½ヴォールト，半切妻屋根，円筒，立方体，三角形など）や材質要素（ステンレス，アクリシン，打放しコンクリートなど）も，都市の風景，都市の表層構成に参加する，浮遊する断片のひとつとなるだろう。もしNWハウスが，現時点で周辺から突出して見えるとしたら，たまたま浮遊する断片群が水平に並存している近隣のなかで，それらが垂直に積み上げられているという違いだけであろう。　　　　　　　　　　　　　　　　（早川邦彦）

KUNIHIKO HAYAKAWA
& ASSOCIATES
Stratum
Nakano, Tokyo
1985-86

Photos: T. Kobayashi

West elevation

First floor shop

Second floor of

Third floor Atl /of

Fourth floor

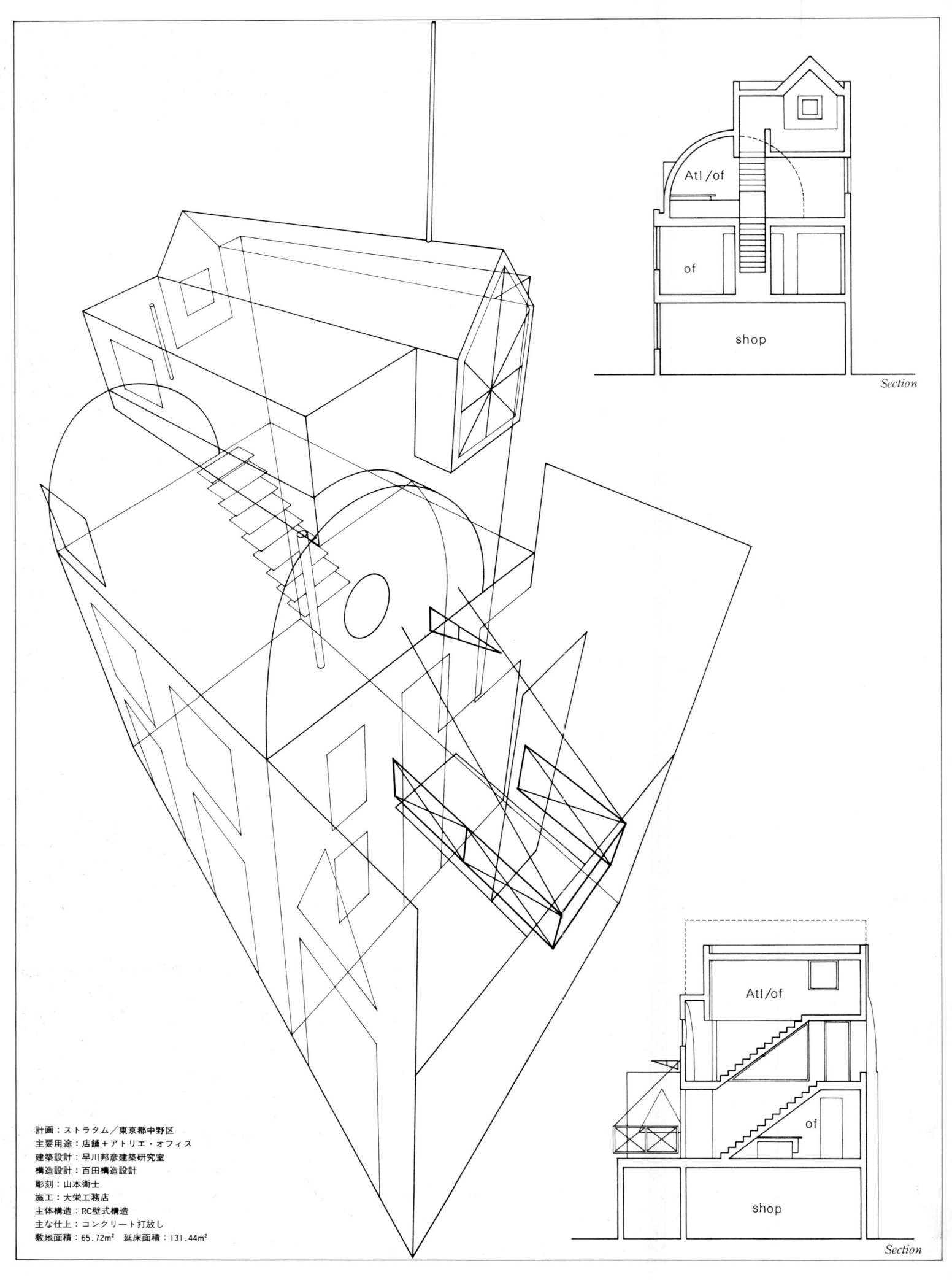

計画：ストラタム／東京都中野区
主要用途：店舗＋アトリエ・オフィス
建築設計：早川邦彦建築研究室
構造設計：百田構造設計
彫刻：山本衛士
施工：大栄工務店
主体構造：RC壁式構造
主な仕上：コンクリート打放し
敷地面積：65.72m²　延床面積：131.44m²

Section

Section

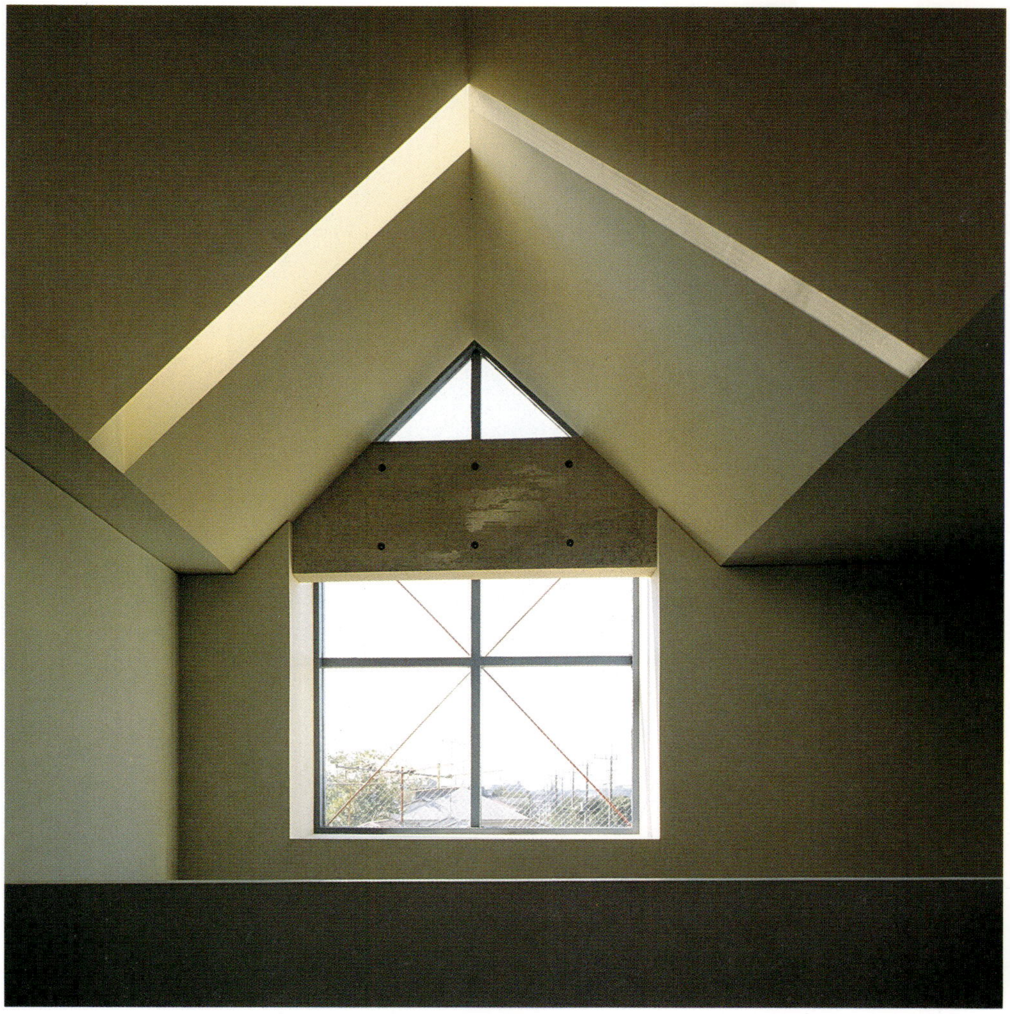

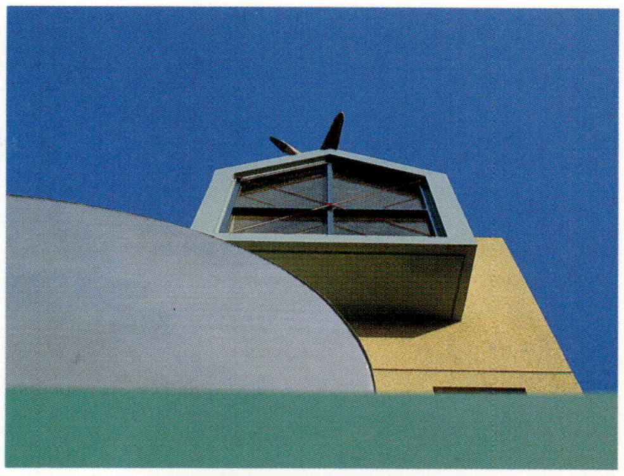

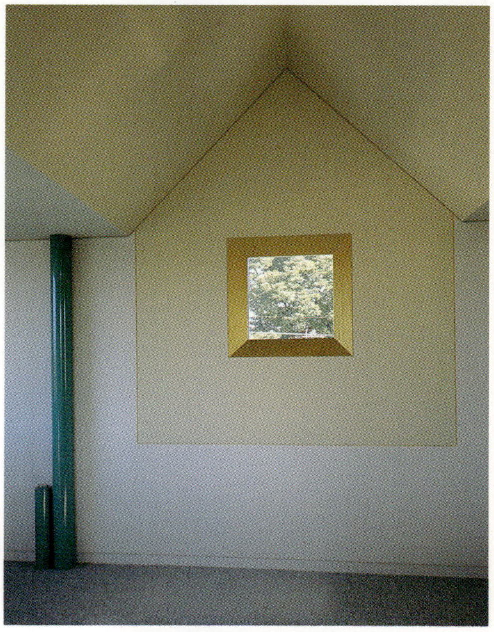

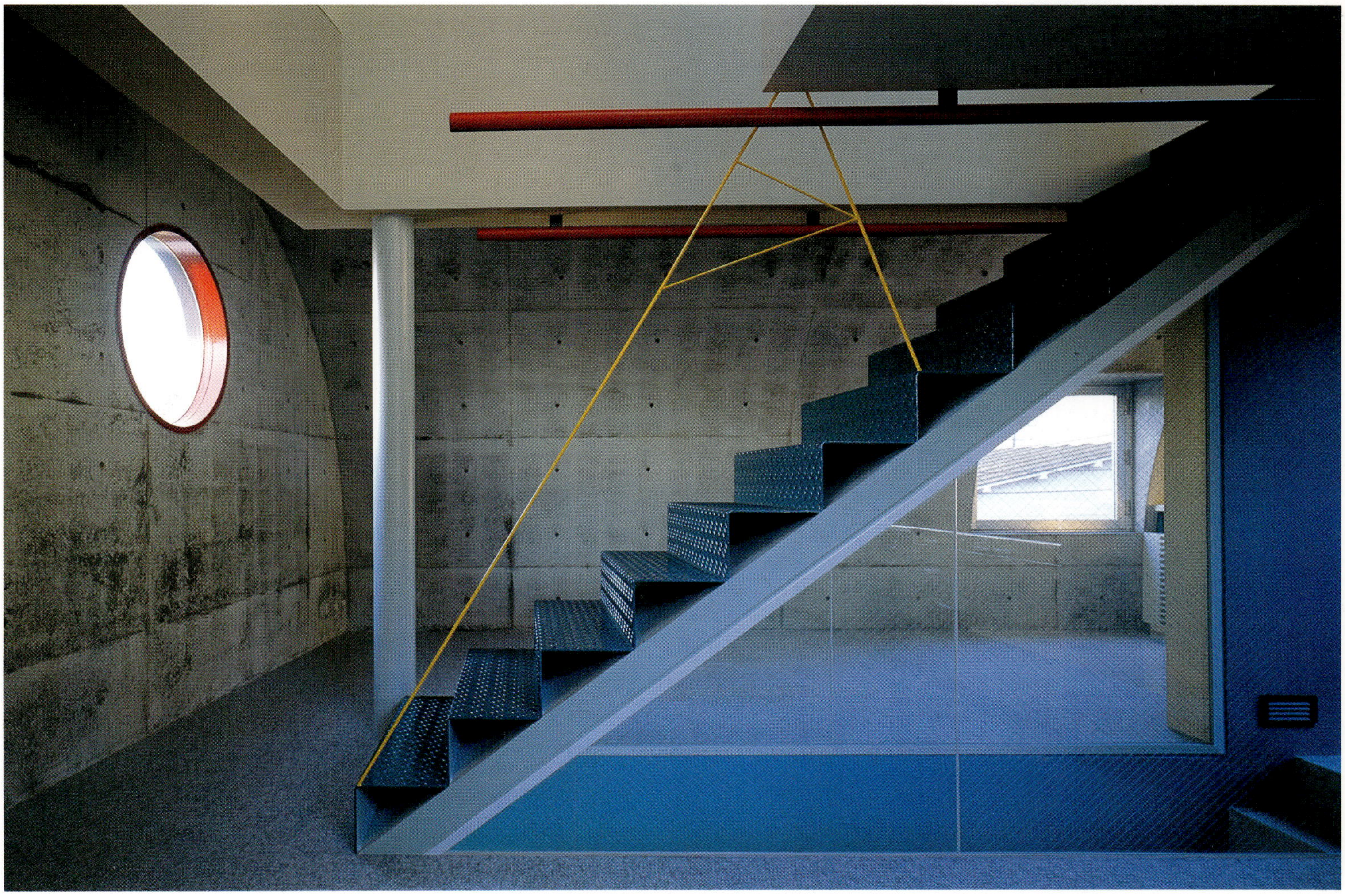

Stratum is located amid shops and houses in an area about ten minutes by commuter train from the subcenter of Shinjuku. This is a *zakkyo biru* with three different functions. A store is on the first floor, an office for the client is on the second floor, and the third and fourth floors can be used either as an atelier/office or as an apartment. In order to get the maximum allowable floor area—in this case the permitted ratio of building volume to lot is 200%—on the 770 square foot site, the floor plan faithfully follows the irregular course of the property line. A *zakkyo biru*, of which this as well as the NW House is an example, is always built on a narrow site to the maximum volume permitted by law and houses spaces with different functions that are stacked vertically; it is a building type characteristic of Japan's cities. It would be only a slight exaggeration to say that *zakkyo biru* account for the greater part of the visible portion of a Japanese city. However, this building type does not yet have a distinctive form. GA Tower, which is presently under construction, is also a *zakkyo biru*, with a handling area for goods on the first floor, offices on the second, third, and fourth floors, and private apartments on the top three floors. Whereas at NW House, various formal elements similar to the floating fragments of the cityscape are allowed to coexist on an equal basis, at Stratum volumes with different configurations are stacked. At GA Tower, spaces with different functions have been given forms that are stereotypes associated with those functions and have been stacked vertically. Although the design approaches are different, these buildings all represent attempts to find an appropriate form for that by-product of the Japanese city, the *zakkyo biru*.
Kunihiko Hayakawa

「ストラタム」は，副都心の新宿から通勤電車で約10分，周辺は商店・住居が混在するなかに建つ。1階は店舗，2階は施主のオフィス，3・4階は住居としても可能なアトリエ／オフィスという3つの異なる機能の組合せにより構成される，いわゆる「雑居ビル」である。770sq.ft.(66m²)の敷地に，最大許容面積(容積200％)を確保するため，平面は菱形をした敷地形状を忠実にトレースした格好になった。「NWハウス」も同様であるが，狭小の敷地のなかに，法的許容面積を最大にとり，異なる機能が垂直に積層した「雑居ビル」は，日本の都市に固有のビルディング・タイプといっていいだろう。極端に言えば，日本の都市の表層の大部分は，このような「雑居ビル」の集積によって構成されている。しかし，われわれは，まだ「雑居ビル」というビルディング・タイプに対する「型」を持ち合わせてはいない。現在工事中の「GAタワー」も，1階に隣接する工場のための荷捌き場，2・3，4階がオフィス，そして上部の3層が個人住宅という構成の雑居ビルである。「NWハウス」では街路に浮遊するさまざまな形態エレメント——断片を等価値に並存させたのに対し，「ストラタム」は異なる形態のヴォリュームを積み上げる手法をとっている。また「GAタワー」は，異なる機能がもつそれぞれのビルディング・タイプのステレオタイプ化した形態を垂直に積み重ねたものとなっている。相互に手法は異なるとはいえ，いずれも日本の都市の副産物ともいえる雑居ビルの「型」を求める試行にかわりはない。
（早川邦彦）

GA Tower project

Photo: T. Kitajima

MARK SIMON
of CENTERBROOK ARCHITECTS
Leonard J. Wyeth, project manager
Crowell Studio/Residence
Long Island
1984

Photos: W. Fujii

Elevations

This small (1300 sq.ft.) house is a composer's studio on the shore in the Hampton dunes of Long Island. Large enough to serve as a vacation house for rental or future sale, it adjoins a permanent residence next door.

Reminiscent of Long Island windmills and lighthouses, an octagonal tower domed with lead-coated copper is the building's core. Hip roofs slope off the tower to the north, protecting it from winter winds. Large double-hung windows face south to gain the sun's warmth. Roofs and walls are of red cedar shingles, and cedar lattice-work abounds in rails and porch overhangs.

Current waterfront codes required that the house be set on poles with the first floor 11 feet above sea level. To hide these and to protect parking and non-habitable storage areas on grade, we applied a skirt of cedar lattice. This skirt becomes a railing for the long ambling stair which leads to the front door and expands into a small sunning deck.

From the deck one enters a studio/living room carpeted for acoustics. Large enough for both a grand piano and sitting area, it has three "piano key" skylights which illuminate the composer's work space without allowing direct sunlight on the piano. The ceiling stretches upward and continues high above a hall to a small kitchenette and dining area. The focus of the studio/living room, however, is a wide set of steps under a tall arch that leads to the bedroom door and a second rambling set of stairs. These, much narrower and steeper than their sister's outside, lead to a tower room, surrounded like a lighthouse by windows and a circular walkway (requested by the composer to pace while creating). Views to the sea here are spectacular. The tower room's space extends up under the dome, with the soffit of the outdoor walk becoming a bed for guests. High at the top is a cupola, letting light in and air out when necessary.

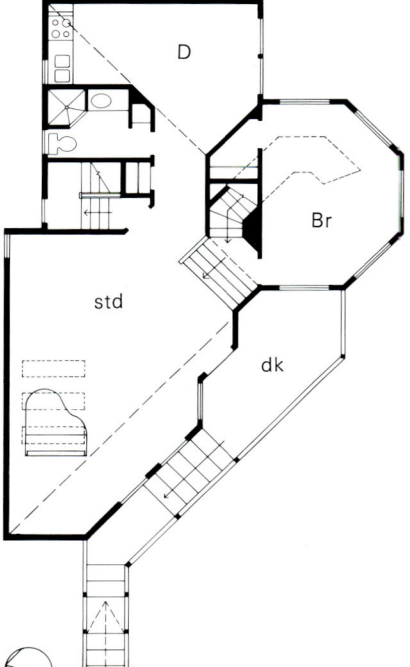

The success of this house, we think, lies in its rambling seaside spirit. Designed with romantic gesture, it reminds some of an old man looking out to sea, his capes flowing behind him. While it fondly remembers old and fast-disappearing Long Island neighbors, it makes no pretense of belonging to any but our own time.

Lower level

Consultant: Besier Gibble Norden, structural
General contractor: M. Clarhe Smith

Upper level

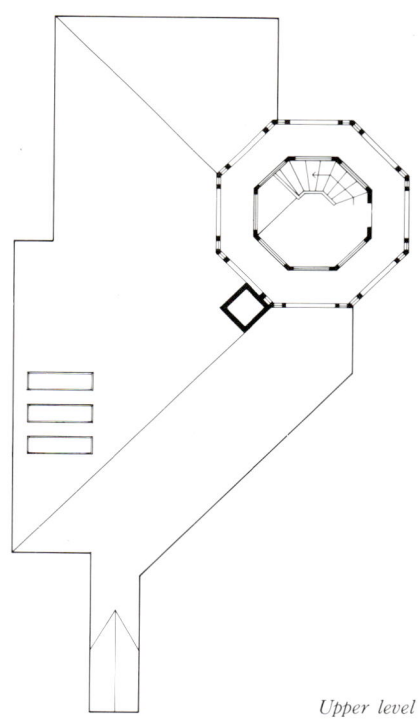

　この小規模な住宅（1300平方フィート）は、ロングアイランドのハンプトン砂漠海岸にある作曲家のスタディオである。賃貸用に、そして将来には売却用にもなる余暇住宅として十分仕える大きさにするため、隣の住居と結びつけられた。

　ロングアイランドに見られる風車、灯台、それに鉛板をかぶせた銅のドームをもつ八角塔の記憶が、建物の中核をなしている。尻下がりの屋根は塔から北へと傾斜し、冬の風の防護となる。壁に掛けられたように見える大きな上げ下げ窓は南に向き、太陽の暖かさを享受する。屋根と壁はレッドシダーのシングル葺きで、シダーの格子細工は、手摺欄干や張出しポーチに氾濫している。

　最近できたウォーターフロント条例によって、住宅は1階が海面より11フィート持ち上がった支柱上につくられなければならない。これらの支柱を隠し、駐車場や非居住の傾斜した倉庫領域を保護するために、われわれはシダーの格子細工によるスカートをはかせることにした。このスカートはフロントドアへと導き、小さな日光浴デッキまで伸びる長くのんびりした階段の側壁ともなっている。

　このデッキから、人は音響的配慮のされたスタディオ／リヴィングルームへとはいる。グランドピアノと座席領域双方に十分な大きさをもち、ピアノに直接自然光が落ちないように作曲家の仕事場を照明する3つの「ピアノ・キー」型のスカイライトがある。天井は上方へと拡大し、ホールの上高く小さなキッチンとダイニングの領域にまで伸びてゆく。しかしながら、スタディオ／リヴィングルームの焦点は、ベッドルームのドアと第2の曲がりくねった階段一式へと続く、丈高のアーチ下に広がる幅広い一連のステップである。これらは外部にある同種の階段よりもはるかに狭く急で、塔の部屋へと人を導いてゆく。複数の窓と周回する歩廊（創作中歩き回るという作曲家の要求によっている）によって、灯台的な環境にされているのだ。ここから望む海は見ごたえがある。塔の部屋の室内空間はドームの下で膨れ上がり、屋外の歩廊下端がゲストのベッドになるという具合だ。頂上はクーポラになり、必要なときに光を入れ、空気を外に出す。

　この住宅が成功していると思われるところは、逍遙的なシーサイドの気分をつくりだしていることである。ロマンティックな身振りでデザインされているため、かつての人々がケープを背になびかせながら海を見ている情景を想い起こさせるだろう。急激に消えゆく優しく古のロングアイランドの近隣一体を回想するものであるにもかかわらず、まさに今日に属し、見せかけ的なものはつくっていないのである。

PAUL RUDOLPH
Tuttle Residence
Rock Hall, Maryland
1980-86

Photos: W. Fujii

Rock Hall, Maryland, is a resort area with many weekend houses, located on the eastern shore of Chesapeake Bay. This residence stands on a 150-acre site facing the water. The client, a breeder of thoroughbreds, wanted the architect to design something that suggested a chateau. The residence is composed of two buildings. One houses the living room and study above guest bedrooms, and the other houses the kitchen, dining room, staff quarters, garage, and service area above the master bedroom suite. These two buildings are linked by a passageway. The entire composition recalls Rudolph's brilliant designs of the '60s.

The exterior finish is copper siding with standing seams; the interior walls are gypsum wall board, and brick and oak are used on the floors.

Consultants: Desimone, Chaplin & Assoc. Consulting Engineers, structural; PA Collins Assoc., mechanical

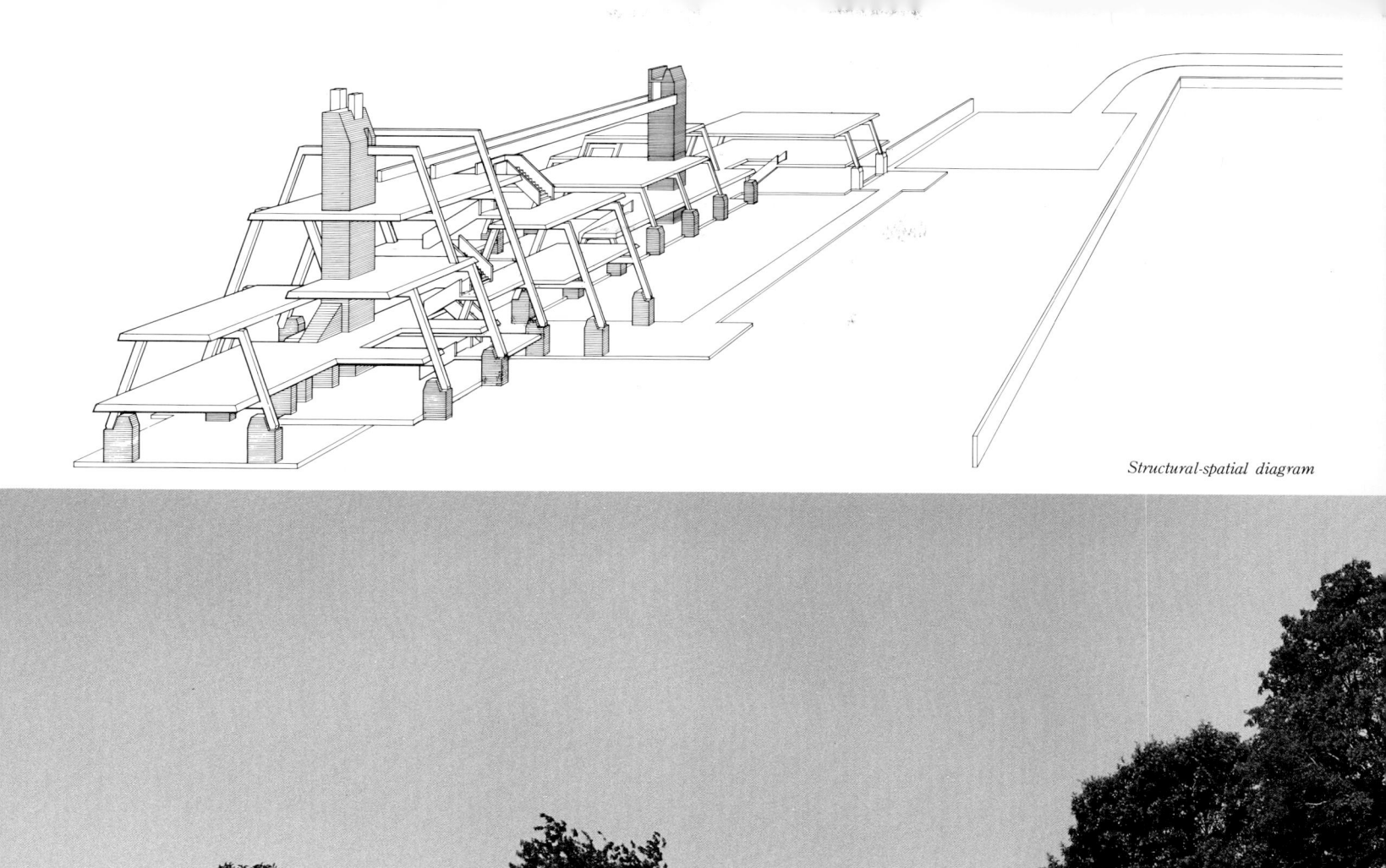

Structural-spatial diagram

First floor

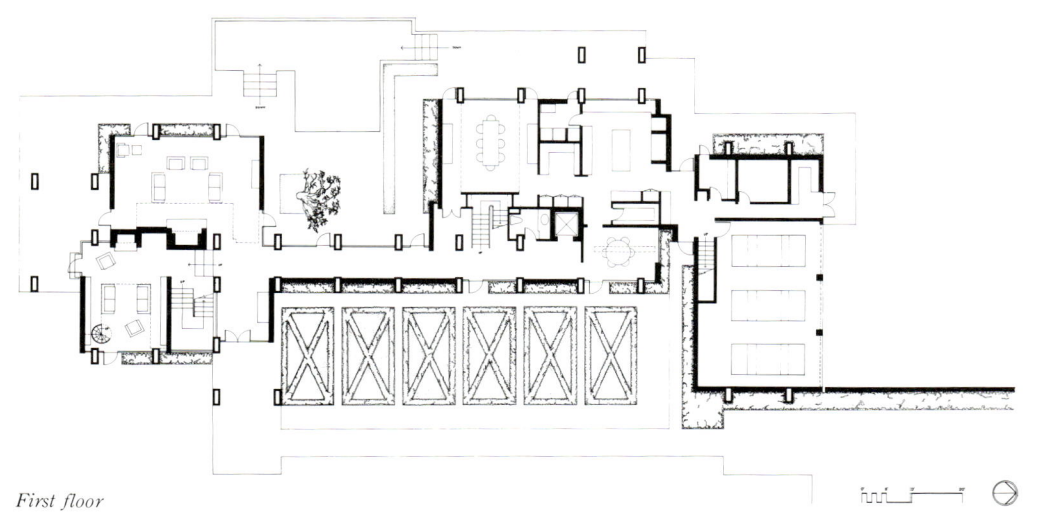

チェサピーク湾の東岸の町，メリーランド州ロックホールは週末住宅の多いリゾート地域である。この住宅は海に面した150エーカーの広大な敷地にあり，クライアントは，サラブレッドを育てる牧場主である。フランスのお城のイメージというのが，クライアントのルドルフに対する要望であった。住宅は2つの棟から成り，一方の棟に居間と書斎，その上にゲストルーム，一方の棟にキッチン，ダイニング，使用人室，ガレージ，サーヴィス部分，その上に主寝室とその付属室が置かれ，この2棟を渡り廊下がつないでいる。全体のかたちは，ルドルフが60年代によくつかった，あの優れた形態を思い出させる雰囲気をもっている。

銅の立ちはぜ継ぎサイディングに内装は石膏ボード，床にはレンガとオークを用いている。

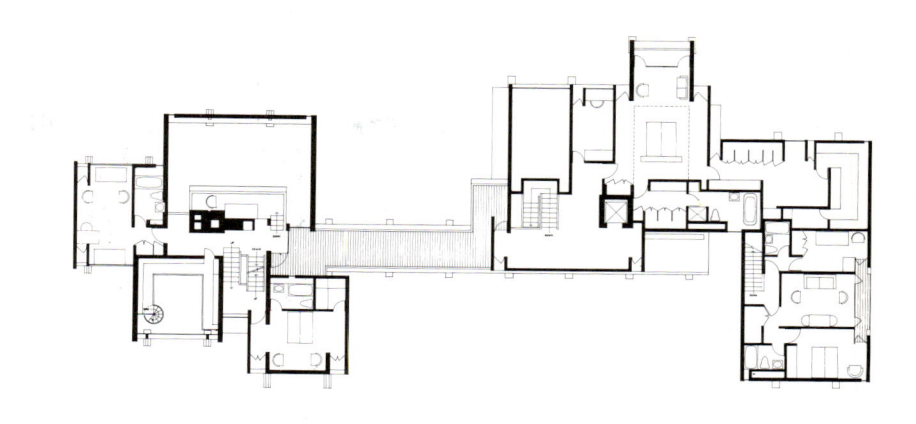

Second floor

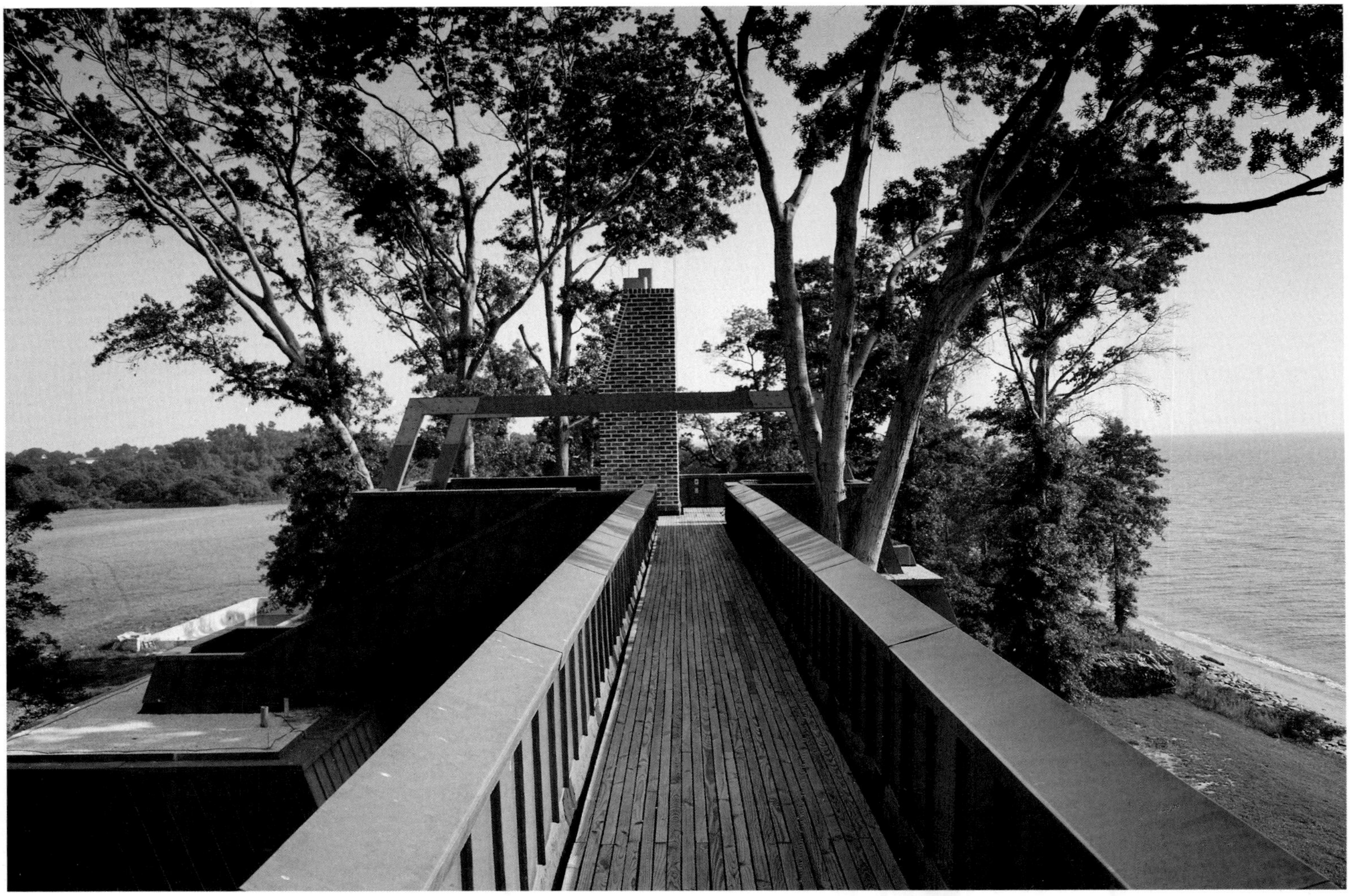
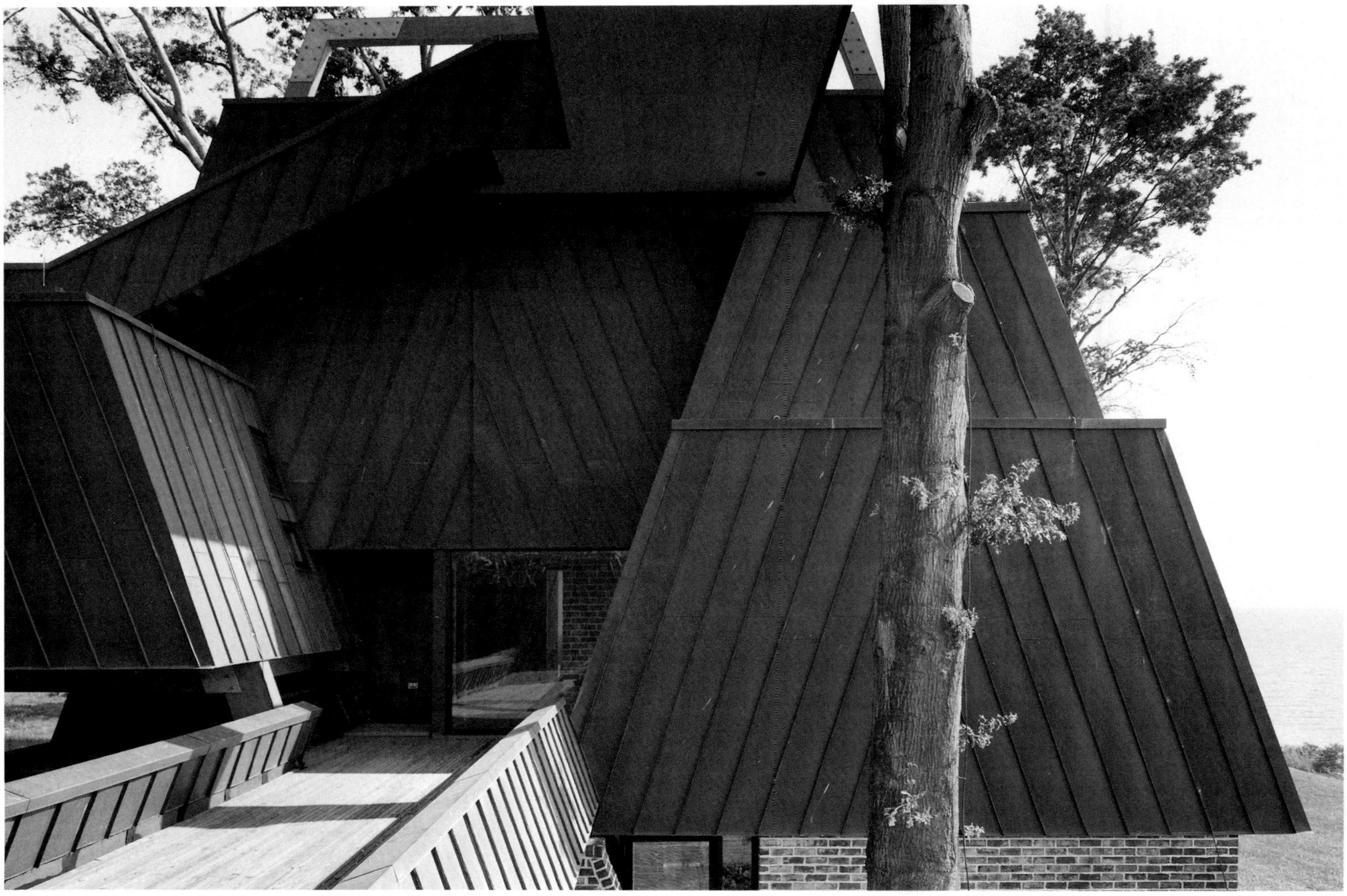

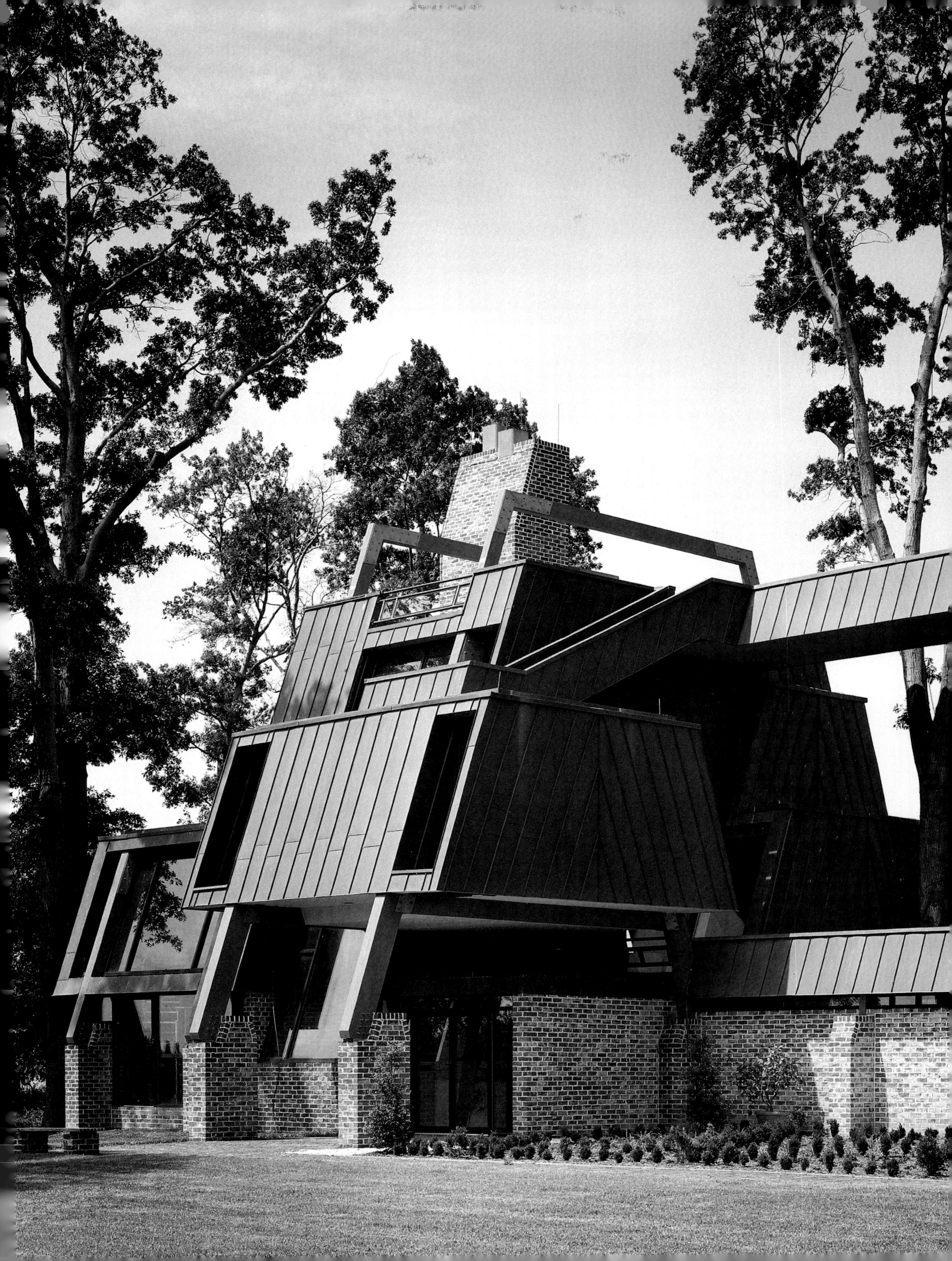

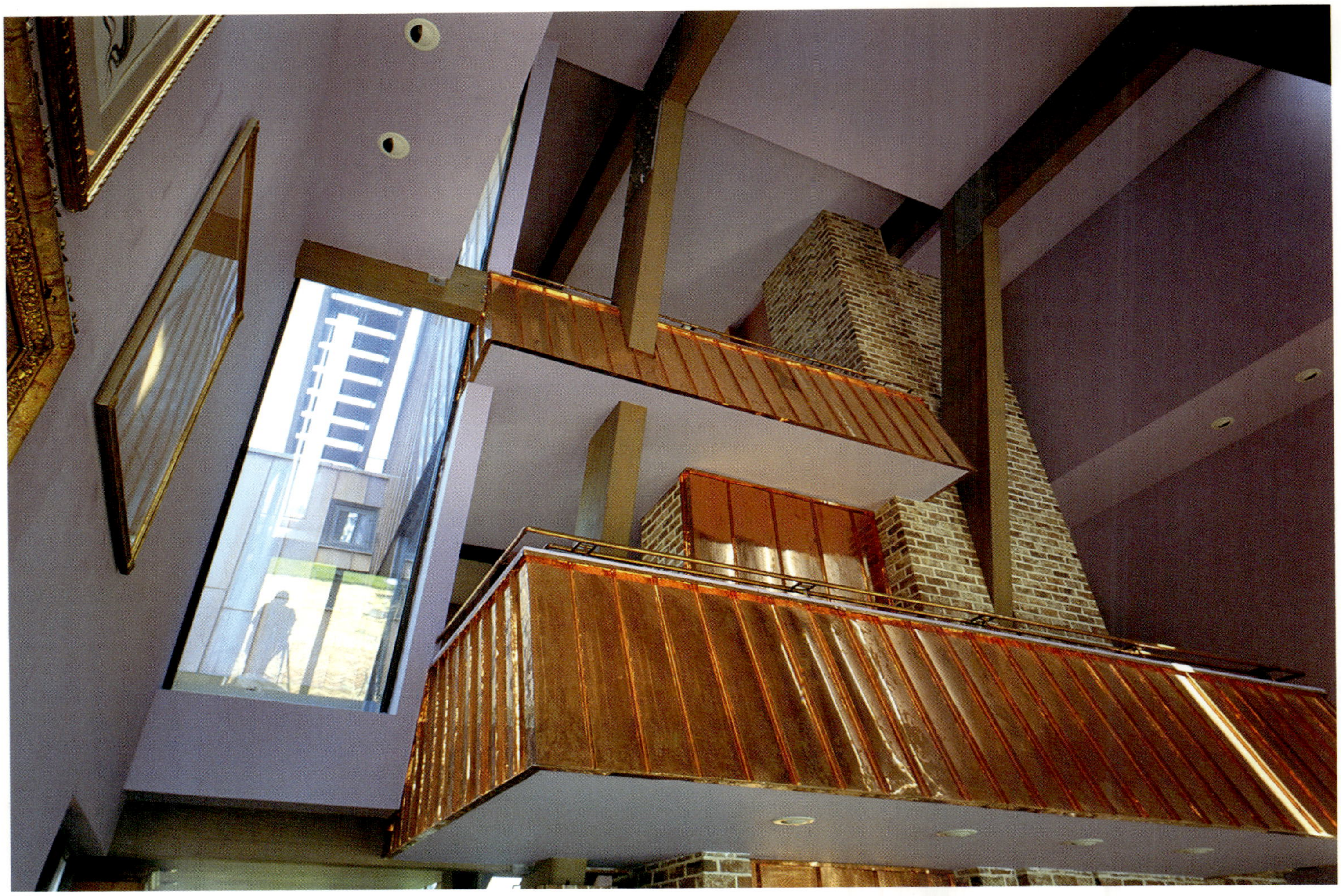

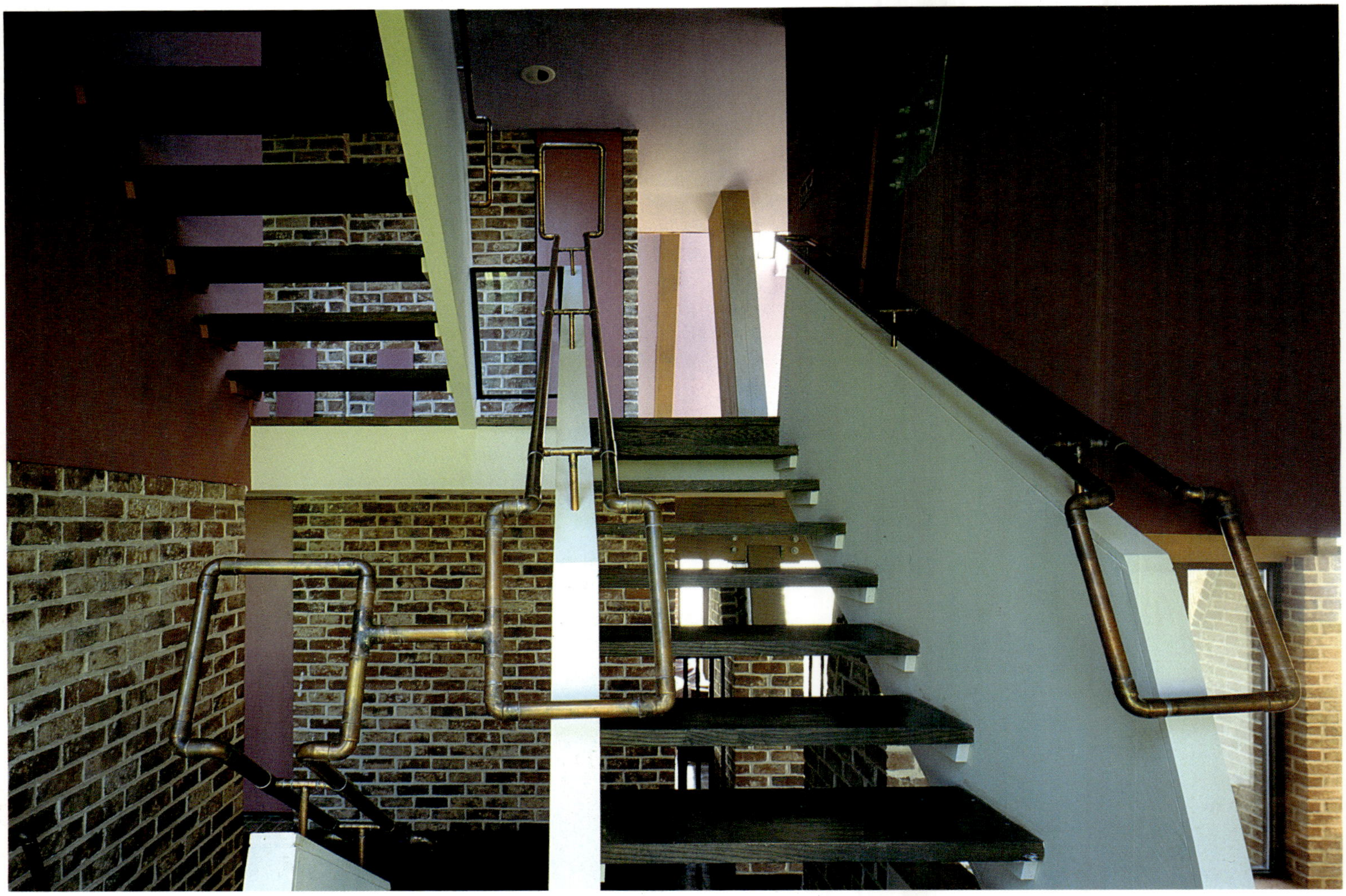

141

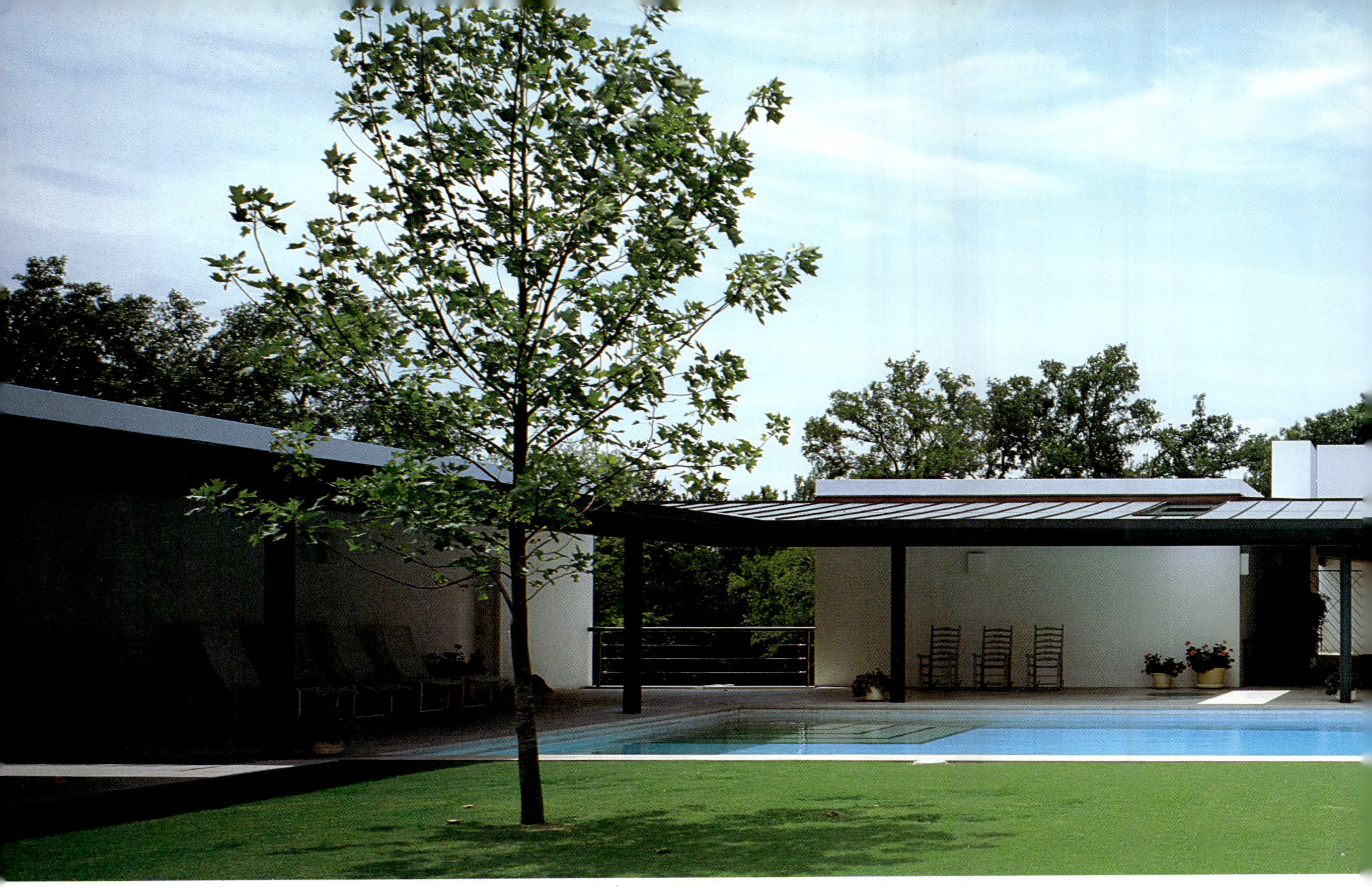

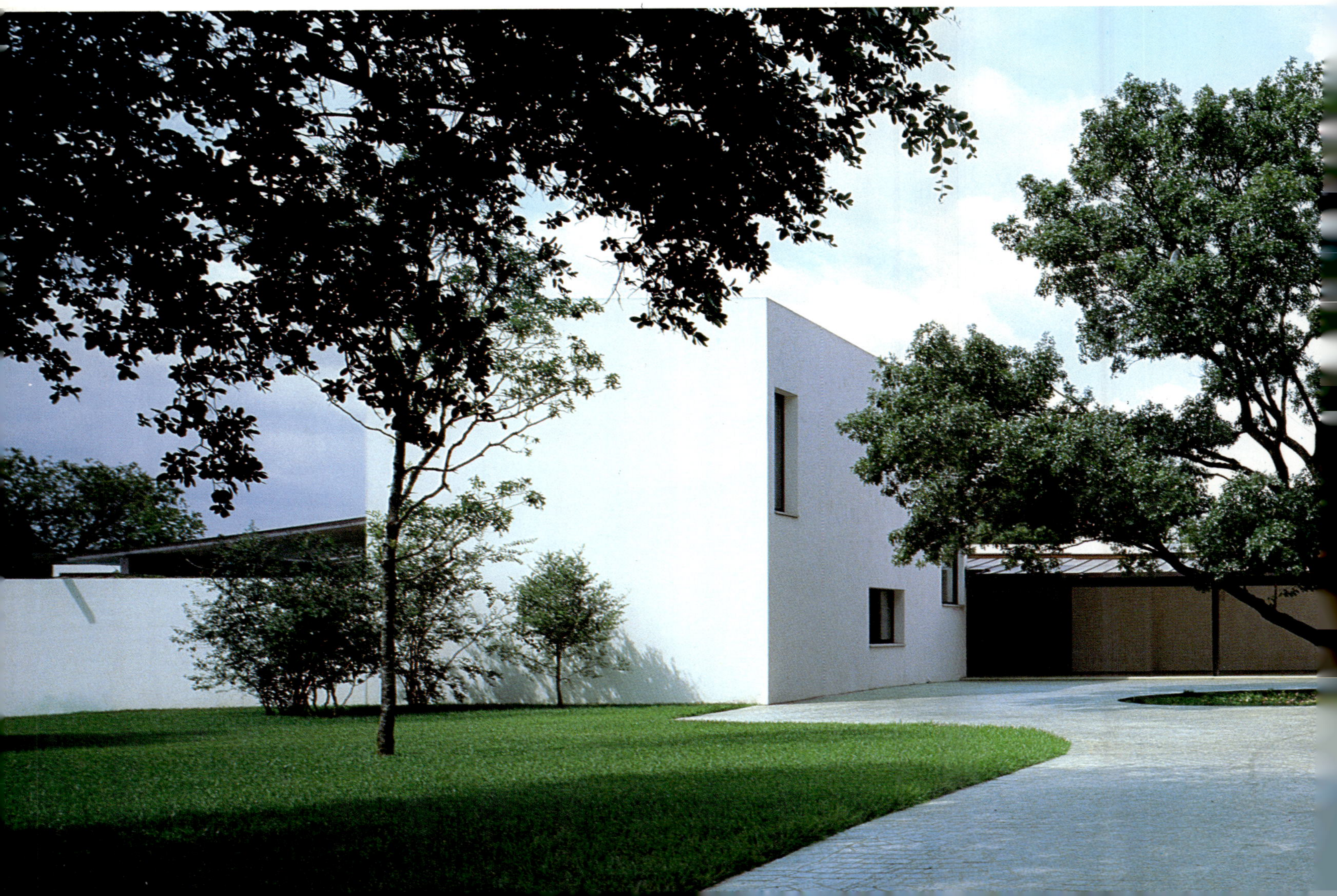

EDWARD LARRABEE BARNES
ARMAND P. AVAKIAN
Residence in Dallas
Dallas, Texas
1983

Photos: W. Fujii

Lower level

Entrance level

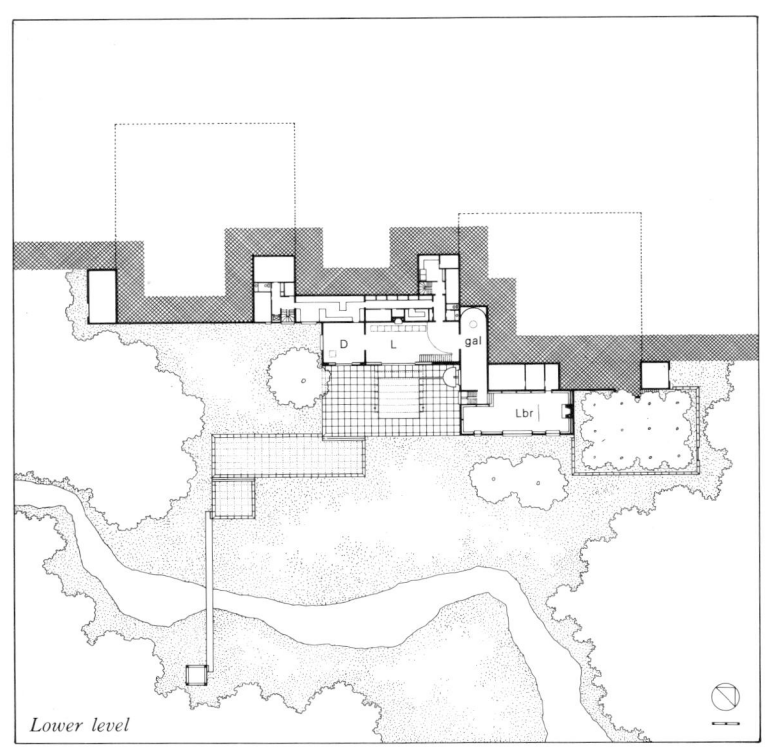

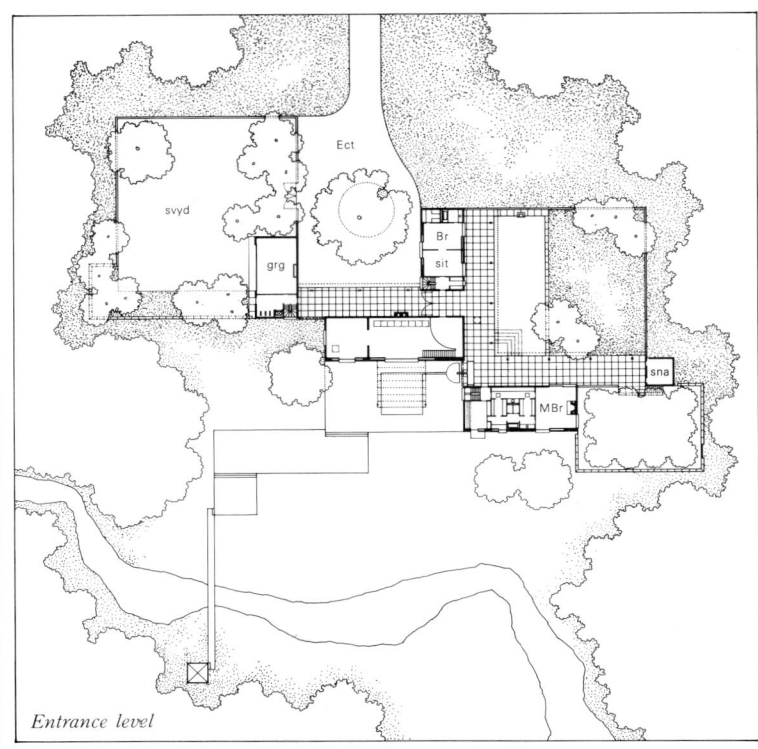

この住宅は敷地を統合することで，美しいアートコレクションの場を設け，家族の居住のためのプライヴァシーとパブリックの領域を共存させ，なおかつ郊外におけるプライヴァシーといったものを保護することを意図して設計された。

リヴィングとダイニングルームは2層分の空間をもち，入口のレヴェルと下のテラスやその向こうにある小川のレヴェルをつないでいる。住宅を通して敷地を下降してゆく動きは，住宅内部および屋外テラスによる多層化したレヴェルによって規定される一連の斜行するヴィスタを生み出す。住宅と自然は相互に組み合わされているのだ。

平面がデザインを生成する。4つの分離されたブロックと3つの中庭が，上のレヴェルを形づくっている。これはゆるやかな「浸透性をもった」計画の反映にほかならない。そして下のレヴェルでは，住宅のすべては連結され，家族を2層分吹抜けの中央のリヴィングへと導いてゆく。

明晰さが，平滑な白いスタッコによって強調されている。

145

Tower level

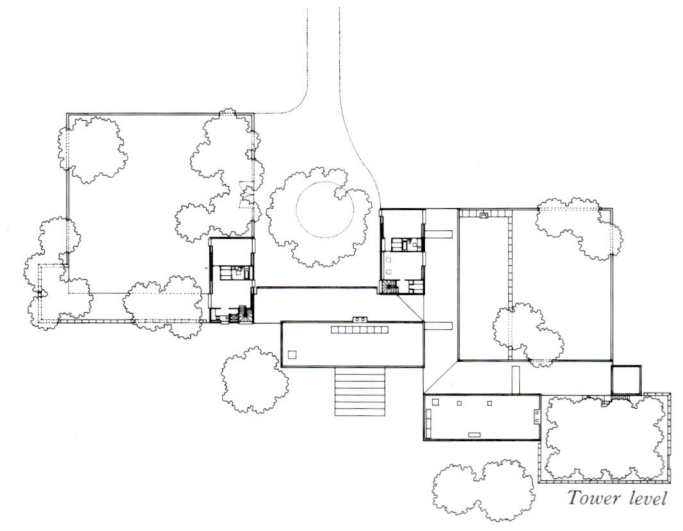

This house was designed to integrate with the site, to provide a setting for a beautiful art collection, to contain both public and private areas for family living, and to preserve privacy in a suburban setting.

The living and dining rooms are two-story spaces that connect the entrance level with the lower terraces and the brook beyond. The movement through the house down into the site is a series of diagonal vistas defined by levels within the house and stepped terraces outside. The house and nature interlock.

It is the plan that generates the design. Four separate blocks and three courts form the upper level. This is a loose "porous" scheme. And yet at the lower level the entire house connects, bringing the family together in the two-story central living room.

Clarity is emphasized with plain white stucco.

Consultants: Severud, Perrone, Szegezdy, and Sturm, structural; Joseph R. Loring and Associates, mechanical; Boyd and Heiderich, landscape; Marguerite Theresa Green, interior; Donald L. Bliss, lighting General contractor: Gene Campbell, Inc.

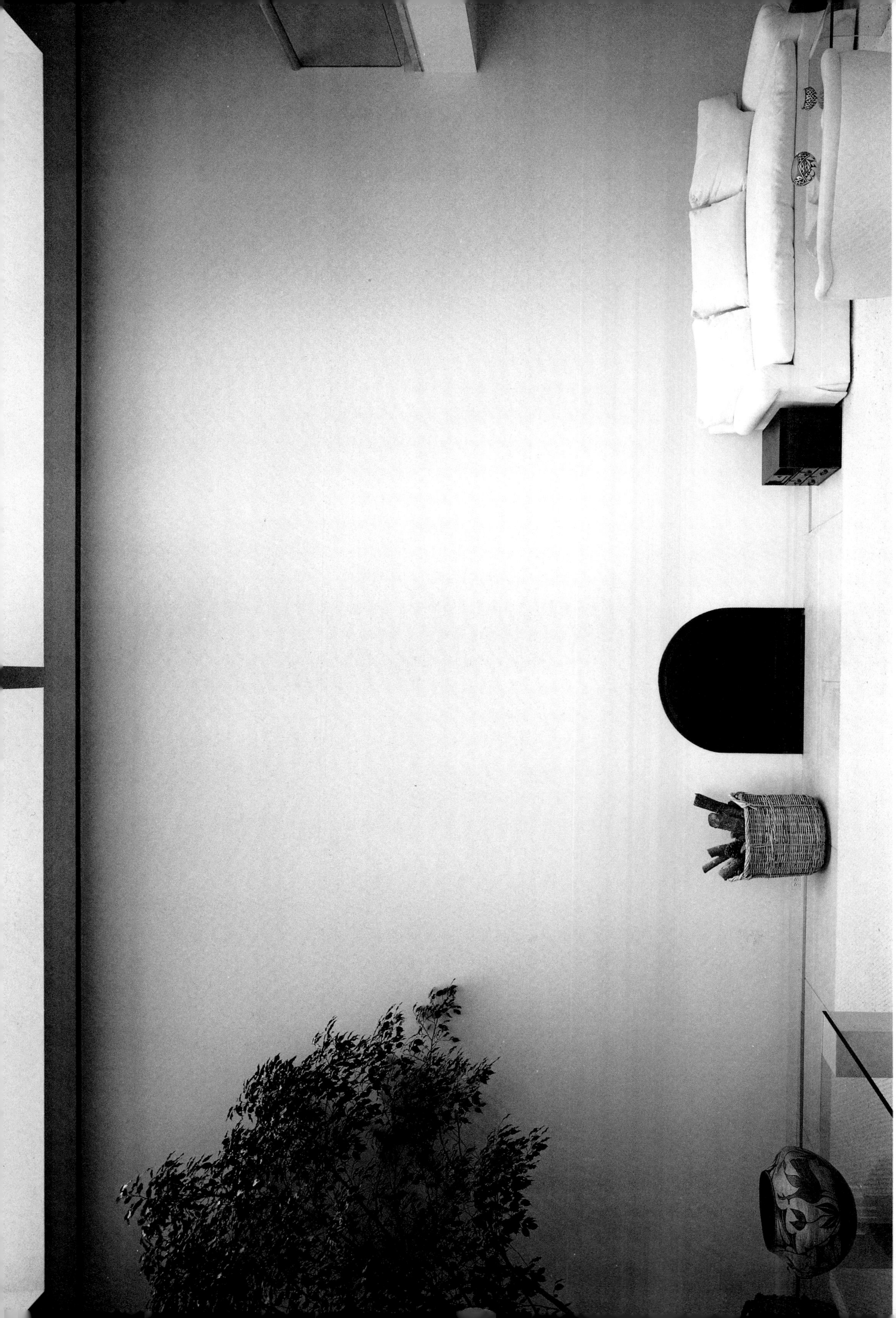

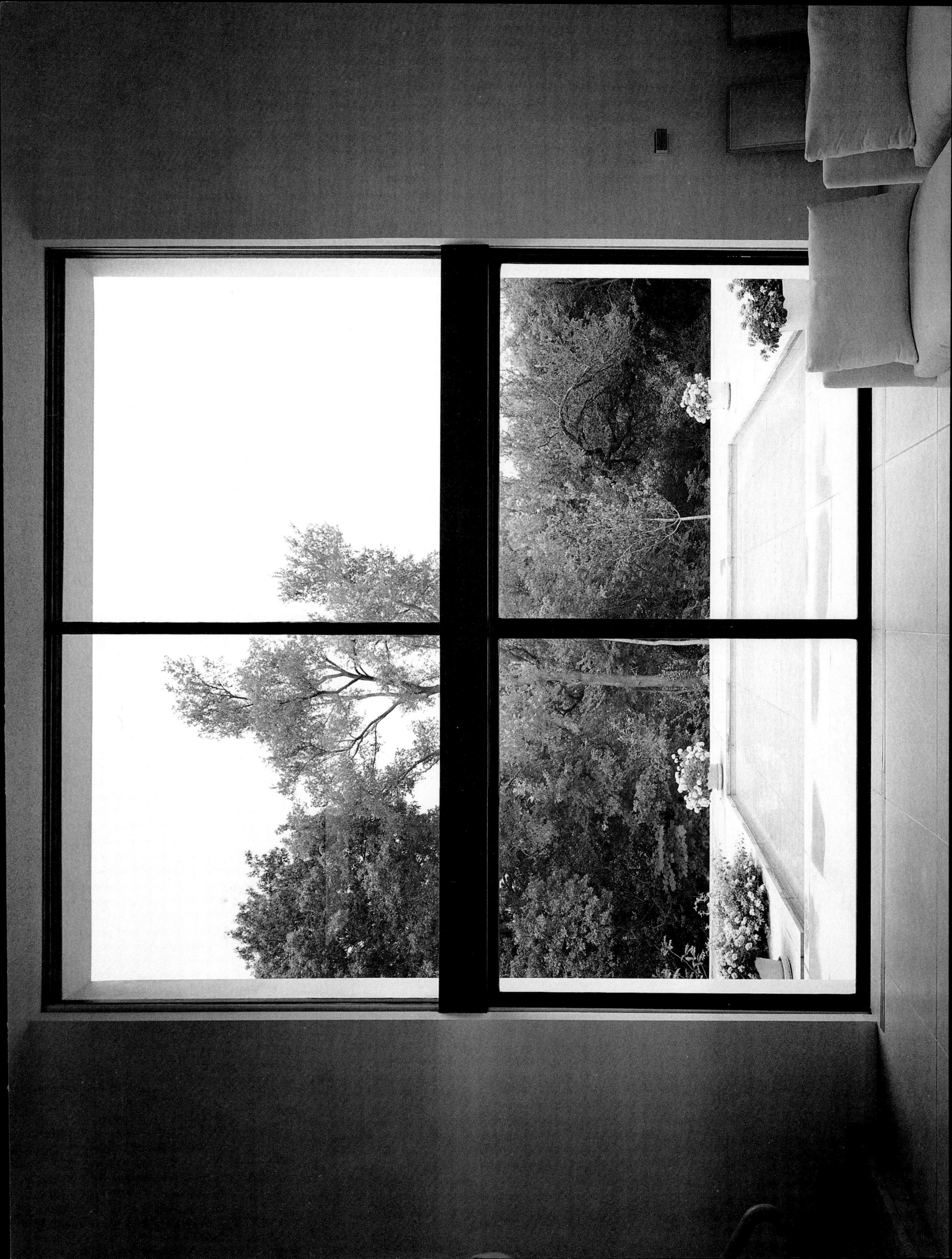

GREG MAXWELL
with CITIGROUP ARCHITECTS
& PLANNERS
Loeken Residence
Seattle, Washington
1985-86

Photos: W. Fujii

The house sits on the brow of a precipice. The site, three hundred feet above Puget Sound, governed the house's orientation, but its axiality and the parti were determined by the client's lifestyle. A psychiatrist who divides her professional time between private practice and community counseling, her personal life is a mix of the physical and the pensive. Because the professional and the personal are at emotional odds, she needed a place that would function both as office and as sanctuary. Consequently, Greg Maxwell with Citigroup Architects & Planners designed her a house with a split personality.

The plan-generated scheme is divided into two perpendicular spines. The primary axis runs east to west from the front walkway/entry through the central living quarters and out onto the rear deck. The secondary axis is the connecting hall between the office and residential interiors. These separate uses are each given distinct material expression. The residence is a primordial memory of dwelling: low to the ground, protective, of the earth, stucco. The office is housed in a high tech tower: white, gridded, enameled steel with guide wires, turnbuckles, and a ribbed steel roof.

This confrontation of preindustrial stucco with the machine esthetic is the principal metaphor for the private and the public self, but there are other motifs worked into the composition as well. The progression from entry through inner space and finally out into the sacrosanct precinct of the rear deck is deliberate, calculated, orchestrated. Staccato lights on the front walkway; the straight lined neon run in the entry; the compound curve/G clef on the living room ceiling; the industrial clerestory that simultaneously inhibits and promotes passage; and ultimately, the deck-which-is-a-runway inviting flight — all read like musical expressions — adagio, allegro, presto, largo — go slow, go fast, go fast cheerfully.

Cheerful attention to detail characterize every surface. Recollection and surprise are

givens. But two elements deserve special recognition. The first, the stair tower, is the center around which the primary and secondary axes pivot. It is also the library. Thus, the eye of this maelstrom is learning, thoughtfulness and repose. The second telling detail, the dining room table is a collaboration between Maxwell and sculptor Tom Lindsey (also w/Citigroup). Although a paraphrasing of the materials and forms used elsewhere, here Lindsey recombines the piano curve and the marble, glass and steel to give Maxwell's purpose new expression. Together, they set this table with exactly what's needed: food for thought.
Victor Gardaya

住宅は絶壁の突出部に設けられている。プジェット・サウンドの上方300フィートにある敷地が住宅自体の方向性を支配しているが，その軸性や建築の基本的な構成は，クライアントのライフスタイルによって決定された。精神科医である彼女は，その職業時間を私的な実践とコミュニティのカウンセリングに分割し，またそのため個人的生活も肉体的なものと瞑想的なものの混合となっている。職業性と個人性が感情的レヴェルで不整合を起こしているため，彼女は，オフィスとしても避難所としても機能する場所をつくることを必要としていた。結果として，グレッグ・マクスウェルとそのグループが，分裂したパーソナリティをはらむ住宅を設計したのである。

計画されたプランは，2本の直交するスパインで分割されている。第1の軸は正面のアプローチ／入口から東西に走り，中央のリヴィング区画を通り，背後のデッキへと出てゆく。第2の軸は，オフィスと住宅のインテリアをつなぐホールとなっている。これらの異なった用途には，それぞれ，顕著な材料上の表現が与えられた。居住することの本源的な記憶である住宅部には，地表面に低く防護的にスタッコが使用され，一方，オフィスはハイテク・タワーとして，ガイドワイヤーやターンバックル，そしてリブになったスティール製の屋根をもつ白い格子の光沢スティールが使われた。

機械美学と前工業的なスタッコとの出会い，それは公的なるものと私的なるものの原理的な隠喩であるが，それと同様にコンポジションに組み入れられた他のモチーフも存在する。入口から内部空間を通って進み，背後にあるデッキの神聖な領域へと至る行程は，慎重に扱われ，計算され，構成されている。正面アプローチに見ることのできる光のスタッカート，入口に走る直線状のネオン，リヴィングルーム天井の複合曲線／ト音記号，パッサージュを助長しつつ同時に抑制する工業的な高窓，飛行を誘う逃避用デッキ……すべては音楽的表現のようにも読める。アダージョ，アレグロ，プレスト，ラールゴ，……ゆっくりと，速く，陽気に速く。

ディテールへの楽し気な配慮は，あらゆる表面を性格づけてゆく。追憶と驚きが立ち現われる。しかし，2つのエレメントが，とくに認識に値するものだ。1つは階段タワーであり，それを中心として第1の軸と第2の軸が旋回する。そこはまた同時にライブラリーでもある。こうして混乱させられた眼は，学び，考え，休息するというわけだ。もうひとつはダイニングルームのテーブルで，これはマクスウェル・グループと彫刻家トム・リンゼイの協同によるものである。素材と形態のパラフレーズが至る所で使われるが，ここでリンゼイは，ピアノ曲線と大理石，ガラス，スティールを再結合し，マクスウェルの意図に新しい表現を与えた。ともに彼らは，まさに必要なものとして，このテーブルをセットした。すなわち，それは思想の食卓にもほかならなかったのだ。
（V．ガルダヤ）

West elevation

East elevation

North elevation

South elevation

North elevation

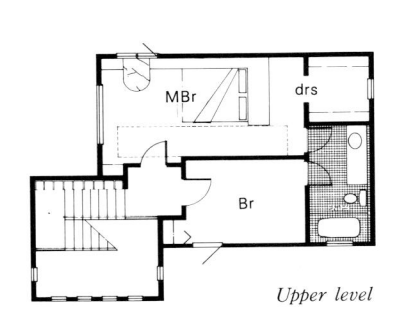

Upper level

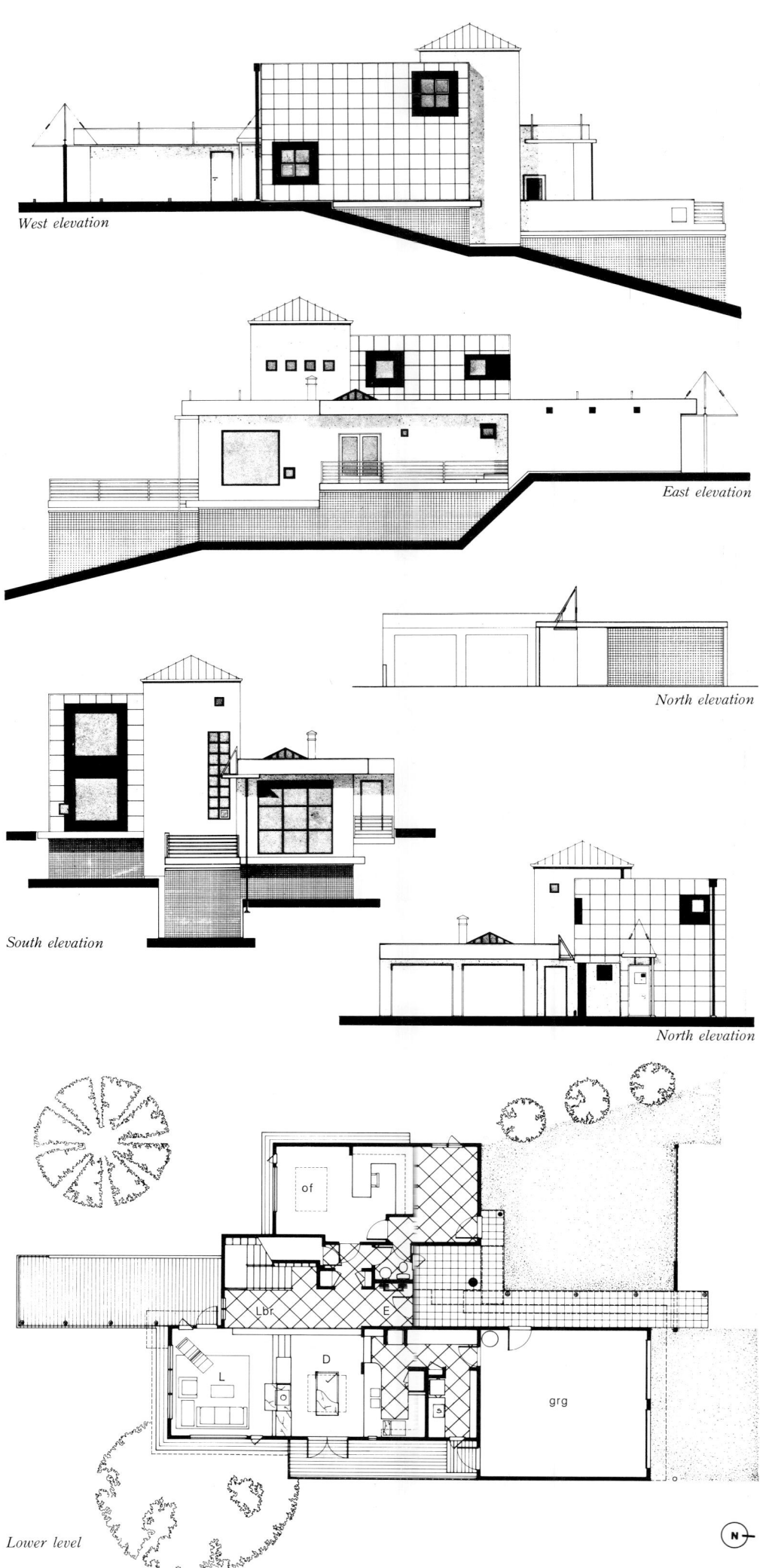

Lower level

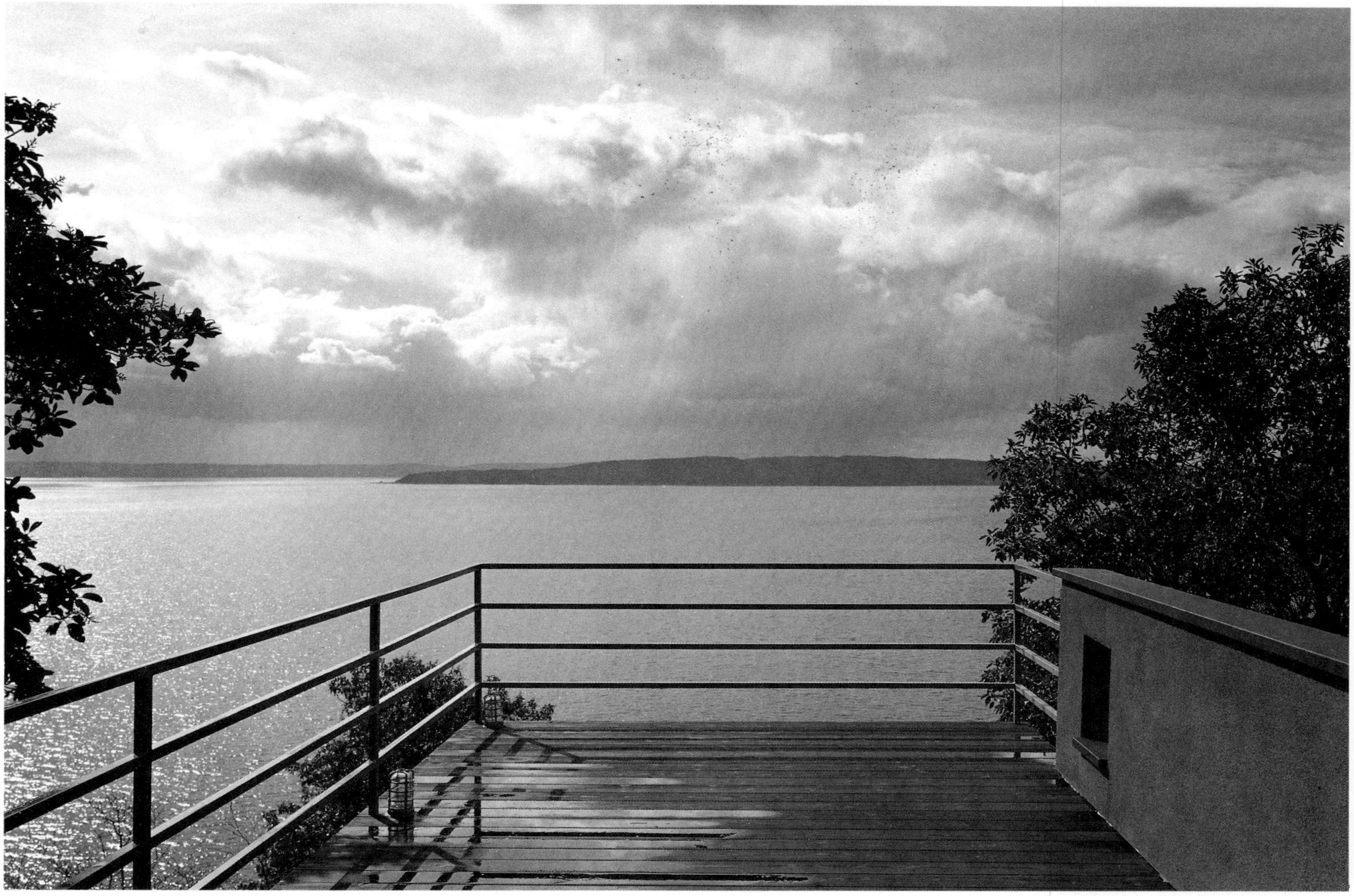

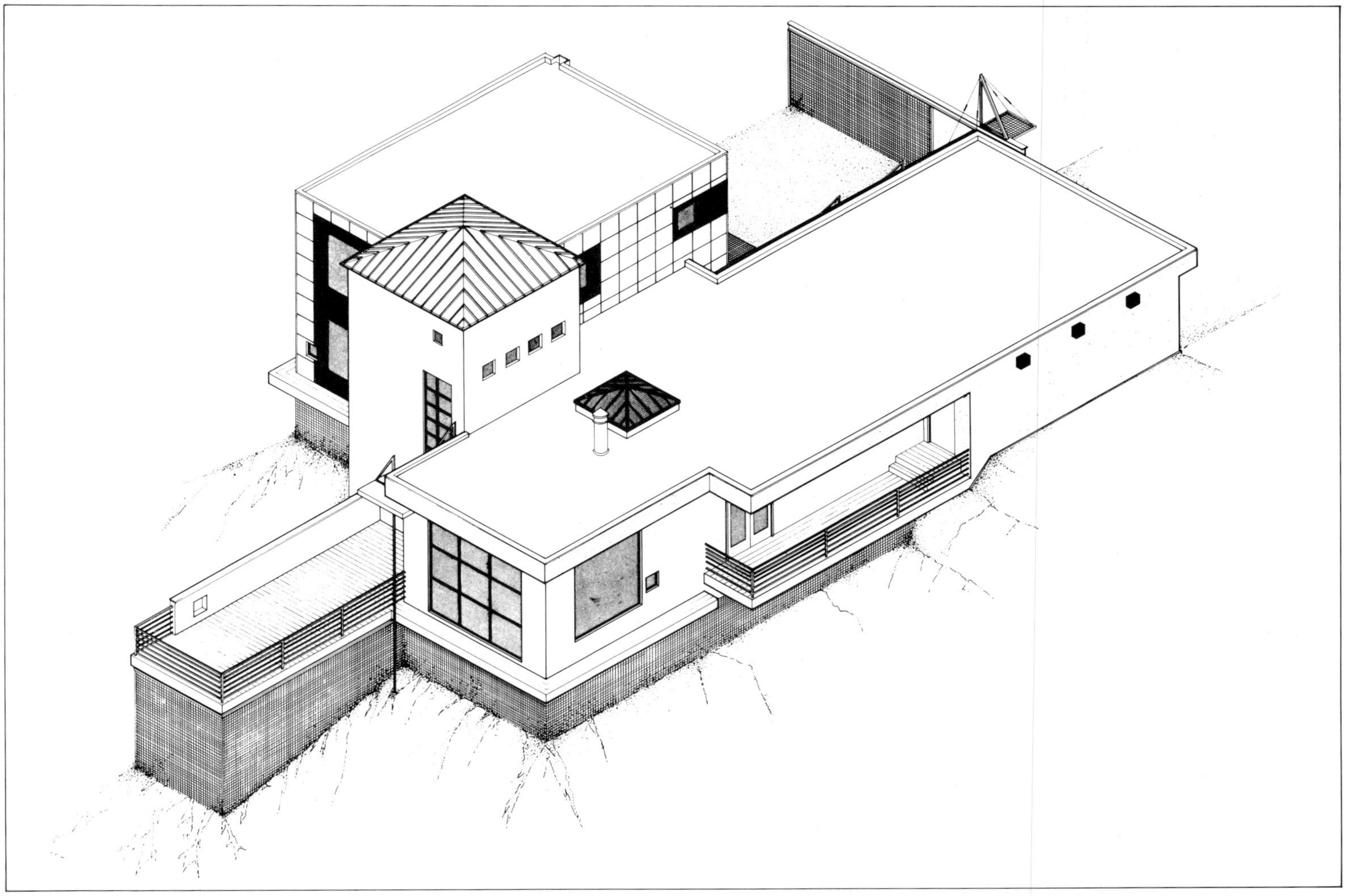

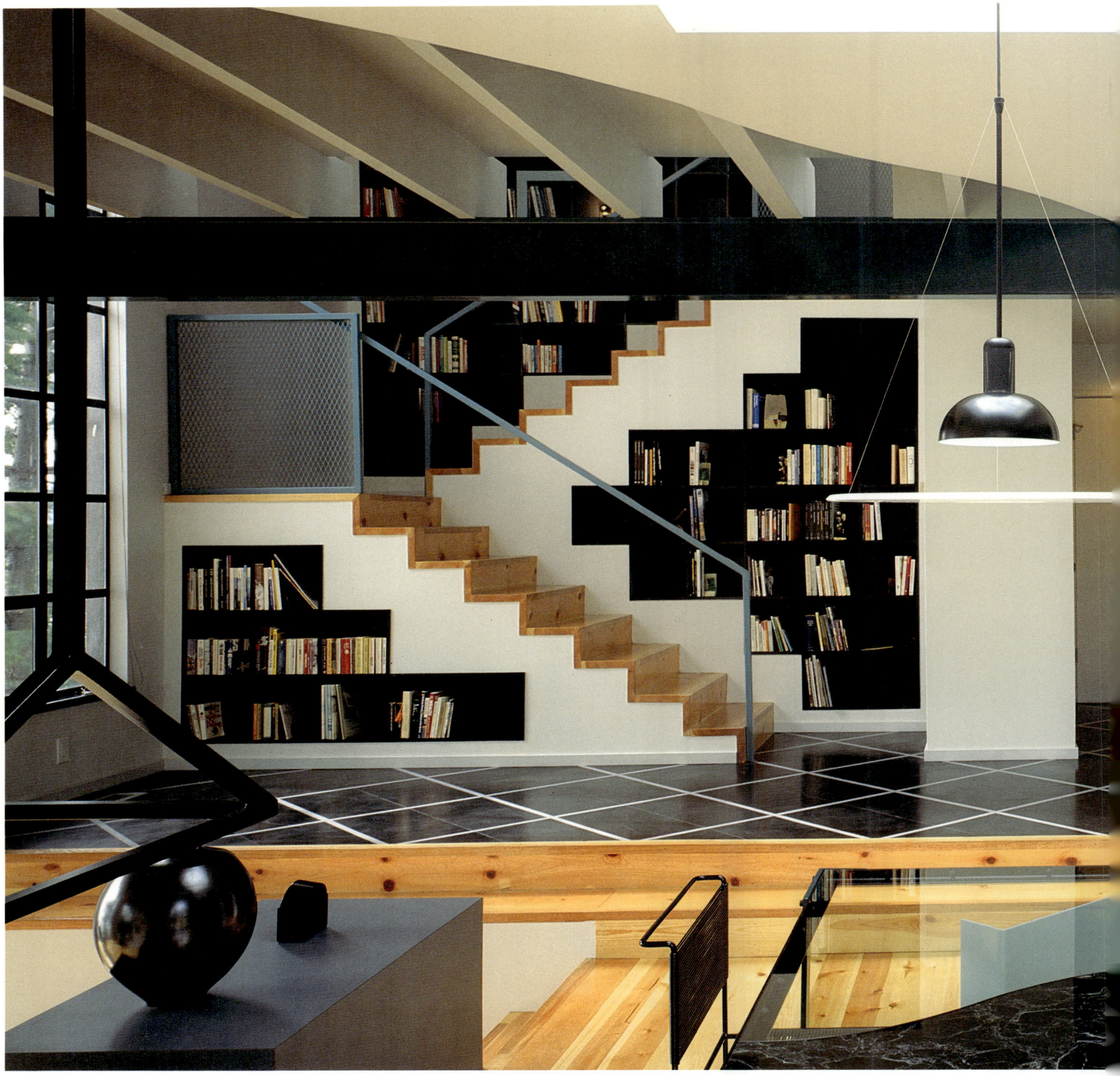

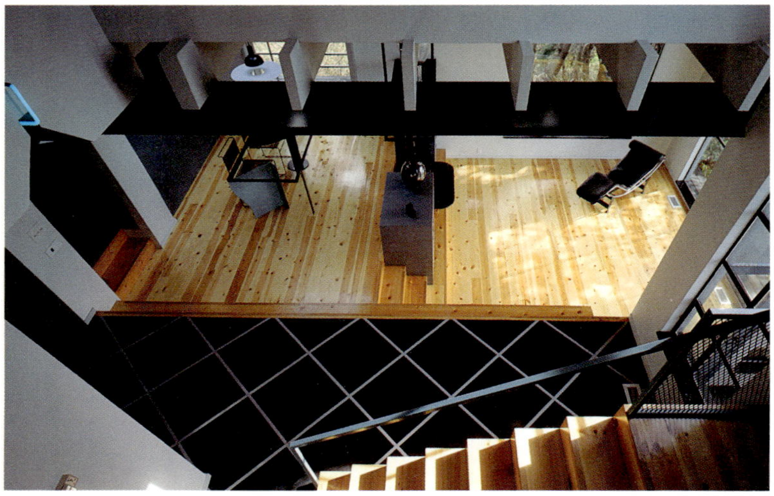

Consultants: Fritz Danz, structural; Tom Lindsey (and Greg Maxwell), table design; Victor Gardaya, narrative
General contractor: Olney & Associates

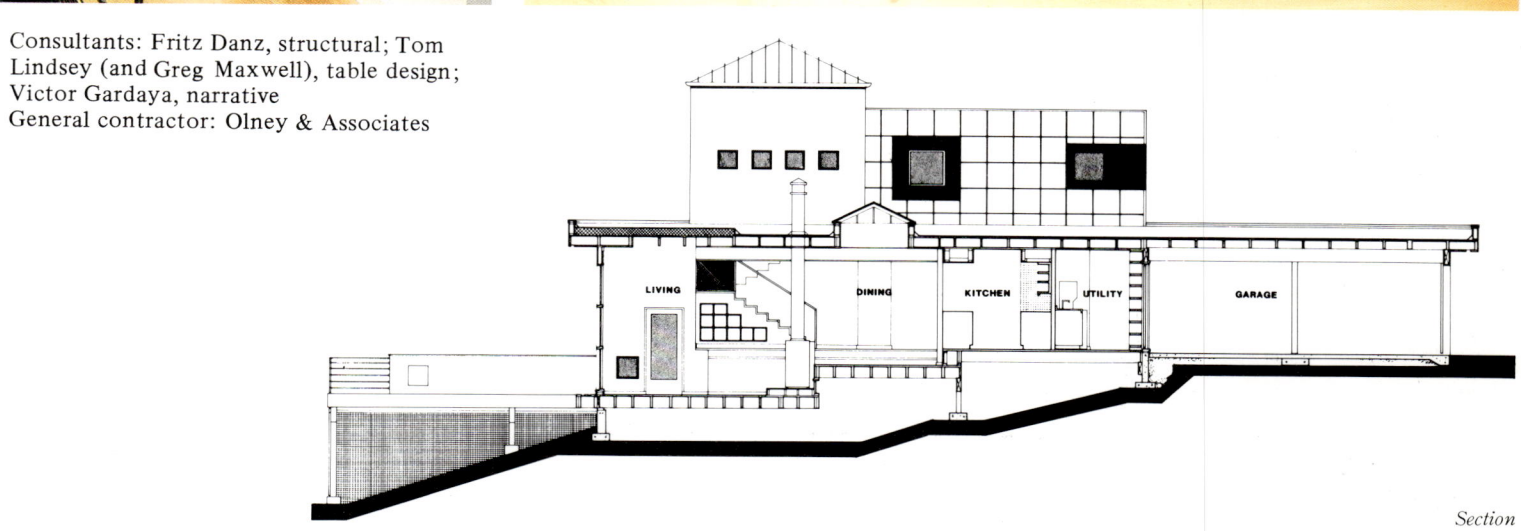

Section

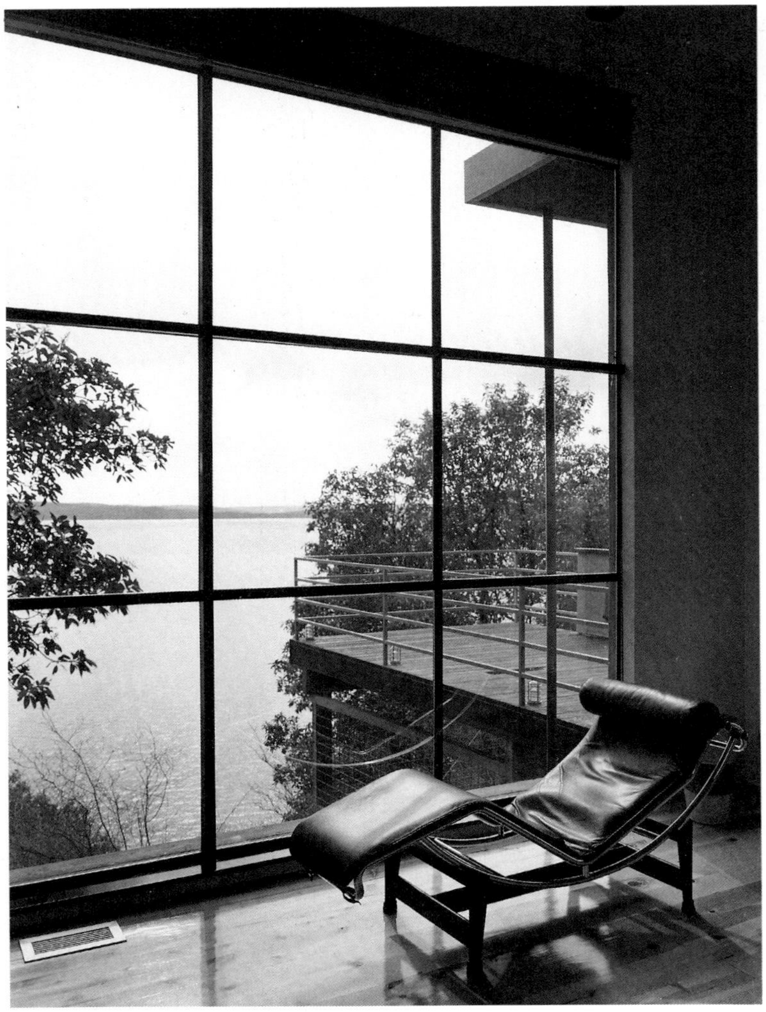
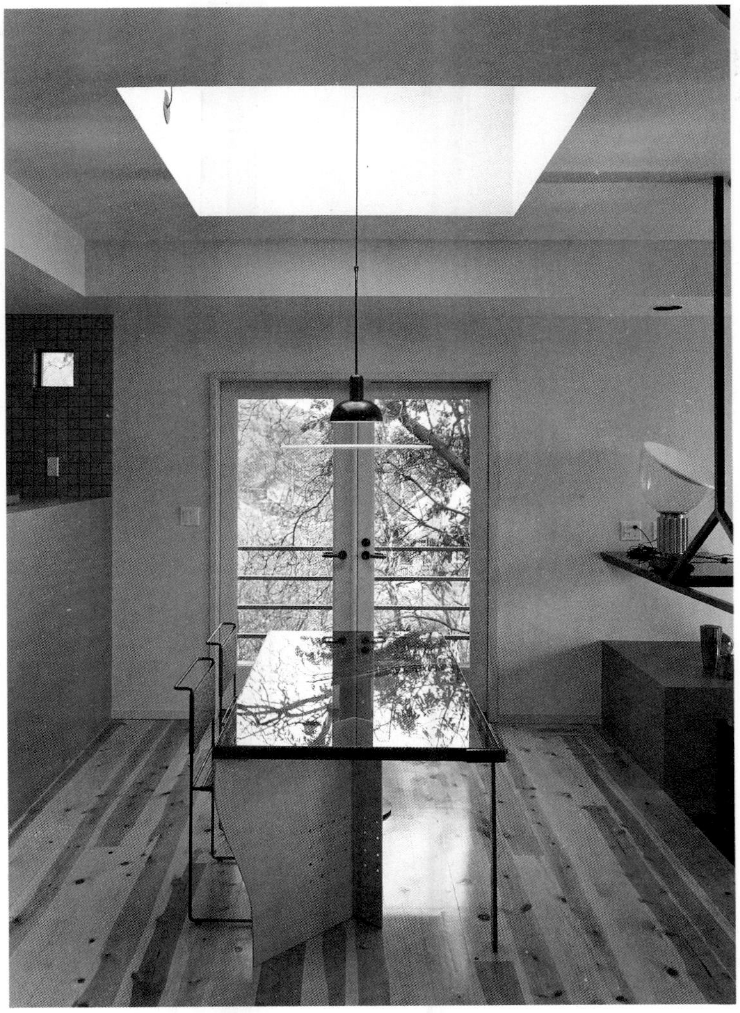
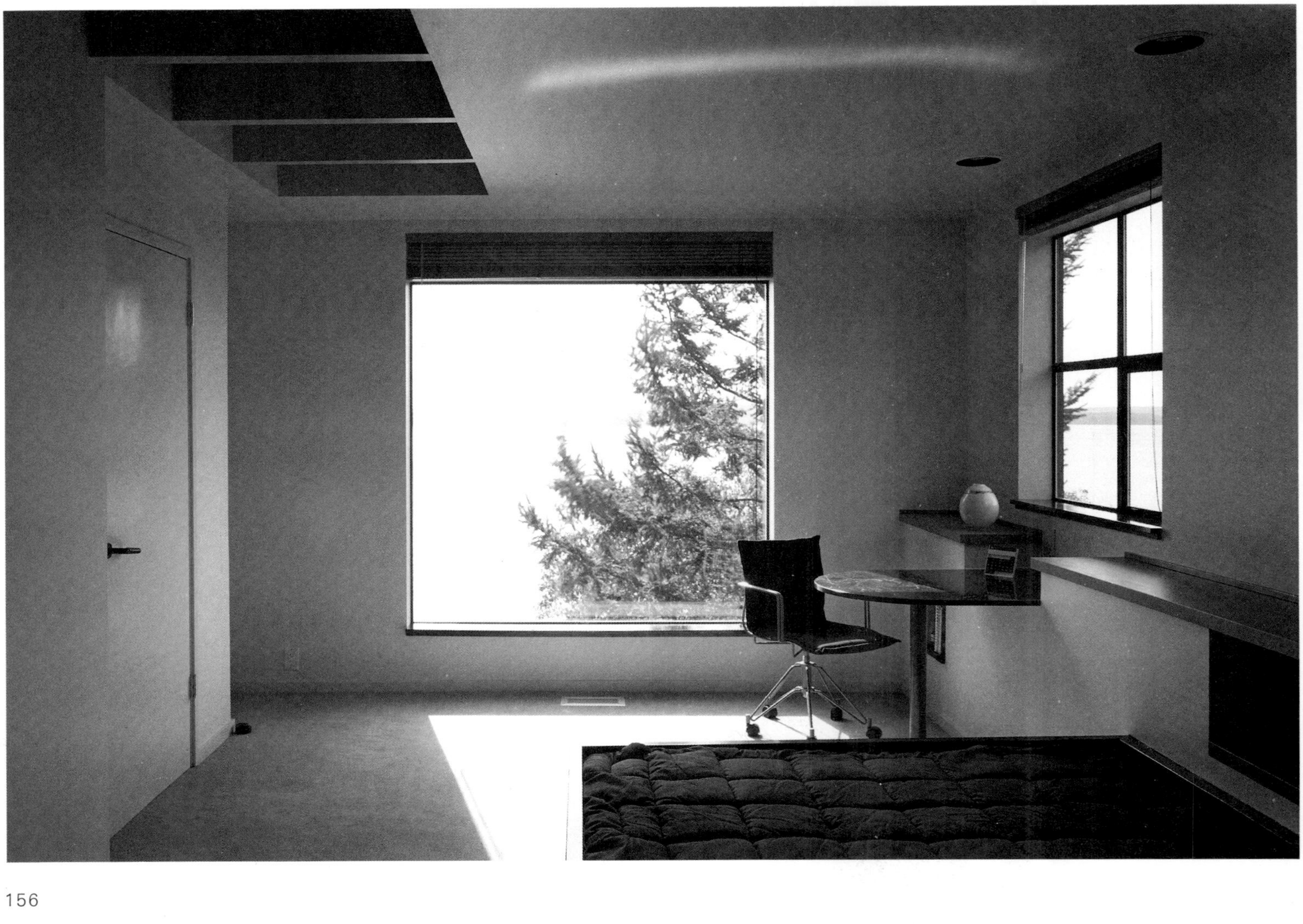

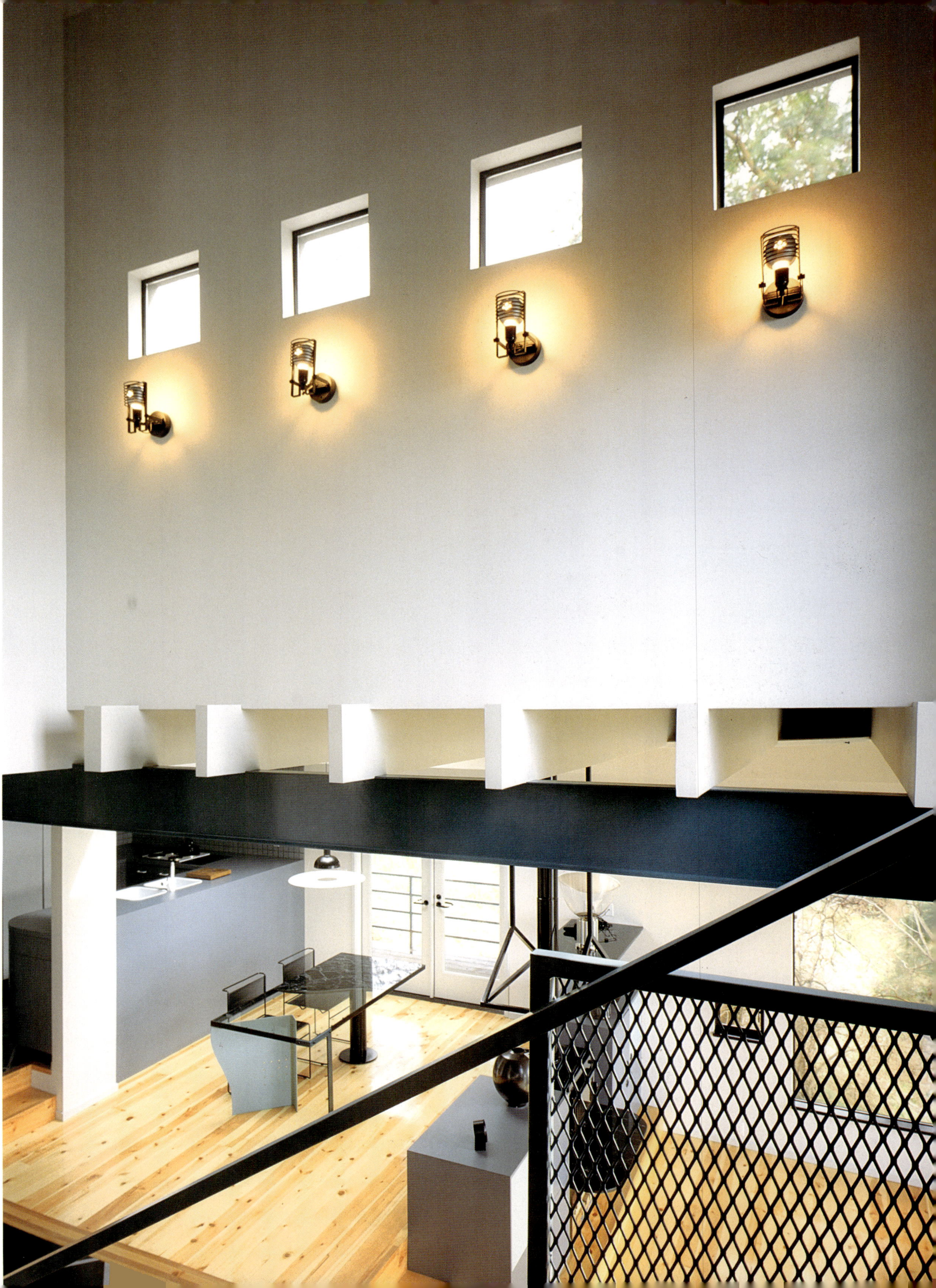

STEVEN EHRLICH
Buchalter-Friedman Residence
Los Angeles, California
1984-85

Photos: W. Fujii

Elevation

Section

Second floor

First floor

Ground floor

Built on a thickly foliated flag lot in suburban Los Angeles, this single-family, two-story (plus basement) house utilizes a series of simple organizational techniques to create a complex interaction of space and light that is exciting, contemplative and serene.

A primary axis, delineated by a vaulted skylight and steel bridge, bisects the building longitudinally providing a powerful identity externally and profuse diffused light inside. A trucated cross axis is implied by the vertical clerestory spaces set like wings on either side of the central portion of the bridge.

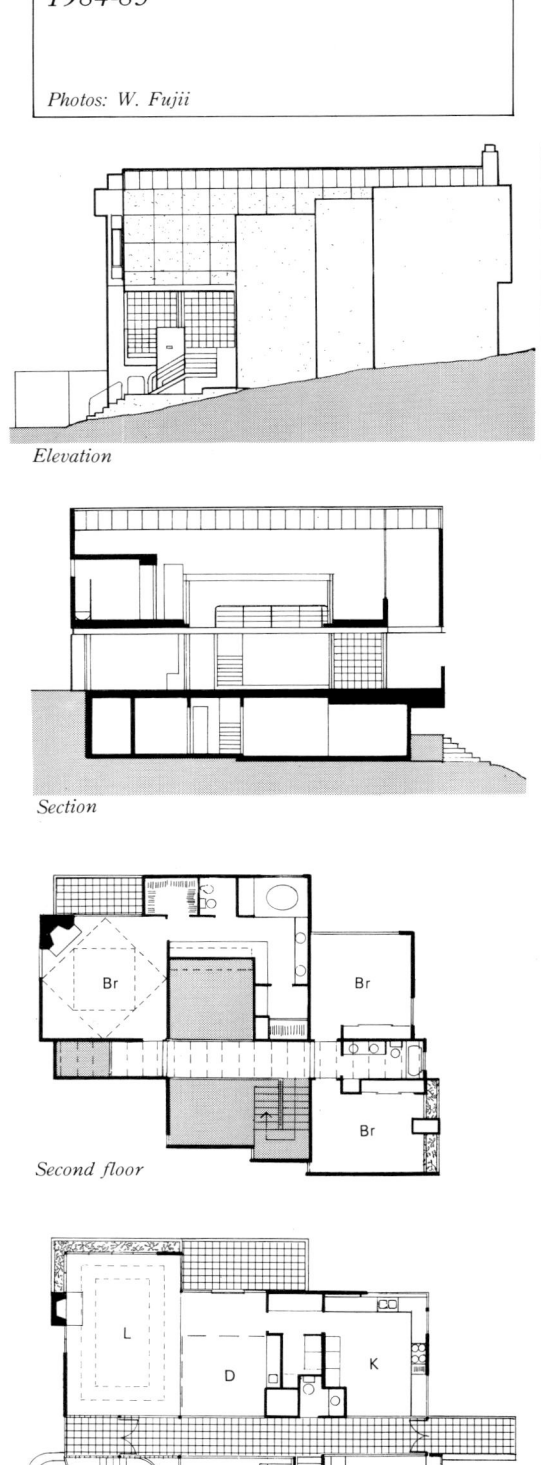

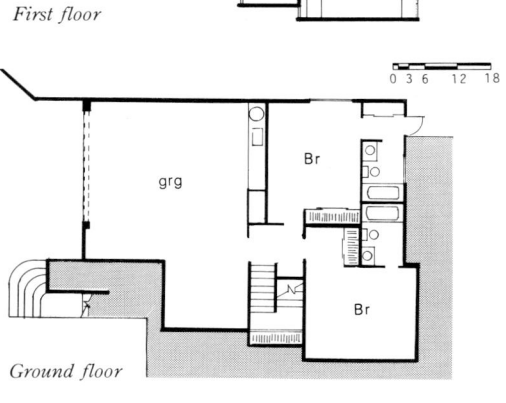

Plan organization is open in the public, first floor, with the living and dining rooms and den grouped close to the entry. The utility areas — kitchen and family room — lie towards the rear yard and pool. On the second floor, the master suite is pulled forward at one end of the bridge with the secondary bedrooms in back.

The house is a collage of stucco, glass and steel frames. The cantilevered steel corner over the entry expresses a multiplicity of form and materials. This subtely painted steel frame follows and emphasizes the galleria. Layering back from the entry, a series of stepped stucco volumes with discrete vertical strip windows, combine with virtually hidden skylights to create beautifully lit art walls.

Special detail was added to certain spaces — living room and master bedroom — with coffered ceilings. Views are oriented towards the surrounding trees, as great care was taken to provide privacy from the nearby, front house.

Consultants: Joseph Pirizelli, structural; Mel Bilow, mechanical; Marlo Wolfe & Ellen Buchalter, interior
General contractor: Ellen Buchalter

Site plan

ロスアンジェルス郊外のイチハツ類の緑に厚くおおわれた敷地に建つこの1世帯2階建て（地下をもつ）の住宅は、エキサイティングで瞑想的かつ静穏な空間と光の複合的相関を創造する一連の単純な組織化術を採用している。

ヴォールト化されたスカイライトとスティールのブリッジによって具体化された主軸は、建物を長手方向に2分し、外部においては力強いアイデンティティを、内部においては拡散した光を生みだしてゆく。切り詰められた交差軸は、ブリッジの中心部両側に翼のように設けられた垂直の明かり採り空間によって暗示されている。

平面の組織は開放的で、1階にリヴィングとダイニング、入口に近接してグループ化された個室がある。キッチン、家事室といったユーティリティ領域は、後庭とプールに向けてしつらえられている。一方、2階では主人のためのスイートが、その背後に第2のベッドルーム諸室をもちながら、ブリッジの一方のエントランスに向けて引き寄せられている。

住宅はスタッコ、ガラス、スティールのフレームの組合せによってできている。入口に突き出したキャンティレヴァーのスティール製隅部は、形態と素材の多様性を表現しているといってよい。この微妙に染められたスティールのフレームは、ガレリアを強調しながら続いてゆく。入口から背後へと多層化しながら分離され、スリットのあけられたスタッコ仕上げの連続する段状のヴォリュームは、隠されたスカイライトとつながっており、美しくアートの飾られた壁面を照らしている。

リヴィングルームやマスターベッドルームといった特別な部屋には、格間天井をもつ特別なディテールが施されている。眺望は周囲の樹林に向けられているが、正面近くにある住宅からのプライヴァシー確保にはとくに考慮がはらわれた。

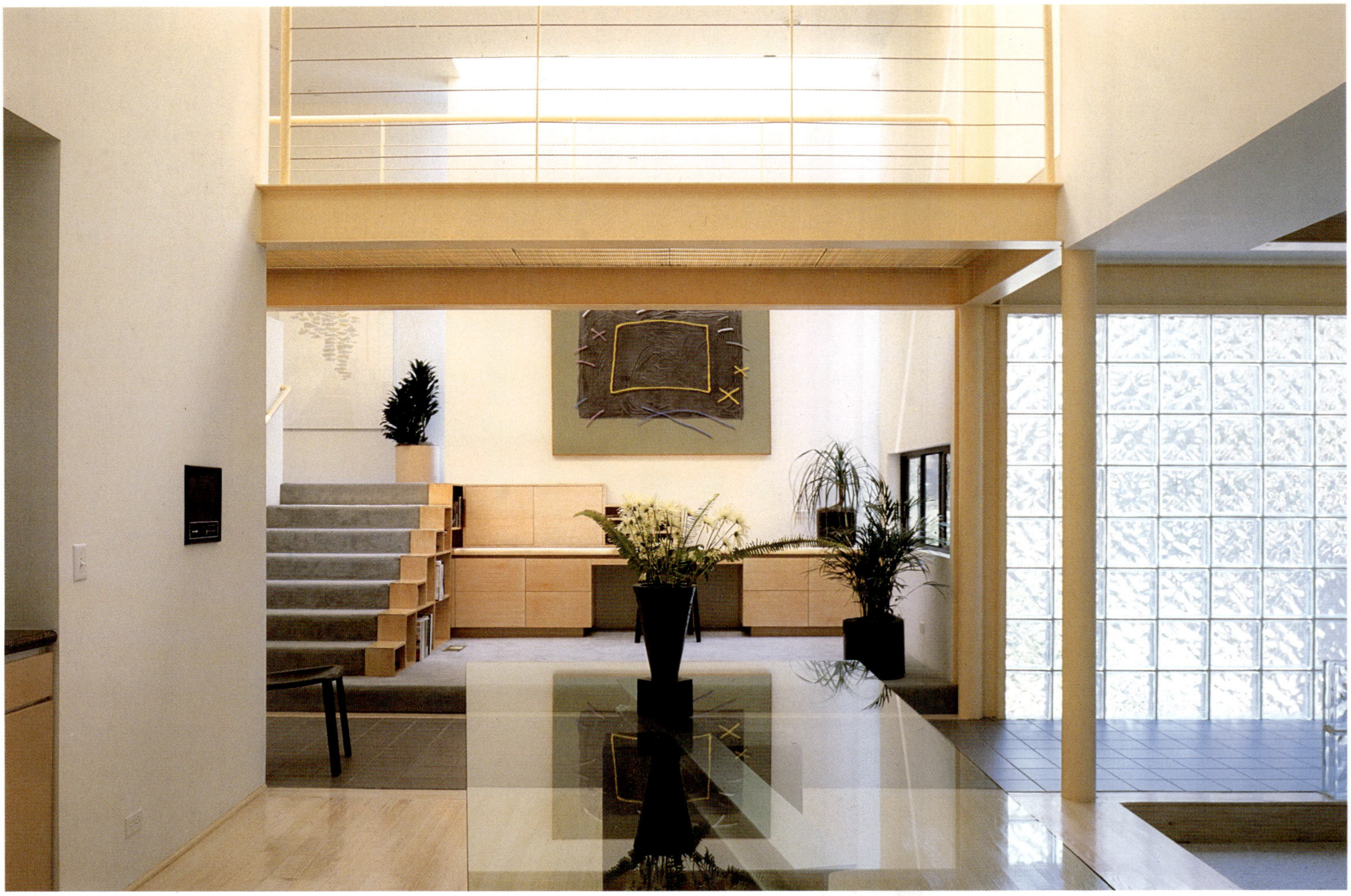

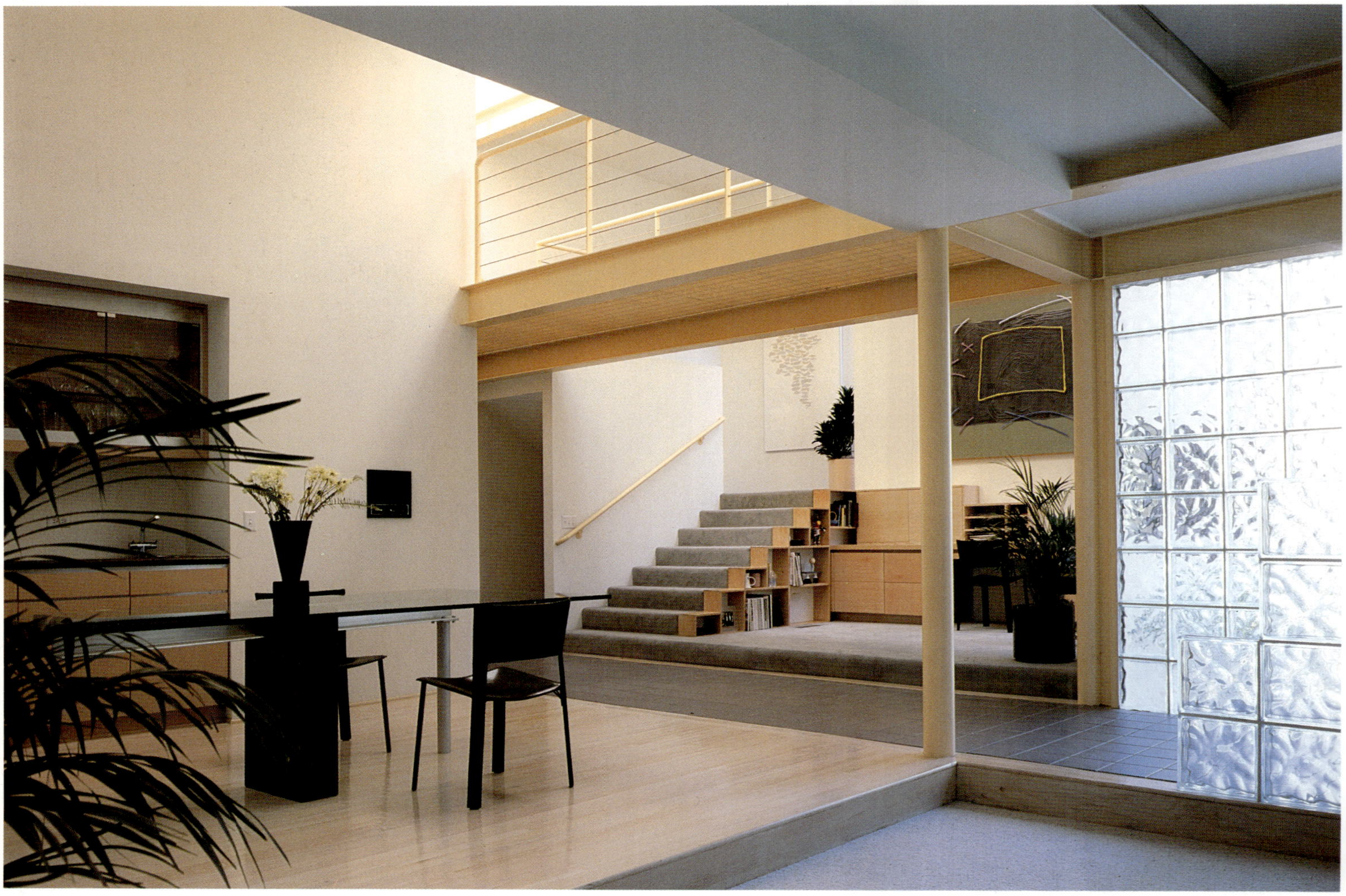

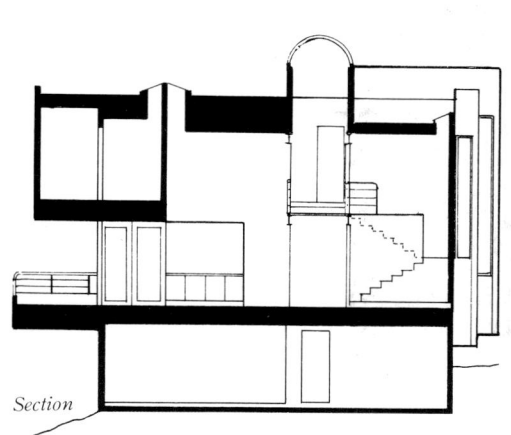

Section

161

CHRISTOPHER H.L. OWEN
Cummin Residence
Ketchum, Idaho
1980-81

Photos: W. Fujii

A year round vacation residence located approximately one mile north of Ketchum, Idaho at an elevation of over 6000 feet. The sloping site is comprised of low scrub bushes, wild flowers and rock outcroppings with views overlooking the Salmon River to the east, Baldy Mountain (the principal skiing slopes of Sun Valley) to the south and the Sawtooth Mountain Range to the north. Most of the surrounding landscape is protected from development.

The program called for a four bedroom house of approximately four thousand square feet, to include a two car garage, workshop, sauna & hot tub.

The house is constructed of wood and steel with a poured concrete foundation and four ply built-up roof. The exterior is stained cedar siding and the interiors are imperial plaster walls with oak and tile floors. Decks are provided on all exposures except the north to take advantage of the sun throughout the day. Due to the very cold winters the house is heavily insulated between 2 x 6 studs. The glass is all double glazed and is provided with insulated and solar shades.

The mechanical system is an electric air to air heat pump in three zones, an economical solution due to very low electric rates from nearby hydroelectric facilities. This provides both heating in winter, air conditioning in summer and humidification—a necessity at this high altitude.

The building in its design recapitulates the intentions of modernism, articulate and precise rather than picturesque and informal. Within a definite design vocabulary it addresses the program and the site. The result a clear interpretation of the owners requirements.

Consultants: Paul A. Gossen, P.E., structural; Tom Polise, mechanical; Diane Kidman Young, interior; C.H.L. Owen & D.K. Young, color
General contractor: Lawrence Warner & Associates

Site plan

　年間を通して余暇に使えるこの住宅は，標高6000フィート余，アイダホ州ケッチャムの北約1マイルのところにある。傾斜する敷地は，低い雑木林，野生の花，露出した岩におおわれ，東にサーモン河，南にバルディ山(サン・ヴァレーの有名なスキー場がある)，北にソートゥース山脈を見晴らすことができる。ほとんどの周辺のランドスケープは開発から守られている状態だ。

　プログラム上の要求は，4つのベッドルームをもつ約4000平方フィートの住宅で，2台分のガレージ，作業場，サウナ兼浴室を備えるというものであった。

　現場打ちコンクリート基礎と4枚の重ね形成板屋根をもつ住宅は，木とスティールによって建設された。エクステリアは，着色シダーの下見貼，インテリアは，オークとタイルの床面に壁は上質プラスターで仕上げられている。北面を除き，デッキはすべて露出され，一日を通して太陽の恵みを享受することができる。極寒の冬のため，住宅は2×6フィートの間柱のあいだに充実した断熱化を施す。ガラスはすべて2重で，断熱性や日除け性を確保している。

　機械システムは，電動式ヒートポンプが3つのゾーンにあり，近くの水力発電所からの送電を利用することによりきわめて安価に経済性を獲得した。これによって，冬期の暖防と夏期の冷房，高地に必要な湿度調整を行なうことができる。

　建物はデザイン上，モダニズムの思念を反復し，ピクチュアレスクなもの，インフォーマルなものよりも，分節化されたもの，精確なるものを表現している。確固としたデザインヴォキャブラリーのなかで，それらはプログラムや敷地に対処する。結果として，そうしたことが，オーナーの要求を明快に解釈したことにもなるのである。

West elevation

East elevation

North elevation

South elevation

Ground floor

First floor

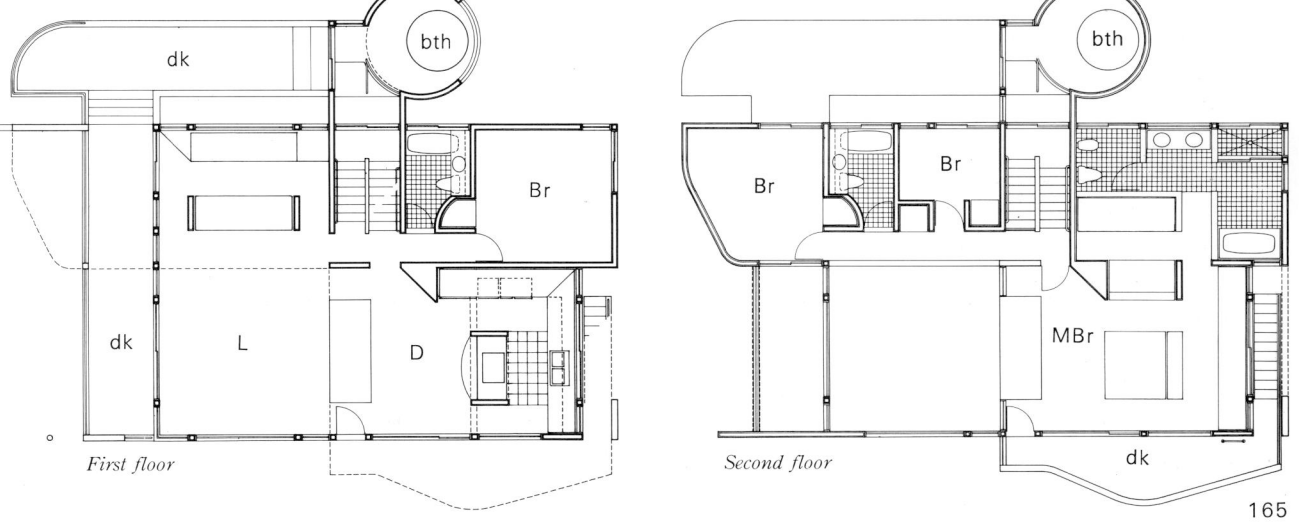

Second floor

Gallery Exhibitions

1. 磯崎新展　Arata Isozaki
   Nov.5-Dec.4, 1983
   Catalogue ¥2,800／Poster ¥1,800

2. マイケル・グレイヴス展　Michael Graves
   Apr.14-May 20, 1984
   Catalogue ¥1,500／Poster ¥1,800

3. ル・コルビュジエ展　Le Corbusier
   June 9-July 15, 1984
   Catalogue ¥2,800／Poster ¥1,800

4. マリオ・ボッタ展　Mario Botta
   Sept.8-Oct.14, 1984
   Catalogue ¥2,800／Poster ¥1,800

5. フランク・ロイド・ライト展　Frank Lloyd Wright
   Oct.27-Dec.2, 1984
   Poster ¥1,800

6. モーフォシス＋モス展　Morphosis & Eric Owen Moss
   Apr.20-May 26, 1985
   Poster ¥1,800

7. グンナール・アスプルンド展　Erik Gunnar Asplund
   June 8-July 14, 1985
   Poster ¥1,800

8. ザハ・ハディド展　Zaha M. Hadid
   Sept.28-Nov.3, 1985
   Poster ¥1,800

9. ピーター・クック展　Peter Cook
   Nov.9-Dec.15, 1986
   Poster ¥1,800

10. リチャード・マイヤー展　Richard Meier
    Apr.19-May 25, 1986
    Poster ¥1,800

11. 現代日本の建築家展　GA Japan '86
    June 14-July 20, 1986
    Poster ¥800

GA Book Shop

GA gallery
〒151
東京都渋谷区千駄ヶ谷3-12-14
3-12-14 Sendagaya, Shibuya-ku, Tokyo, 151, Japan
telephone：03-403-1581

GA DOCUMENT

80年代を迎えた世界の現代建築の動向は非常に複雑な様相を呈し、新しいデザインの波がアメリカ、ヨーロッパを始め世界各地から生まれようとしています。
GA DOCUMENT は、こうした時代の現代建築の姿を紹介する全く新しいスタイルの建築誌です。当社のモットーとする現地取材をフルに活用し、300×297mmの大型サイズの誌面に、写真・図面・解説・論文をダイナミックに構成しています。

GA DOCUMENT is a totally new architectural magazine which documents the latest developments and significant works from all over the world as they happen and as realistically as possible in a generous format (300 × 297mm) similar to our GA series, illustrated with abundant color and black & white photographs which supplement critical essays by prominent architectural critics and historians.

サイズ300×297mm／総112～132頁、カラー20～40頁／各巻￥2,900　12号, 16号——￥3,800　15号——￥4,800
Size 300 × 297mm／112-132 total pages, 20-24 color pages　　**品切**：Out of print: nos. 1-6

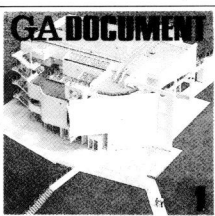

1
論文：V・スカリー／K・フランプトン　インタヴュー：P・ジョンソン
作品：R・マイヤー, アセニウム, 計画2案／I.M・ペイ, ケネディ図書館；ニューヨーク・コンヴェンション・センター／A・エリクソン, 地方裁判所／H・ヨーン, 計画5案／C・ペリ, 計画3案／ヴェンチューリ／DMJM／L・レオ／他
Critics: V. Scully／K. Frampton　　Interview: Philip Johnson
Works & Projects: R. Meier *The Atheneum; Two projects*／I.M. Pei *J.F. Kennedy Library; N.Y. Exposition & Convention Center Project*／A. Erickson *Provincial Law Courts Complex*／C.F. Murphy Assoc. *Five projects*／C. Pelli *Three projects*／Venturi, Rauch & S.-Brown／DMJM／L. Leo *Umlauftank;DLRG* and others
24 color pages, 12 gravure pages／132 total pages

2
論文：C・ノルベルク＝シュルツ　リポート：ビエンナーレ1980
作品：磯崎新, 筑波学園センター・ビル計画／NEG／M・ボッタ, クラフト・センター；図書館／R・マイヤー, 美術館コンペ当選案／K・ローチ, デンバー舞台芸術センター；計画2案／G・バーカーツ, ガラス博物館；ドゥールース図書館／W・ホルツバウアー, ハウジング／L・バラガン, 礼拝堂　他
Critic: C. Norberg-Schulz　Report: The Biennale 1980
Works & Projects: A. Isozaki *Tsukuba Civic Center Project; N.E.G.*／M. Botta *Library, Craft Center*／R. Meier *Museum for the Decorative Arts Competition*／Roche & Dinkeloo *Denver Center; Two projects*／G. Birkerts *Museum of Glass; Duluth Library*／W. Holzbauer *"Wohnen Morgen"*／L. Barragán *Chapel* and others.
28 color pages／128 total pages

3
論文：B・ゼヴィ　フォーラム：ビエンナーレ対論——C.N.＝シュルツ VS. K・フランプトン
作品：P・ジョンソン, ガラスの教会／R・ボフィル, タリエールのスタジオ：湖畔のアーケード；計画2案／H・シリアーニ, ノアジーII／H・ヨーン, ゼロックス・センター／P・アイゼンマン, 住宅11号ODD／J・ポートマン, ホテル計画案／CRS／W・ケスラー／D・ヒサカ／B・フラー, アメリカ館（Expo'67）他
Critic: B. Zevi　　Forum: C. Norberg-Schulz／K. Frampton
Works & Projects: P. Johnson *Crystal Cathedral*／R. Bofill *Taller's Studio; Les Arcades du Lac; Two projects*／H. Ciriani *Noisy II*／C. F. Murphy Assoc. *Xerox Centre*／P. Eisenman *House El Even Odd*／J. Portman *Times Square Hotel*／CRS／W. Kessler／D. Hisaka／B. Fuller *Montreal Dome* and others.
24 color pages／120 total pages

4
論文：P・ゴールドバーガー／P.C・サンティーニ／T.A・ギル／D・スチュワート
作品：C・スカルパ, ヴェローナの銀行／H・ラーセン, トロンヘイム大学／R・マイヤー, ハートフォード・セミナリー／グワスミー＆シーゲル, コロンビア大学イースト・キャンパス；計画2案／C・ムーア／A・ファン・アイク／原広司, 末田美術館, 鶴川保育園, 森工房／他
Critics: P. Goldberger／P.C. Santini／T.A. Gill／D. Stewart
Works & Projects: C. Scarpa *Banca Popolare di Verona*／H. Larsen *University of Trondheim*／R. Meier *The Hartford Seminary*／Gwathmey Siegel *East Campus Complex (Columbia University); Two projects*／C. Moore／A. van Eyck／H. Hara *Art Gallery; Nursery School; Lithography Workshop* and others.
30 color pages／120 total pages

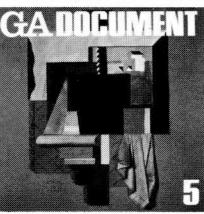

5
インタヴュー：M・グレイヴス　論文：P・ゴールドバーガー／P.C・パパデメトリオー
作品：ショールーム特集——M・グレイヴス, 磯崎新, ヴィネーリ・アソシエイツ／J・スターリング, ライス大学建築学部／F・ゲリー, カブリロ水族館；サンタモニカ・プレース；ロヨラ法律学校／F・イゲーラス, ホテル・ラスサリナス／J.A・コラレス, バンコ・パストール本社／他
Interview: Michael Graves　Critics: Paul Goldberger／Peter C. Papademetriou
Works: M. Graves *Sunar showrooms*／A. Isozaki *Hauserman showroom, Chicago*／Vignelli Assoc. *Hauserman showroom, L.A.*／J. Stirling *Rice Architecture School*／F. Gehry *Cabrillo Marine Museum; Santa Monica Place; Loyola Law School*／F. Higueras *Hotel Las Salinas*／Corrales, Molezun *Banco Pastor*
40 color pages／112 total pages

6
インタヴュー：M・ボッタ　論文：三宅理一
作品：M・ボッタ, フリブール州立銀行；計画2案／H・ホライン, アプタイベルク美術館／ミッチェル・ジオラ, イタリアにおける教育施設3作／タフト・アーキテクツ, YWCA／R・マイヤー, 計画2案／H・シリアーニ, 「ラ・クー・ダングル」, 「ノアジーIII」／S・デ・オイツァ, ビルバオ銀行／他
Interview: Mario Botta　Critic: Riichi Miyake
Works & Projects: M. Botta *Fribourg State Bank; Two projects*／H. Hollein *Abteiberg Museum*／Mitchell／Giurgola *Three works in Italy*／Taft Architects *YWCA; Three projects*／R. Meier *Two projects*／H. Ciriani *La Cour d'Angle; Noisy III; Quartier Republique, Chambéry*／F.J. Saenz de Oiza *Banco de Bilbao*
36 color pages／120 total pages

7
インタヴュー：アルキテクトニカ, マイアミの集合住宅4作, 計画案10題／H・ヨーン, ファースト・ソース・センター, アーゴン国立研究所, シカゴ商取引所増築, ワン・サウス・ワッカー, 計画案10題／安藤忠雄, 「フェスティバル」, BIGIアトリエ・ハウス, 六甲の集合住宅／P・ルドルフ, フォートワース・シティ・センター／他
Interview: Arquitectonica
Works & Projects: Arquitectonica *The Imperial, The Atlantis, The Palace, The Babylon, 10 projects*／Murphy／Jahn *U.S. Post Office, First Source Center, Argonne Program Support Facility, Chicago Board of Trade Addition, One South Wacker, 10 projects*／T. Ando *Rokko Housing, BIGI Atelier House*／P. Rudolph *Fort Worth City Center* and others
48 color pages／132 total pages